Race and Social Policy

Social policy is *not* blind. It has been at the forefront of perpetuating structural inequality in many of the systems charged with serving and protecting. The impact of race on social policy is linked to historical (intended and unintended) patterns of discrimination that have resulted in disparate impact for many across their life course. This book uses critical race theory to examine key social policies. The chapters give primacy to addressing the experiences of African Americans in navigating systems that are flawed by structural racism and yet too often attribute individual pathology rather than systemic injustice to the worsening life circumstances they find themselves in. Using scholarship, personal, and professional experiences, the contributors offer valuable insight on differential treatment and the resulting missed opportunities to address historical barriers that, if not addressed, will continue the cycle of harm for marginalized members in society.

The Covid-19 pandemic along with the loss of Black lives through carceral injustices have amplified the national discourse about race and social policy. Additionally, critical race theory has been championed by many as a framework for understanding the structural inequalities that plague our nation. Others have assailed the theory as promoting hate, guilt, and divisiveness. The contributors use critical race theory in combination with other theoretical frameworks to provide context for the persistent and pernicious injustices that have historically plagued society. Their work offers context with the goal of policy changes aimed at eradicating systemic injustices that negatively impact quality of life.

Race and Social Policy is a significant new contribution to understanding and addressing systemic and structural racism, and it will be of interest to researchers and advanced students of social work, politics, public policy, and sociology. This book was originally published as a special issue of the journal *Social Work in Public Health*.

Sandra Edmonds Crewe is Dean and Professor of Social Work at Howard University, USA. Her scholarship addresses social justice, and policy and program initiatives aimed at improving the quality of life for African Americans, especially older African Americans. Dr. Crewe has extensive practice experience in assisted and affordable housing.

Race and Social Policy

Edited by
Sandra Edmonds Crewe

LONDON AND NEW YORK

First published 2023
by Routledge
4 Park Square, Milton Park, Abingdon, Oxon, OX14 4RN

and by Routledge
605 Third Avenue, New York, NY 10158

Routledge is an imprint of the Taylor & Francis Group, an informa business

Chapters 1–12 © 2023 Taylor & Francis

All rights reserved. No part of this book may be reprinted or reproduced or utilised in any form or by any electronic, mechanical, or other means, now known or hereafter invented, including photocopying and recording, or in any information storage or retrieval system, without permission in writing from the publishers.

Trademark notice: Product or corporate names may be trademarks or registered trademarks and are used only for identification and explanation without intent to infringe.

British Library Cataloguing-in-Publication Data
A catalogue record for this book is available from the British Library

ISBN13: 978-1-032-33502-5 (hbk)
ISBN13: 978-1-032-33508-7 (pbk)
ISBN13: 978-1-003-31992-4 (ebk)

DOI: 10.4324/9781003319924

Typeset in Minion Pro
by codeMantra

Publisher's Note
The publisher accepts responsibility for any inconsistencies that may have arisen during the conversion of this book from journal articles to book chapters, namely the inclusion of journal terminology.

Disclaimer
Every effort has been made to contact copyright holders for their permission to reprint material in this book. The publishers would be grateful to hear from any copyright holder who is not here acknowledged and will undertake to rectify any errors or omissions in future editions of this book.

Dr Ruby Morton Gourdine was a key contributor to this book. She was a member of the Howard University faculty of the School of Social Work for 30 years and a staunch advocate for social justice. This book is dedicated to her memory and her contributions to scholarship that elevated the Howard University Black Perspective in Social Work Education.

Contents

Citation Information	ix
Notes on Contributors	xi

1 Race and Social Policy: Confronting Our Discomfort   1
 Sandra Edmonds Crewe and Ruby M. Gourdine

2 The Intrapsychic Psychological Binds of Poverty and Race: The Intersection of Mind and Milieu   12
 Janice Berry Edwards

3 Banging on a Locked Door: The Persistent Role of Racial Discrimination in the Workplace   22
 Tracy R. Whitaker

4 Tilted Images: Media Coverage and the Use of Critical Race Theory to Examine Social Equity Disparities for Blacks and Other People of Color   28
 Gracie Lawson-Borders

5 The Last Stages of Gentrification: Washington, DC, Mayoral Elections and Housing Advocacy   39
 Lorenzo Morris

6 Education Policy and Outcomes Within the African American Population   61
 Martell L. Teasley

7 We Treat Everybody the Same: Race Equity in Child Welfare   75
 Ruby M. Gourdine

8 Game Changers: A Critical Race Theory Analysis of the Economic, Social, and Political Factors Impacting Black Fatherhood and Family Formation   86
 Brianna P. Lemmons and Waldo E. Johnson

9 Inequities in Family Quality of Life for African-American Families Raising Children with Disabilities   102
 Carl Algood and Amber M. Davis

10 Justice Is Not Blind: Disproportionate Incarceration Rate of People of Color 113
   Janie L. Jeffers

11 The Task is Far from Completed: Double Jeopardy and Older African Americans 122
   Sandra Edmonds Crewe

12 Racism and the Christian Church in America: Caught between the Knowledge of Good and Evil 134
   Annie Woodley Brown

Index 145

Citation Information

The following chapters were originally published in the journal *Social Work in Public Health*, volume 34, issue 1 (2019). When citing this material, please use the original page numbering for each article, as follows:

Chapter 1
Race and Social Policy: Confronting Our Discomfort
Sandra Edmonds Crewe and Ruby M. Gourdine
Social Work in Public Health, volume 34, issue 1 (2019) pp. 1–11

Chapter 2
The Intrapsychic Psychological Binds of Poverty and Race: The Intersection of Mind and Milieu
Janice Berry Edwards
Social Work in Public Health, volume 34, issue 1 (2019) pp. 12–21

Chapter 3
Banging on a Locked Door: The Persistent Role of Racial Discrimination in the Workplace
Tracy R. Whitaker
Social Work in Public Health, volume 34, issue 1 (2019) pp. 22–27

Chapter 4
Tilted Images: Media Coverage and the Use of Critical Race Theory to Examine Social Equity Disparities for Blacks and Other People of Color
Gracie Lawson-Borders
Social Work in Public Health, volume 34, issue 1 (2019) pp. 28–38

Chapter 5
The Last Stages of Gentrification: Washington, DC, Mayoral Elections and Housing Advocacy
Lorenzo Morris
Social Work in Public Health, volume 34, issue 1 (2019) pp. 39–60

Chapter 6
Education Policy and Outcomes Within the African American Population
Martell L. Teasley
Social Work in Public Health, volume 34, issue 1 (2019) pp. 61–74

Chapter 7
We Treat Everybody the Same: Race Equity in Child Welfare
Ruby M. Gourdine
Social Work in Public Health, volume 34, issue 1 (2019) pp. 75–85

Chapter 8
Game Changers: A Critical Race Theory Analysis of the Economic, Social, and Political Factors Impacting Black Fatherhood and Family Formation
Brianna P. Lemmons and Waldo E. Johnson
Social Work in Public Health, volume 34, issue 1 (2019) pp. 86–101

Chapter 9
Inequities in Family Quality of Life for African-American Families Raising Children with Disabilities
Carl Algood and Amber M. Davis
Social Work in Public Health, volume 34, issue 1 (2019) pp. 102–112

Chapter 10
Justice Is Not Blind: Disproportionate Incarceration Rate of People of Color
Janie L. Jeffers
Social Work in Public Health, volume 34, issue 1 (2019) pp. 113–121

Chapter 11
The Task is Far from Completed: Double Jeopardy and Older African Americans
Sandra Edmonds Crewe
Social Work in Public Health, volume 34, issue 1 (2019) pp. 122–133

Chapter 12
Racism and the Christian Church in America: Caught between the Knowledge of Good and Evil
Annie Woodley Brown
Social Work in Public Health, volume 34, issue 1 (2019) pp. 134–144

For any permission-related enquiries please visit:
http://www.tandfonline.com/page/help/permissions

Notes on Contributors

Carl Algood, University of Maryland, Baltimore, Maryland USA.

Annie Woodley Brown, Howard University School of Social Work, Washington DC, USA.

Sandra Edmonds Crewe, Howard University School of Social Work, Washington, DC, USA.

Amber M. Davis, Johns Hopkins University, Baltimore, Washington, DC, USA.

Janice Berry Edwards, Howard University School of Social Work, Washington, DC, USA.

Ruby M. Gourdine, Howard University School of Social Work, Washington, DC, USA.

Janie L. Jeffers, Howard University School of Social Work, Washington, DC, USA.

Waldo E. Johnson, School of Social Service Administration, University of Chicago, USA.

Gracie Lawson-Borders, Cathy Hughes School of Communications, Howard University, Washington, DC, USA.

Brianna P. Lemmons, Diana R. Garland School of Social Work, Baylor University, Waco, USA.

Lorenzo Morris, Department of Political Science, Howard University, Washington, DC, USA.

Martell L. Teasley, College of Social Work, University of Utah, Salt Lake City, USA.

Tracy R. Whitaker, Howard University School of Social Work, Washington, DC, USA.

Race and Social Policy: Confronting Our Discomfort

Sandra Edmonds Crewe and Ruby M. Gourdine

ABSTRACT
The election of President Barack Obama, our first U.S. black president, for many was accompanied by the hope of a postracial society. This hope was short lived. This growing racial tension was particularly prominent in the U.S. 2016 presidential election that magnified the racial, ethnic, and class divisions in our country. An ethical responsibility of social workers is to address social justice issues and work individually and collectively to address them. Although mindful that social policy and subsequent legislation do not always change the hearts of people, dialogue adds knowledge that in turn opens the opportunity for change. The introduction begins this important dialogue.

According to Whitney Young, "An ancient Greek scholar was once asked to predict when the Greeks would achieve victory in Athens. He replied, 'We shall achieve victory in Athens and justice in Athens when those who are not injured are as indignant as those who are' And so it shall be with the problem of human rights in this country."„ (Young, 1968, p. 4).

The election of President Barack Obama, our first U.S. black president, for many was accompanied by the hope of a postracial society. This hope was short lived. Shortly into his first term, it was clear to most that racial tension was escalating. Even the most powerful person in the world could not eradicate the deep-seated racism that paraded across our televisions and social media. This growing racial tension was particularly prominent in the U.S. 2016 presidential election that magnified the racial, ethnic, and class divisions in our country. It has often been stated that conversations about politics and faith were taboo in certain settings. We would also add race to this taboo list. For too many, race is an uncomfortable conversation that is avoided. Yet others have built their careers around addressing the persistent disparities and inequities in our society. Many social workers and their professional organizations have been among those who have called attention to the growing influence of race on practice. Unfortunately, others have silenced the topic of race and racism and have stood watch over policies that are biased and perpetuate the inequity that is on the faces of the individuals and communities that we serve. The authors believe strongly that social work has an obligation to address race and social welfare practice and policy. Although mindful that social policy and subsequent legislation do not always change the hearts of people, we believe that the dialogue adds knowledge that in turn opens the opportunity for change.

Race according to Ta-Nehisi Coates (2015) in his widely acclaimed book, *Between the World and Me*, is a "defined-indubitable feature of the natural world. Racism – the need to ascribe bone-deep features to people and then humiliate, reduce, and destroy them – inevitably follows from this intolerable condition" (p. 7). The stigma of race (Crewe & Guyot-Diagnone, 2016) too often takes root in social policy, and these roots can strangle the quality of life of marginalized and vulnerable households. Of particular concern is how racism intersects with gender to create layers of vulnerability that is born by women with children who are forced to rely upon safety net and protection programs.

As guest editors, we have had extensive experience with social policy and its power to right inequities and drastically improve quality of life for marginalized groups. Simultaneously, we have seen social policy as a destructive force when it has not been vetted to ensure that the failures are not the result of systemic bias. Dr. Gourdine has experience with the courts, child welfare agencies, medical services, and the public-school system and Dr. Crewe with public and assisted housing and the ancillary programs supporting the residents. Our practice experiences wedded with our scholarship have provided important context in shaping this special edition. Another driving force for this special edition is our coming of age during the Civil Rights era. Experiences desegregating public schools and social welfare agencies offer additional context to our view of race and racism. Separate but equal, freedom of choice, separate Black and White professional associations and organizations, Uncle Tom, Civil Rights, Jim Crow, Black power, restricted covenants, and more are influential parts of our life-course perspective. We also have the shared Howard University School of Social Work experience that is undergirded by the Black perspective. This educational perspective that most of the authors in this special edition have been exposed to articulates six principles including social justice (Howard University School of Social Work, 2016).

Throughout history there have been race men and women who have created institutions to champion the dismantling of racism. Despite their phenomenal successes, racism still infiltrates the systems that are created to ensure quality of life. There is the longstanding tension between serving the worthy versus unworthy poor that continues to promote practices that cause harm (in some cases irreparable) to persons of color. Without regard to the field of practice, questions of disparities, equity, opportunity, and responsibility inform our thinking and the creation of policies and related programs and services. It is often race that determines our approaches to the social problems of the day. Prominent scholar and provocateur Cornell West (1993) succinctly characterized the problem in the title of his seminal book *Race Matters*. Despite the generations of social workers who have grappled with issues of race, the schism seems as entrenched as ever and race continues to be a social determinant of access to positive outcomes. A 2016 Pew research report on views of race and inequality states:

> By large margins, black adults are more likely than whites to say that blacks are treated less fairly than whites across key areas of American life. For example, 64% of black adults say blacks are treated less fairly than whites in the workplace, compared with 22% of whites who say the same – a 42-percentage-point gap. Blacks are also considerably more likely than whites – by margins of at least 20 points – to say that blacks are treated less fairly than whites in dealing with the police, in the courts, when applying for a loan or mortgage, in stores and restaurants and when voting in elections. (Stepler, 2016, p. 1)

Social work is not immune from these divides in beliefs about the treatment of Blacks as well as other racial or ethnic minorities. The all-too-regular encounters with racism on television and through social media have heightened the discussion about race, yet the discussion has not necessarily translated into social welfare practice and policy that acknowledges and takes corrective action to address the disturbing numbers that place too many persons of color in toxic situations. In the mid-1930s and 1940s, the founding dean of the Howard University School of Social Work, Dr. Inabel Burns Lindsay, called the profession of social work on its inconsistency in practicing social justice values (Crewe, Brown & Gourdine, 2008). Dr. Lindsay firmly believed that having a conference at a location that did not allow African Americans should never have been a battleground in social work—but it was. Her article "The Negroes and the National Conference of Social Work" Lindsay, 1941) was an exposé on the profession. Although placing itself on high moral ground as a profession that advocated for justice for all, historically too often social work has been an active player in carrying out the discrimination that took place in the larger society. James Dumpson, former dean of Fordham University and former director of Council on Social Work Education affirms this enigma:

> Social work has been referred to as the 'civilizing and humanizing profession' and at times has served as a barometer for our society. And if the profession has taken on a role of pointing out hypocrisies in our

national life, Black social workers particularly have taken on the added role of holding the profession accountable for the discrepancies between what we say we stand for as a profession and what we do as a profession. (Gourdine & Brown, 2016, pp. 59–60)

The efforts African American social work pioneers like Lindsay and Dumpson place in context is the reason the authors selected critical race theory (CRT) as a framework to discuss race within the context of social welfare policy and practice. The collective voices of African American scholars is purposeful and intended to add personal context to the problems of the profession in addressing racism and disparities that confront workers and client systems.

In reviewing the definition of social policy, the source of the contradiction becomes clearer. According to Barker (2003) social policy is defined as:

> The activities and principles of a society that guide the way it intervenes in and regulates relationships among individuals, groups, communities, and social institutions. These principles and activities are the result of the society's values and customs and largely determine the distribution of resources and level of well-being of its people. Thus, social policy includes plans and programs in education, health care, crime and corrections, economic security, and social welfare made by governments, voluntary organizations, and the people in general. It also includes social perspectives that result in society's rewards and constraints. (p. 405)

When society's values are incongruent with the values of oppressed racial communities, then it is consistent that the policies and programs that emerge are often out of sync. Despite the good intentions of many, the genuine caring for and about fellow human beings, the divides are engrained in a manner that create the constant need for a widening of our attention to all groups rather than the laser focus that is needed to address the racial and ethnic groups most infected and hurt by racism. Statements affirming "All Lives Matter" versus alignment with "Black Lives Matter" mask the resistance to focusing on those most negatively impacted by our actions or inactions. When we focus on "all" we somehow simultaneously find ourselves in the position of "creaming" to ensure that we are guaranteed successes. Additionally, our seemingly over-reliance on evidence and outcomes, may force us to look to those we feel that our policies and practices can help rather than force use to look closely at our failures—that we too often mislabel as solely the failures of the individuals to take advantage of resources available through the various social welfare systems.

This special journal edition provides insight into social welfare policy through the lens of CRT. It avoids the pitfall of being "colorblind" as we respond to the African Americans and other communities of color. A child welfare worker's quote "we treat everyone the same" that appears in Dr. Gourdine's article exemplifies the colorblind mentality that permeates the workforce and really signals the miseducation around cultural competence. It also forces our attention on inequality that has persisted despite social welfare policies that have been put in place presumptively to make life better. The authors invite critical thinking about their topics through the lens of race and critical race theory that their discourse has not been diluted by language such as "diversity" that too often provides a way of including everyone at the expense of neglecting those in greatest need such as African Americans and other persons of color. Collectively they argue that race is a critical factor that influences how we treat people and we formulate policy. Ladson-Billings and Tate (1995) in their article on CRT cite Delgado's premise that "racism is not a series of isolated acts, but is endemic in American life, deeply ingrained legally, culturally, and even psychologically" (p. 52). Thus, CRT offers a lens that makes some uncomfortable in examining social welfare and social work education. Yet this lens allows a critique of policy and practices that gets us out of our comfort zone and moves us to a paradigm that opens rather than closes doors of opportunity for historically racially oppressed groups. It rejects personal failure as the dominant force driving the statistics that place African Americans, Latinos, and other groups of color in the lowest quartile of achievement and success as measured by the greater society. Examples of this include education, health, income, poverty, wealth, and the list goes on. CRT does not disregard the successes that have been made in closing gaps, it simply guides us to more critically focus on who has not been served well and how race is central to their situation. It seriously invites self-assessment of the biases we bring in serving our client systems.

As we prepare the next generation of social workers and scholars, we do them a disservice when we avoid the topic of race. It is paramount to the content of human behavior and the social environment to be informed by racial oppression and its pernicious effects on first the individuals harmed and second the society as a whole. The articles assembled provide context that inform "discourse and dissent" that are critical to enlightened social work education. The inclusion of authors from other disciplines represents the important partnerships and collaborations needed to break the cycle of disparities and inequalities that plague our current social welfare enterprise.

As noted earlier, the current climate in the United States and the 2016 U.S. presidential, state, and local elections create the urgency to address race and racism in social welfare policy. The shattered if not abandoned dream of a postracial society has created the opportunity to delve more into race and its impact on those we serve. The polarization in the recent election lends speculation and perhaps some level of fear that racial inequity will be magnified during the next 4 years. The social policies that have been a safety net for American's most vulnerable citizens is being threatened, and it appears policies will most benefit the already financially secure. Also, there is deep concern that the conservative tidal wave will invade the Supreme Court and influence social policy in the next several decades. America has changed from an industrial society to one that is seeking its place in the global community with a bias toward the needs of the middle class. As former Congressman Ronald Dellums (personal communication, October 28, 2015) states, a focus on poverty, has been replaced by the political primacy given to the political party. With a global economy, American businesses seek to relocate their business to other countries so they can pay lower wages, increase profit margins, and receive preferable tax breaks. The United States must complete for jobs with liveable wages. Poverty rates are soaring (Whitaker & Simpson, 2016). The Patient Protection and Affordable Care Act (Obama Care) is under siege. Homelessness is part of the urban landscape, and waitlists for affordable housing are on the rise. It is within this toxic political environment that our authors present salient issues that confront our communities across the nation. It is the hope of these authors that our humanity rests in the value we place on eradicating racism and enacting social policy that addresses past disparities and recognizes that the problems extend beyond the hallways of personal responsibility to the hallways of city halls, state capitols as well as the halls of congress.

Collectively these authors (contributors) address topics that are critically important to the quality of life of African Americans and other oppressed and marginalized groups. Using CRT as the framework, they have presented conceptual and empirical knowledge to draw attention to race and social policy that is designed to provide discourse on how race and racism inform or affect people that we are obligated to serve. The authors hope that the narrow focus on race and more specifically African Americans will draw attention to the disturbing data that profiles the failure of the systems, and the intersectionality of the systems, in addressing the needs of historically oppressed groups. Noted in Berry Edwards' article is the subject of poverty and the intersection with race and mental health. She interweaves how income can affect the psyche and how these struggles affect not only lifestyle but the mental health of families. She uses case studies to demonstrate her point. Whitaker addresses income in a different vein. She focuses on how race affects employment including how something as innocuous as a name can determine if you are interviewed or offered employment. These conscious or unconscious biases are typically harmful to people of color and especially African Americans. Lack of employment contributes to low social economic status and subsequently societal ills. Despite laws to address employment bias, it still occurs at alarming rates

Given the increased focus on interprofessional approaches to problem solving, the guest editors invited contributors from other professions. These contributors represent communications and political science. Lawson Borders (communications) writes about how housing is portrayed in the media and how housing or lack of it can be detrimental to people seeking housing and their ability to acquire it. The media certainly shapes how the public perceives housing access. Morris (political science) writes on the important topic of gentrification. He presents a case study that explores how the political process affected the gentrification in the District of Columbia, the nation's capital. He details voting patterns and the actions of mayors over several decades that have resulted in a housing crisis for the poor and basically is pricing out middle- to low-income African American residents.

Education and child welfare are two of the major arenas that continue to show disparate impact for African Americans and other minority groups. Teasley addresses the educational system and the impact of educational policies have on academic achievement among African Americans. He documents reforms that have resulted in successful outcomes. Additionally, he explores other prominent policies and practices in terms of whether they are helping improve academic performance. Similarly, Gourdine addresses the ongoing disparities in the child welfare system. These disparities result in disproportionate number of African American children entering the system and remain there longer. In recent years, there is more attention given to the issue of equity in the provision of child welfare services. Some researchers indicate the disparities are the result of greater need by African American families, but others cite poverty and racial bias as contributors to the problem. Most research does not indicate that abuse and neglect occurs more often among African Americans, however this is a widely believed misconception that drives practice.

Lemmons and Johnson provide an account of the history of fatherhood and challenges they face as they parent their children. They cite mass incarceration as contributory to African fathers being absent in their children's lives. Jeffers covers the criminal justice system and cites Michelle Alexanders' treatise on mass incarceration (The New Jim Crow) and its impact on African Americans and offers models that can address the policies that lead to mass incarceration such as differential sentencing practices. Interestingly enough father absence and incarceration of parents are reasons that African American children enter the child welfare system.

Children with disabilities are another important group that is victimized by the intersection of race and disability status. Dr. Carl Algood and Amber Davis provide historical context regarding the protective legislation for children with disabilities. They address the added vulnerabilities of African American parents who struggle with caring for their children. They cite this as "simultaneous oppression." Using a research study of 123 African Americans with disabled children, they document parental strengths and coping skills.

Crewe (2018) addresses the effectiveness of social policy in eradicating poverty and access to resources among the aged African Americans. Using the seminal 1964 Double Jeopardy Report by the National Urban League, she chronicles how the aged Black has fared given the enactment of the Civil Rights and Older Americans Act. She notes the monumental gains in education and great headway in health care with a closing of the gap in longevity. Unfortunately, however, 50 years later, older African American are twice as likely to be in poverty.

Much has been written in social work literature about the affirming role of spirituality and religion in the Black community. Despite the strong bonds to religion and faith among African Americans, the broader faith based community itself is not immune to racism. The final article by Dr. Annie Brown addresses the history of racial discrimination as people practice their religion. Her historical account places in context how religion can be used to justify prejudice and bias and concludes with her efforts to begin an earnest conversation about race and helping others understand how race was created and used to justify behavior against racial groups defined as inferior even though religious tenets would not support this behavior.

These contributing authors have used their scholarship and interaction with the various client systems to document how race has influenced the outcomes of diverse groups. Unfortunately, all report gaps that signal the need for more collective focus on improving the quality of life for persons oppressed by systemic injustices. It is important to note that the authors appreciate the strengths of the Black family as well as other marginalized families. Dr. Robert Hill's seminal works, "Strengths of the Black Family (1972) and (Hill, 1999) "Strengths of African American Families: Twenty-five Year Later" remain relevant today. Resilience is evident in all of the articles. Yet an over-reliance on resilience (Davis, 2015) can have the unintended consequence of neglecting culturally informed and unbiased social policy that can assist is advancing the quality of life. Race and racism is ubiquitous, and the solutions partially rely upon an acceptance of racism as a coconspirator to many of the social ills that we are committed to solving. CRT helps to understand this but more importantly, the authors hope that understanding will propel actions to identify promising practices that will usher in policies and practices that are responsive to the narratives that are presented. We are all accountable for being aware of racism and bias in social policy. By identifying barriers and proposing solutions, progress can be made. As you read the articles, we hope that an action list will emerge and you will follow up. Whether the action is to teach about the impact of race/racism or to call attention to the pejorative impact of social policy on a segment of the client system—each of us has a critically important role. In closing, we individually and collectively each have two options—to be a part of the problem or to be a part of the solution. Our social work ethics demand that we commit to being a part of the solution to eradicate racism and other social injustices that permeate society today. In the words of Whitney Young Jr., "the task that we are faced with in regards to the intersection of race and social policy is to "support the strong, give courage to the timid, remind the indifferent, and warn the opposed" (Boswell, 2012).

Conclusion

Race and social policy-racism is a public health problem

We end this special edition by placing the articles in the context of social work and public health through the lens of CRT. The authors used CRT as a framework for understanding how social policy, or perhaps more accurately, the impact of colorblind social policy has on African Americans and other oppressed populations. Whether conscious or unconscious, social policy and its implementation in the United States continues to divide groups among racial lines—thus CRT allows the authors to examine their topics and stray from the traditional theoretical lens that sometimes down play race. Derek Bell (1994) states that CRT is by its nature disruptive to the usual discourse, and in the words of Audre Lourde (2007) it does not rely on the master's tools to dismantle the master's house. Thus, racism is inextricably linked to the disparities and lack of equity experienced by African Americans and reported by the authors. From child welfare to aging; from motherhood to fatherhood; from criminal justice to housing; from religion to politics; and from employment to school performance, race plays a role and consequently racism impacts the quality of life at every stage and phase of life. The authors assert that racism is a public health problem and sought to identify others with shared views. Baker & Simmons (2015) in their book, *The Trouble with Post-Blackness*, state "to be black now for the Black Majority is to live shorter lives, work disgusting menial jobs, suffer unemployment when such jobs fail, endure explicitly and implicit insults" (p. 253.) This quote adds context to the lingering health and economic disparities that exist today Others agree that racism is a tour de force in perpetuating poor outcomes for blacks in America. The following additional quotes help to affirm the salience of a focus on public health and racism.

- Structures of racism and privilege continue to put a serious toll on the African American community's health – and contribute to the fact that black Americans are still dying younger than white Americans. Here's why racism is a serious public health issue" (Culp-Ressler, 2014, p. 1).
- "Racism is a 'wicked' public health problem that fuels systemic health inequities between population groups in New Zealand, the United States and elsewhere" (Came & Griffith, 2018, p. 1).
- "The Editorial Board of the *Harvard Public Health Review* recognizes that racism has driven health inequities among historically underserved and marginalized populations nationwide, evidenced not only in the extraordinarily disparate rate at which Blacks are killed at the hands of the police compared to Whites, but also through inequities in environmental exposures, limitations in access to health care, and other factors that affect optimal health and well-being.... As public health professionals, it is our responsibility to address racial injustices

through research, discourse, and reform. And at this critical juncture, reneging on such responsibility is not an option" (Harvard Public Review Editorial Board, 2015, p. 1).
- "Racism is a complex and multifaceted construct…. According to Gilmore, racism is 'the state-sanctioned and/or extralegal production and exploitation of group-differentiated vulnerability to premature death.' (Gilmore, 2007, p. 247) If whole segments of our society are systematically blocked from the possibility of optimal health and this differential risk is structured along racial or ethnic lines, then it can be said that racism is at work. Taking seriously both our field's charge to facilitate optimal health for all and Gilmore's definition of racism, it seems to me we can only achieve the goals of Public Health if we treat racism as a Public Health problem" (Ford, 2017, p. 1).

Although there was extraordinary optimism that the election of President Barack Obama would bring relief to the hardships of Blacks, the United States continues to be mired in harmful racial politics. Despite two consecutive terms of the Obama presidency, the country seems more racially divided than ever. The civility of politically correct dialogue has been replaced with blatant attacks on "otherness" that reaffirm privilege rather than the core values of social work that affirm the dignity and worth of all persons. Scholars in this special edition have noted that racism is exacerbated by laws, policies, and practices that result in disparate treatment. The range of circumstances that highlight this point is evidenced in education, the criminal justice system, family formation, employment opportunities, social services such as child welfare and services to families with disabilities. Through examining selected topics and associated policies and practices, a compelling case is presented to reexamine all policies and practices through a lens of harm and hurt—who fares well and who does not? Although most authors were social workers, authors from other disciplines broadened the perspective. Although CRT was the organizing framework, authors also referenced other theories such as ecological theory, life-course perspective, restorative justice, intersectionality, and more to address social welfare policies that negatively affect the quality of life of African Americans and expose them to disability and premature death. The authors explain the trajectory of how we moved from one policy to another and described how laws and policies that were designed to help disenfranchised groups were either ignored, amended, or rolled back to resist the democratic tenet of fair treatment for all its citizens. All the authors concluded that there are ways in which we can combat the existing policies that are detrimental to people of color and used a strengths perspective in looking at ways to address the inherent problems associated with a policy or practice. Collectively, the authors present antiracism as critical to ensuring equity and eradicating disparities across social welfare policies. The authors presented the following key themes:

- Race affects one's ability to have economic security and can affect one's mental and emotional health. The pathways to financial security require the ability to secure and maintain employment. Racial bias can prevent one from being considered as an employee and for people of color poor employment histories are factors that prevent stable employment. These decisions are based on assumptions and both conscious and unconscious bias that belie a person's ability, knowledge and skills because they are members of a racial/ethnic group.
- Local and national politics can affect communities of color. The author notes that the District of Columbia has now gone from a city nicknamed "the chocolate city" to being highly gentrified and increasingly segregated city where the Black population fell from 70% to 49% in several decades. The election of Black politicians during this period could not prevent the inevitable change. Behind the change was the discussion of housing and its availability to low income residents. Additionally, negative media images of Blacks perpetuate the racial divide in our country.
- Education is sometimes referred to the new civil rights issue of the current century. Although achievements are noted there continues to be a significant lack of achievement among low income people of color, especially African American children who are among the least

successful in our educational systems. Policies such as "zero tolerance" have an enormous effect on communities of color as noted in their high school dropout rates.
- Race-based policies have affected family systems as well. The policies have interrupted family formation as well as economic security and other well-being indictors. In the last decade and a half, there have been high rates of African American children entering foster care/out of home care. Thus, the issue of racial equity is now a popular refrain and efforts are underway to address the disparities in child welfare. Additionally, the narrative of "dead beat" dads and their inaccessibility to parent children is too often accepted as factual. Researchers, and practitioners report efforts that prevent family formation or the attempts they are making to maintain relationships with their families. Research has documented that these fathers have shown that they are involved in their children's lives despite systemic barriers in making those relationships more viable. Authors have also noted that families raising children with disabilities are often faced with intersecting stigmas associated with race and disability. Older Blacks also often face lifelong disadvantage because of the intersection of race, age, and poverty. For example, many older Whites have multiple sources of income and social security is a supplement to these other sources. For many older Blacks, social security is the primary source of income and often the fragile family systems require that their incomes support younger family members.
- The criminal justice system in the United States has encapsulated many African Americans particularly the men in what is commonly referred to as the "prison industrial complex." The United States incarcerates more individuals than any other country, and recent events in this country have demonstrated the unfair treatment or excessive force by the police toward Black men and women. Even when injury or death occurs the police officers are seldom held accountable for their actions. This situation has resulted in the "Black Lives Matter "movement that has become highly politicized as evidenced by those who oppose the movement and emphasize that all lives matter despite the overwhelming evidence that the problems are mostly located in the Black community. A particularly relevant point in the discourse about race and public health is the harsher sentencing for crack vs powder cocaine. Thus, racism contributes to the disproportionality in the criminal justice system. More recently, attention is given to the difference in approach to addressing the opioid epidemic. Crack addiction mostly affected Blacks, and opioid addiction mostly affects Whites. Crack addiction was criminalized as compared with opioid addition being viewed through a public health lens. President Trump proclaimed the opioid crisis a public health emergency under federal law and referred to it as a "national shame and human tragedy." When crack additional swept the country it was cast as a Black problem and criminalized, and no public compassion was evident. In fact, American citizens feared Black communities and the violence that resulted from crack epidemic and swiftly moved to mass incarceration and the destabilization of families (Sweet, 2018). Although it is possible that lessons were learned, it is equally plausible that racism accounts for the different approaches to addition. What is equally concerning is that this differential practice is another way of reinforcing among African Americans that their lives—their well-being is marginalized. Like the Tuskegee experiments, this disparity will be passed on from generation to generation and add to the longstanding narrative that Blacks are never viewed by the system as being as good as Whites. Jackson (2015) discusses the "twice as good as whites' rhetoric was about recognizing that American society was a place where whites and blacks could perform the same actions and come out with very different results" p. 200. The danger of differential social policy surrounding the crack cocaine vs opioid addiction is that it reinforces the half-as-good stereotype and reinforces the system is against you—so why try conundrum.
- Religion has also a historic role in promoting persistent racial and gender disparities. This volume included an article that presented the history of religion and its role in promoting racism within their ranks and the resulting racial problems based upon a person's religion or spiritual practices. It demonstrates the efforts within the church communities to combat racism and its recommendations for the churches to embrace their Christian values that promotes the

equalization expressed in the quote "God loves all children" as evidenced in Biblical and humanistic terms. Recently there were accounts that the Trump administration's separation of undocumented immigrant parents from their children when they were attempting to illegally enter the country was grounded in religious doctrine. Religion and social policy are inextricably linked and race is a part of this mix. This is very important given the role that faith has in well-being and quality of life for African Americans.

Collectively, the authors have provided convincing evidence that we are not in a postracial society. On the contrary, they present compelling evidence that today the divide between the haves and have-nots has widened and that too often race is the common denominator. The purpose of this discourse is to create a new narrative that exposes systemic disparities and rejects the paradigm of blaming the victim. Collectively, the scholars and practitioners have sought to focus on resilience as they expose the pernicious effects of race in America. In the words of Ta-Nehisi Coates (2015):

It is truly possible to understand yourself as the essential below of your country. It breaks too much of what we would like to think about ourselves, the world we move through and the people who surround us. The struggle to understand is our only advantage over the madness. (p. 106)

Thus, the agenda for this volume is to bring awareness to disparities. Through this awareness, the coeditors hope that advocacy will be intensified to identify and end racism in all its forms. By shining the spotlight on the selected areas of race and social policy in this special edition, we offer a starting point for the difficult conversations that need to take place.

The core values of social work include social justice and the dignity and worth of the person. The scholars provide important context that identifies barriers to honoring these elusive yet critically important values. DuBois asserted in 1903 that "The problem of the twentieth century is the problem of the color line: the relation of the darker to the lighter races of men in Asia and Africa, in America and the islands of the sea" (p. 8, Today, despite civil rights legislation—this still holds. Our challenge is to continue the struggle to eradicate social injustice by exposing unfair and unjust social policy and practices that result in poor health and social outcomes We firmly believe that racism that contributes to inequality and lack of equity represents a public health crisis in our country today. Effective interventions require that social workers acknowledge the detrimental effects of racism on individuals, communities, as well as society, and work across levels to address the damage and eradicate the injustices that continue to harm. Although we recognize the strengths and resilience that many African Americans and other oppressed populations have shown over time, social policy should not and cannot continue to overly rely on resilience and neglect its responsibility to lessen barriers that too often penetrate the strengths and cause breakdowns that result in irreparable harm. We have observed the power of policy changes in improving quality of life for many. Because we have witnessed in our lifetimes some of the positive results of systemic change, we are committed to continuing the pressure to examine and remove barriers that are rooted in racism; this is the new narrative we seek—the realization that racism is a public health problem and that social work has a role in addressing the problem in our many spheres of practice. The articles in this special edition (Fong, Lubben & Barth, 2018) are aligned with many of the 12 grand challenges for social work by the American Academy of Social Work and Social Welfare . Although racism is not uniquely identified as a challenge, it cuts across all of them and is core to some of them such as extreme economic inequality, closing the health gap, and equal opportunity and justice. The focus of these challenges includes examination of social policy and the application of evidence-based research that offers alternative practices. Heyman and Congress (2018) in their book *Health and Social Work* calls for social work to:

> address the very fabric of society that produces health inequity, those social and structural factors that are viewed as distal from health problems, but comprise the predictors of inequality. These include housing, education, financial resources, neighborhood environments, social media access, expanding community assets. (pp. 323–324)

Our authors in this special edition through using CRT have singled out race and racism as structural problems that undergird the deeply ingrained poor outcomes for African Americans. The hard reality is that hard-fought struggles resulted in great strides and moderate made over the past 50 years, however the picture for many African American families is still dismal: African American men make up approximately 50% of incarcerated individuals, 33% of African American children live in poverty, life expectancy is shorter for African Americans, and more (Hattery & Smith, 2007). What is touted as "zero tolerance" for the breaking of policies too results in widening equality gaps.

All authors in this special issue are informed by the Black perspective that undergirds social work education at Howard University. Evolving overtime from the sociocultural perspective, the Black perspective emphasizes sensitivity to the needs of African Americans as well as other oppressed and marginalized populations. Robert Smith's (2018) political intellectual biography, *Ronald W. Walters and the Fight for Black Power (1969–2010)*, also discusses the importance of a black perspective. He states that Dr. Walters felt that a Black perspective was key to the elimination of Black oppression and that a Black perspective required an appreciation and significance of the African American culture. Dr. Walters, a former Howard University professor and renowned political scientist/activist and friend of social work, stated that of equal importance was the belief in the "criticality of racism" (p. 219) to a Black perspective. Although appreciating that the Black perspective is also embraced by the Whites, Dr. Walters understood the importance of Blacks bearing the responsibility in pointing out racism because of their historical and lived experiences that made them perceptively tuned to the environmental cues. It is this sense of responsibility that we recruited Black authors to address different aspects of race and social policy in the United States. It has been our intent to redirect the language of personal responsibility (Reed, 2018), zero-tolerance (Winn & Winn, 2016), and more to the systems that bear responsibility for the cover up of the negative consequences of race. At the Howard University School of Social Work, a task force was convened in 1970 in the aftermath of the Civil Rights movement to revitalize the curriculum to address historical oppression and transform the curriculum to reflect the experiences of African Americans (Gourdine & Brown, 2016). The Black Perspective was adopted as a educational philosophy that challenged rather than blindly adopted the blueprint of the white community. The articles in this special edition on race builds upon the thinking that "the Black Perspective must assure Black people the possibility of building a better social milieu than the one which was handed to them by the White power structure„ (Gourdine & Brown, 2016, p. 74). We hope that this collective effort will raise awareness and collective responsibility to examine social policy and advocate for changes that will eliminate structural barriers that continue the inequities that plaque our society..

Disclosure statement

No potential conflict of interest was reported by the authors.

References

Barker, R. L. (2003). *Social work dictionary* (5th ed.). Washington, DC: NASW Press.
Bell, D. A. (1994). Who's Afraid of Critical Race Theory? *University of Illinois Law Review, 4*, 893–910.
Boswell, B., (Executive Producer), Khalafian, C., & Hamilton, T., (Directors). (2012). *The power broker: Whitney's young's fight for civil rights* [PBS Documentary]. Arlington, VA: Bluegate LLC.
Came, H., & Griffith, D. (2018). Tackling racism as a "wicked" public health problem: Enabling allies in anti-racism praxis. *Social Science and Medicine, 199*, 181–188. doi:10.1016/j.socscimed.2017.03.028
Coates, T. (2015). *Between the world and me* (1st ed.). New York, NY: Spiegel & Grau.
Crewe, S. E. (2018). The task is far from completed: Double jeopardy and older African Americans. *Social Work in Public Health*, 33, 7/8. online
Crewe, S. E., Brown, A. W., & Gourdine, R. M. (2008). Inabel burns lindsay: A social worker, educator, and administrator uncompromising in the pursuit of social justice for all. *Affilia, 23*(4), 363–367. doi:10.1177/0886109908323974

Crewe, S. E., & Guyot-Diagnone, J. (2016). *Stigmatization and labelling. Encyclopedia of social work*. National Association of Social Work. doi:10.1093/acrefore/9780199975839.013.1043

Culp-Ressler, T. (2014). *Why racism is a public health issue*. Retrieved from https://thinkprogress.org/why-racism-is-a-public-health-issue-b01056c63e44/

Davis, L. E. (2015). *Why are they angry with us? Essays on race.*Chicago, Ill: Lyceum Press .

DuBois, W. E. B. (1903). *The souls of black folk*. Chicago, IL: McClurg & Company.

Fong, R., Lubben, J., & Barth, R. (eds.). (2018). Eradicate Social Isolation in Grand Challenges for social work and society: Social progress powered by science. New York: Oxford Press

Fong, R., Luben, J. E., & Barth, R. P. (Eds.). (2018). *Grand challenges for social work and society*. New York, NY: Oxford University Press.

Ford, C. L. (2017) *UCLA center for the study of racism, social justice and health is racism a public health issue?* Retrieved from https://www.racialhealthequity.org/blog/racism-is-a-public-health-issue

Gilmore, R. W. (2007). *Golden gulag: Prisons, surplus, crisis, and opposition in globalizing California*. Berkeley, CA: University of California Press.

Gourdine, R. M., & Brown, A. W. (2016). *Social action, advocacy and agents of change: Howard University School of Social in the 1970's*. Baltimore, MD: Black Classic Press (Imprint Editions).

Harvard Public Health Review Editorial Board. (2015). *Racism is a public health problem*. Harvard Public Health Review (v. 3). Retrieved from http://harvardpublichealthreview.org/hphr-editorial-racism-is-a-public-health-problem/

Hattery, A. J., & Smith, E. (2007). *African American families*. Los Angeles, CA: Sage Publications.

Heyman, J. C., & Congress, E. P. (Eds.). (2018). *Health and social work: Practice, policy and research*. New York, NY: Springer Publishing.

Hill, R. (1972). *The strengths of the African American families*. New York, NY: National Urban League.

Hill, R. (1999). *The strengths of African American families: 25 years later*. Lanham, MD: University Press.

Hill, R. B. (1999). *The strengths of african american families: Twenty-five years later*. Lanham, Md: University Press of America.

Howard University School of Social Work. (2016, December 1). *The black perspective: Our guiding philosophy*. Retrieved from: http://www.howard.edu/schoolsocialwork/about/default.htm

Jackson, J. L. (2015). Half as good. In H. Baker & K. Simmons (Eds.), *The trouble with post-blackness* (pp. 194–208). New York, NY: Columbia University Press.

Jr. H. Baker. & Simmons, K. M. (Eds). (2015). The trouble with post-blackness. New York Columbia University Press.

Ladson- Billings, G., & Tate, W. F. (1995). Toward a critical race theory of education. *Teacher's College Record, 97*(1), 47–68.

Lindsay, I. B. (1941). The Negroes and the national conference of social work. *Opportunity, 120*, 269–271.

Lourde, A. (2007). *Sister outsider*. Berkley, CA: Crossing Press.

Reed, A. (2018). *Without justice for all: The new liberalism and our retreat from racial equality*. New York, NY: Routledge.

Smith, R. C. (2018). *Ronald W. Walters and the fight for black power 1969-2010*. Albany: State University of New York Press.

Stepler, R. (2016, June 27). *5 key takeaways about views of race and inequality in America*. Retrieved from http://www.pewresearch.org/fact-tank/2016/06/27/key-takeaways-race-and-inequality/

Sweet, T. (2018). *The Opioid crisis and the effects of racism during the crack epidemic*. American University Journal of Gender, Social Policy & the Law. Retrieved from http://www.jgspl.org/opioid-crisis-effects-racism-crack-epidemic

West, C. (1993). *Race matters*. Boston, MA: Beacon Press.

Whitaker, T., & Simpson, J. (Eds.). (2016). *Poverty: Research & reflections from the black perspective*. Washington, DC: Howard University School of Social Work and the E. Franklin Frazier Center for Social Work Research.

Winn, L. T., & Winn, M. T. (2016). There's nothing for us here: Black families navigating the school/prison nexus 60 yers after Brown. In P. Noguera, J. Pierce, & R. Abrams (Eds.), *Race, equity and education: Sixty years from Brown* (pp. 245–266). Switzerland: Springer International Publishing.

Young, W. M. (1968). *Keynote address at the 1968 AIA convention in Portland, Oregon*. Retrieved from http://isites.harvard.edu/fs/docs/icb.topic753413.files/14_Outsiders%20in%20the%20Profession/Young%201968%20AIA%20speech.pdf

The Intrapsychic Psychological Binds of Poverty and Race: The Intersection of Mind and Milieu

Janice Berry Edwards

ABSTRACT
Race and poverty are poignant factors in how individuals and communities experience the world. The reality is that more people of color than White people live in poverty (Milner, 2013). How these inequalities intersect with the mind and environment is of compelling importance. The experiences of race and living in poverty are riddled with innumerable stressors and barriers, and as a result are subject to the experience of a range of mental health issues. Those that live the experience of trauma related to race and poverty suffer disproportionately from a host of hardships that contribute to psychological distress that can have a profound effect on mental health and serve as intrapsychic binds. These internalized weights require therapeutic supports to alleviate the internal oppressive circumstances by those that are immersed in the experience on a daily basis. This article explores the intersection of these psychological binds and their effect on human behavior.

Poverty in the United States is frequently considered to be influenced by the economic fluctuations and accompanying insecurity experienced by many in American society. With the dramatic changes and the "economic apartheid" that occurred after the "great recession" of 2008 and its lingering effects, individuals and families have experienced a myriad of stressors and multiple strains in their adjustment to the devastating impact of financial insecurity and the socioeconomic changes in the changing fiscal climate. Kochhar and Fry (2014) and Gould and Dastrup (2012) report that African American and Hispanic families were hardest hit by this recession. The U.S. Census Bureau stated that "in 2014, there was no statistically significant change from 2013 in either real median household income or the official poverty rate" (DeNavas-Walt, Proctor, & Smith, 2014, p. 1). An examination of the poverty statistics reveals that the rate of poverty among Blacks and Hispanics was well over 20%. These statistics reflect the reality that more people of color than White people live in poverty, as pointed out by Milner (2013). In citing Munin's (2012) poverty statistics, Milner (2013) suggests that Blacks and Hispanics make up a larger percentage of people in poverty than their overall proportion in the entire low-income population, which places Blacks and Hispanics at a double disadvantage of adverse intrapsychic effects from their experience of living in poverty. This article aims to advance an understanding of the effect of the milieu on the minds of individuals who experience the intersection of poverty and race.

Race and poverty are poignant factors in how individuals and communities experience the world. The experience of living with scarcity, as pointed out by Shah, Shafir, and Mullainathan (2015), "taxes the mind," and for people who are "mired in poverty, it captures and compromises the mind" (Feinberg, 2015, p. 19). The psychological responses and interpersonal issues embedded in the mind of individuals experiencing the brunt effects of poverty are fixed emotional processes in the intrapsyche of the individual. The contextualizing of the intrapsychic experience and intersubjective space is critical to the understanding of the dynamics between the internal and external psychological spaces. It also must be considered in collaboration with instinctual energies, which are greatly influenced by the environment. As Winnicott (1971, 2013) so astutely explained, for healthy development to ensue, an environment where one is able to feel aliveness safely is critical. Our clients experience the intersectionality of multicultural, multiethnic, multiracial, and economic circumstances. As the theory of intersectionality suggests, we interact in "relationships among multiple dimensions and modalities of social relationships and subject formations" (McCall, 2005, p. 1171). For McCall (2005), this intersectionality involves the acknowledgment that social relationships are complex, multiple, and intersected. McCall stresses that in our analysis of the "multiple" in intersectionality that we not focus solely on dimensions within categories but also on dimensions across categories. Davis (2008) defines *intersectionality* as "the interaction between gender, race, economics, and other categories of difference in individual lives, social practices, institutional arrangements, and cultural ideologies and the outcomes of these interactions in terms of power" (p. 68).

In this article, I suggest that intersectionality is useful in understanding the intrapsychic psychological binds and the social milieu. This focus expands and enriches our understanding of the client. In the practice of clinical social work, we bear witness to these complexities, and it is essential to factor this understanding into the practitioner's clinical perspective of the client's narrative and experiences, and consequently, it is essential to the development of a comprehensive understanding of the client and the client's lived experience. Use of the client's narrative can further illuminate the unresolved traumatic experiences associated with dimensions of poverty, the intrapsychic psychological binds, and the complexities of the intersection of the mind and milieu. It is clinically important to develop an informed appreciation for how clients experience the effect of poverty, of living on the economic margins, and the context of their vulnerable circumstances. These conditions can challenge their adaptive abilities, options, and overall outlook on life and are influenced by their internalized narrative of poverty. This narrative provides the necessary understanding of how the circumstances of poverty are personally experienced, which is critical for proper clinical assessment. It is a compelling framework for the helping process as it contextualizes the intrapsychic experience and the effect of this experience.

Poverty can devastate those who experience it. Its effects can be detrimental to mental well-being with the potential to create great difficulties and weaken and eventually sabotage individuals, families, and communities. Poverty is not only a form of deprivation but is also a form of alienation and isolation. It is a traumatic experience that not only affects the individual but also influences the community's mental well-being. In our work with clients, the clinical understanding of clients and the context of their lived experience is a perspective that cannot be overlooked, "poverty has an inextricable psychological impact on people which could be seen as an under emphasized dimension of poverty itself" (Maclay & Marsden, 2013, p. 694). Poverty and the association of mental health problems as a result of living in poverty are well documented. Studies indicate that those living in poverty experience the psychological distress of depression at a disproportionately high rate (Bruce, Takeuchi, & Leaf, 1991; Siefert, Bowman, Heflin, Danziger, & Williams, 2000). Psychological conditions of mood disorders such as anxiety and substance abuse are also associated with poverty (Zilberman, Tavares, Blume, & El-Guebaly, 2003), and anxiety (Brown & Moran, 1997; Miranda & Green, 1999). Trauma associated with poverty can manifest in depression, anxiety, and post-traumatic stress disorder (PTSD) (Vest, Catlin, Chen, & Brownson, 2002; Vogel & Marshall, 2001).

A range of traumatic experiences can be a part of the client's experiential narrative of living in poverty and have the potential to manifest in these conditions, such as living in neighborhoods where there are high rates of crime and community violence; being an eye witness to crime, or being in the physical proximity and vicinity of gunshots and violent crime, such as murders, and stabbing; interpersonal relationship violence; and sexual victimization (Bassuk, Buckner, Perloff, & Bassuk, 1998; Bausman & Goe, 2004; Belle, Doucet, Harris, Miller, & Tan, 2000; Cunradi, Caetano, & Schafer, 2002; Grote, Zuckoff, Swartz, Bledsoe, & Geibel, 2007; Vest et al., 2002). Many struggle on a daily basis with the acute and chronic daily stressors that accompany living with scarcity and/or inadequate resources, such as lack of transportation, discrimination, inability to pay bills, access to health care, insufficient resources to provide for children, hunger and food insecurity, unemployment, and unstable housing (Evans & English, 2002; Siefert, Heflin, Corcoran, & Williams, 2001).

To develop the clinical appreciation for how poverty affects the mind-set of the individual it is imperative that we listen to the highly personalized accounts of the effect of these experiences. Practitioners must also understand that these accounts are shaped by history and have become internalized in the intrapsyche of the client and can influence behavior. Winnicott (2013) understood the importance of physical presence, emotional attitude, environment, and the profound impact on intrapsychic organization (Abram, 2008). Winnicott (2013) placed a particular emphasis on how the interaction of individuals' environment affects their intrapsychic development. Winnicott purports that the external world makes an impression on the structure of the individual's internal world, and as a result, he brought to the fore the importance of the environmental effect on human development and the psychical organization of the individual. Winnicott (1971, 2013) explained that for healthy development to ensue, there must be an environment where the infant is able to feel this aliveness safely—a nest where his or her psyche and soma can be integrated into a unified sense of self (Abram, 2008).

Developmental theories and attachment theory suggest that with respect to social and emotional development, the strain of the experience of poverty fundamentally shapes the psychology of the individual and plays a role in the development of psychological distress. It also places the individual and child at a greater risk for the development of psychiatric disorders (Ainsworth, Blehar, Waters, & Wall, 1978; Avan & Kirkwood, 2010; Bowlby, 1982). Psychological distress resulting from economic hardship has been proposed as a factor in the relationship between poverty and parenting behaviors (Lempers, Clarke-Lempers, & Simons, 1989; McLoyd, 1990). McAdoo (1988) proposed that poverty creates stresses and frustrations that constrain parents from providing adequate care and disrupts the formation of emotional bonds. It has been suggested that adults living in poverty have often experienced adversity during their own childhood, which impairs their capacity to meet the needs of their children because of their own scarred developmental experiences, consequently leaving them unprepared and unable to meet the needs of their own children (Egeland, Jacobvitz, & Sroufe, 1988). McLeod and Nonnemaker (2000) suggest that African American children are more likely to live in persistent poverty. The effects of this experience and the accompanying stress and strain trickle down to the child and can become embedded intrapsychic memories of the child that are carried forward across the life span.

The role of the bidirectional interaction with the environment and the effect on the cognitive aspects of the individual have been emphasized by several theorists (e.g., Bronfenbrenner, 1999; Costello, Farmer, Angold, Burns, & Erkanli, 1997; Miller & Korenman, 1994). Strong research evidence demonstrates the multiplicity of chronic and acute stressors that face people living in poverty (Banyard, 1995; Evans & English, 2002; Mickelson & Kubzansky, 2003). Poverty is associated with a range of mental health problems (Fryers, Melzer, & Jenkins, 2003; Poole, Higgo, & Robinson, 2013; Sareen, Afifi, McMillan, & Asmundson, 2011; Siefert et al., 2000; Substance Abuse and Mental Health Services Administration, 2011; Wan, 2008). These disorders include depression (Siefert et al., 2000), PTSD (Vest et al., 2002; Vogel & Marshall, 2001), substance abuse (Zilberman et al., 2003), and anxiety (Miranda & Green, 1999). The correlation between sustained low income, poverty, and poor health has been well established. Groups whose incomes are low are disproportionately exposed to social and psychological conditions that have adverse effects that affect the individual's physical and psychological well-being (Geronimus, Bound, Waidmann, Hillemeier, & Burns, 1996; Haan, Kaplan, & Syme, 1989; Link & Phelan, 1996; Lynch, 1996). Physical and mental health can be affected directly through the effects of poverty, urbanicity, and inadequate housing and sanitation or indirectly through social factors such as threatening and socially chaotic environments, violent and disrupted neighborhoods, and the promotion of behavior and other psychosocial characteristics that can have deleterious effect on health (Lynch, Kaplan, & Salonen, 1997).

Research indicates that individuals living in poverty are more likely to be in poorer physical health and their psychological and cognitive functioning may be compromised, all factors that might benefit from medical intervention that most often is not received (Gallo & Matthews, 2003). An examination of the causal factors related to the chronicity of physical health and psychological issues indicates that these factors are connected to the many barriers to the access of care for the physical and psychological issues. These barriers to healthcare can include such factors as race, ethnicity, culture, acculturation, language, gender, physician availability, educational level, and the educational level of one's parents (Stiehm, 2001). Stiehm (2001)states that "these factors influence the likelihood of gaining entry into the healthcare system and the amount of services that will be received once entry is achieved" (p. 280). The perceived stigma associated with mental illness can be a barrier because it deters people from seeking treatment (Scholle, Haskett, Hanusa, Pincus, & Kupfer, 2003). There are "indirect economic barriers to healthcare such as the cost of taking time off from work to seek healthcare services, the distance to or between available healthcare providers and the availability of adequate transportation" (Stiehm, 2001, p. 280).

Case study #1

Ufomi is a 46-year-old African American male from New Orleans, Louisiana (the Lower Ninth Ward). His trade is food preparation; specifically, he was a chef at a federal building. Since 2005, Ufomi has had one quadruple heart bypass and has also been hospitalized for suicidal ideation twice since 2012. Given his health challenges and his displacement as a result of Hurricane Katrina, he has found himself in need of social service support for job placement. In his intake, he told his social worker that he feels like he is being shut down by the system that he helped to build. He said that in New Orleans, he escaped gun violence as a child and has buried a daughter and one grandchild from gun violence. He said he'd "lived the life so they didn't have to." He survived Katrina and moved to Utah after the storm and then chose to relocate to Washington, DC, for the benefits. He said that he has become isolated from his family because they do not understand that he feels stuck—even though he has been able to relocate. He believes, in contrast to his family members' opinion, he has witnessed disasters all of his life and he is tired of being his "own rescuer." Adding to this, he told the intake worker that he is not able find a good job even when he tries because

> people don't want to call me by my name, Ufomi. Nor, do they want to hire me because of my Adinrka symbol on my neck. They don't understand that I changed my name like the Panthers did in the 1960s because I felt like I was more than Jimmie Lee, Jr. I felt like Ufomi embodied where I wanted to push myself—past what I saw, I wanted to get away from the caged thoughts of the people in my neighborhood and do better. So I went to trade school. I got a good government job and worked for 10 years. Then I retired and Katrina happened. No, I have gone back to what I worked 10 years to escape. People don't want to see that. They see the tattoo on my neck, my age.... I'm a black man with locs and they assume that I have always been broke. They don't know that I just feel broken!

Questions for analysis

(1) How has Ufomi's lived experiences informed his self-concept? How does his demography situate how society views him? What is the praxis between his self-concept and the embedded narrative of trauma?
(2) Given the historical context of trauma, how do we illustrate how race and poverty are embedded in his personal narrative?
(3) What biological, psychological, physical, emotional, familiar, and racial factors contribute to his help seeking during the intake process?
(4) In what ways, if any, does the discourse of resilience permeate through the lens of his inter psyche, or does his admission of brokenness exacerbate his former social practice?

As with the intrapsychic binds of psychological development, race also has a significant intrapsychic effect on the individual. As suggested by Taylor, Henderson, and Jackson (1991), the experience of being of a particular race and being subjected to racism as well as the internalization of racism can affect one's mental well-being. For persons of color, "racism is a reality of everyday existence" (Brown, Keith, Jackson, & Gary, 2013, p. 83). The toxic experience of racism is overt and covert, and individuals are subjected to a range of "personal assaults, denials, and expulsions of opportunities, or it can consist of subtle and elusive personal injuries, slights, or rude behaviors" (Brown, Keith, Jackson, & Gary, 2013, p. 83). The relentless and chronic exposure to racism leaves indelible memories that not only have the potential to shackle the mind, but also because of the associated stress has a detrimental effect on physical and psychological health.

With respect to physical health, the experience of racism can lead to cardiovascular challenges, such as high blood pressure and cardiac reactivity. Epidemiological studies by Sutherland and Harrell (1986), James, LaCroix, Kleinbaum, and Strogatz (1984), and Krieger (1990) found that racism was positively related to high blood pressure. Kessler and Neighbors (1986) found that poor African Americans are more likely to experience psychological distress than Whites. In a study conducted by Williams and colleagues (1997), African Americans who experienced racism reported issues of difficulty with their psychological well-being. In citing Adams (1990) and Pierce (1995), Harrell (2000) states that "racism can traumatize, hurt, humiliate, enrage, confuse, and ultimately prevent optimal growth and functioning of individuals and communities" (p. 42). The effect of racism on persons of color includes what Lazarus and Folkman (1984) refer to as race-related transactions between "unique person-environment transactions involving race" (p. 44). It is this persistent experiential transaction that serves to have only detrimental effects and lodges in the intrapsyche of the individual.

Persons of color, and in particular African Americans, have experienced exposure either directly or indirectly to the unforgiveable crimes of racism—crimes of the dehumanizing institution of slavery, the oppression of the post-Jim Crow world, police brutality, and the excruciating effects of racism and segregation. These experiences, memories, and vicarious traumas experienced from the narratives associated with these emotionally injurious experiences are embedded in the psyches of African Americans and other persons of color. The detrimental psychological effects of these internalized events can serve to further oppress. Internalized oppression has been found to cause psychological and emotional pain that also correlates with health problems, domestic violence, depression, and PTSD (Gump, 2010; Lago, 2011; Walker, 2004; Williams, 2008; Wilson, 2009). African Americans who lived this traumatic history are vulnerable to having transmitted their trauma to subsequent generations (Bowers & Yehuda, 2016; Caruth, 2010; Yehuda et al., 2015). Transmission may come from the narrative process of the trauma or the observation of the traumatic reaction.

There is growing evidence suggesting that trauma symptoms and PTSD are inherited through genetic material (Yehuda et al., 2015). According to this research, trauma and stress cause genetic adaptations that are carried forward in the process of sexual reproduction. Support for this mechanism of transmission is the research that has demonstrated an association between preconception trauma and epigenetic alterations in trauma-exposed parents and their offspring in human samples (Yehuda et al., 2015). The research suggests that "stress-exposed parents may confer vulnerability via genetic risk factors, i.e., their offspring may inherit the same or similar genetic risks that have an impact on their own stress vulnerability" (Yehuda et al., 2015, p. 232). Genetic transmission can also occur causing "behavioral alterations stemming from the development of stress-related psychopathology" (Yehuda et al., 2015, p. 232). This scholarship suggests an intergenerational transmission of genetic vulnerability among African Americans to the trauma of slavery and its aftermath.

With the undergirding of the genetic vulnerability and the intrapsychic embedding of internalized experiences with racism, African Americans are predisposed to stress and physical, behavioral, and cognitive problems, as well as psychopathology. When experiencing the interpersonal forms of racism—the interactions between individuals and the interactions with the social milieu (systemic racism)—with the purposeful exclusion of access to the labor market and material symbolic resources within society (Berman & Paradies, 2010; Hamilton & Carmichael, 1967; Paradies, 2006), psychological and health-related responses that have long-term effects on well-being remain significant despite attenuation over time (Paradies et al., 2015).

Case #2

Darrin Patterson is an 87-year-old African American male from Hot Coffee, Mississippi. His parents were sharecroppers who lived to their mid-seventies and died of natural causes. His family's sharecropping turned into a family business in the 1950s. The income from the family farm was barely enough to provide for his 15 brothers and sisters. Because he is illiterate, his youngest sister managed the business side of the business for 40 years. They have worked past their retirement years, and the brother and sister business partners have decided to give their business to their grandchildren. Darrin's grandson, Pete, is a graduate in agricultural engineering from Tuskegee University. Pete agreed to take over the family business in an effort to honor his grandfather's wishes but has made several costly financial decisions that forced the business and Darrin into bankruptcy.

Darrin has never had one drink or smoked. As a Seventh-day Adventist, he believes in consistent exercise and adheres to a strict vegetarian lifestyle. He has recently been prescribed Lisinopril Oral, baby aspirin for stroke prevention, and efinaconizole because his health is declining.

Questions for analysis

(1) Given Darrin's upbringing in the post-Jim Crow south, how does the clinician process his journey from share cropper to business owner to bankruptcy?
(2) In what ways might the generational gap between Darrin and his grandson Pete situate historical traumas of race, education, and income?
(3) What biological, psychological, physical, emotional, familial, and racial factors contribute to Darrin's lack of coping mechanism related to his trauma?
(4) In what ways, if any, does the discourse of the generational shift permeate through the lens of Darrin's inter psyche as it relates to race and poverty? Is this the same for Pete?

Case #3

Idilin is a 15-year-old, female Indigenous American whose family lives on a reservation in Colorado. She aspires to be a computer engineer. Since age 10, two of her friends, Reign and Ryan (twins), have been placed in foster care. Reign and Ryan's parents have had domestic issues since as long as she can remember. She remembers her friends saying that her mother often cries at night and they "hear stuff banging often." Idilin is often worried for her friends' safety as well. She has recently been caught stealing alcohol and her mother has begun to explain that she should pray to the ancestors for direction and guidance. At 15, she has had two abortions but when asked, she says that she has never had a boyfriend. With probing, she told the counselor that she "goes to the truck stop of the reservation to make extra money to save for summer programs." Idilin is currently in her sixth day of in-patient psychiatric treatment and is a self-labeled "cutter."

Questions for analysis

(1) How has Idilin's lived experiences inform her self-concept? How do her age and demography situate how society views her? What is the praxis between her self-concept and the embedded narratives of trauma?
(2) Given the historical context of trauma, how does the clinician come to understand how race and poverty are embedded in her personal narrative?
(3) What biological, psychological, physical, emotional, familial, and racial factors contribute to her hospitalization?
(4) In what ways, if any, does the discourse of resilience apply to her inter psyche still in development?
(5) How do we avoid retraumatising this client in the therapeutic dyad?

Case # 4

Tashanna is 13-year-old African-American who lives in the Bronx, New York, with her four brothers and her father. Tashanna's mother died when giving birth to her youngest brother Tashanna was age 5. As a result, her father has worked three jobs to provide for the family. He served in the Afghanistan war and is a functional alcoholic. He drinks to cope with his PTSD and the loss of his wife. Tashanna is dating a boy who lives in her neighborhood, and he is pressuring her to have sex with him—all of her other friends have had sex. She does not think she is ready to have sex with him. Nor, does she want to risk getting pregnant. Her three older brothers each have multiple children, by different women. Tashanna thinks that getting pregnant may affect her ability to open a childcare facility for children in her neighborhood. She worries about sharing her aspirations with her family or friends because she is a below-average student in school and may possibly have to repeat the eighth grade. Her academic performance can largely be attributed to her undiagnosed dyslexia undiagnosed vision problems. She has always been socially anxious, but the pressure of underperforming in school and her worries about having sex with her boyfriend have caused her to develop stomach ulcers, chest pain, and patches of her hair to falling out.

Questions for analysis

(1) In what ways can the clinician help Tashanna become more empowered to make decisions about her current and future situations?
(2) In what ways have biological, psychological, physical, emotional, familial, and racial factors contributed to her health problems?
(3) How can she develop her sense of self and ability to make decisions that may seem countercultural?
(4) Given the historical context of trauma, how do we illustrate how race and poverty are embedded in her personal narrative?

Traditional psychotherapy, with its focus on the intrapsychic, has not addressed the condition of marginalized groups such as poor, ethnic minorities. This article aims to conceptually advance an understanding of the effect of the milieu on the mind of individuals who have the lived experience of poverty and race. In the clinical setting, clinicians must be mindful of the praxis of the preconception of trauma, the experience of trauma, and the aftermath of traumatic experience. In the dialogue with the client, the triad of these experiences and the residual effect of singular or multiple traumas become mitigated as the client tells their narrative. As the client processes these emotions and experiences, he or she becomes aware of the exchange of the systemic impact, the generational experiences, and the specific trauma that initiated psychotherapeutic intervention. This becomes the praxis of intersectionality as theory and lived experience. The cases presented problematize and illustrate where the narrative of trauma is couched between issues of segregation, social isolation, and embedded psychological responses that are carried through the lifespan of the individual based on experiences that are related to the unique person–environment transactions involving race and poverty.

The questions from the case studies guide the clinician to draw from the client's narrative anecdotal information that is embedded in the intrapsyche. This chronicle contextualizes the experience of the client and provides the necessary insight for the psychotherapeutic process of healing. The future implications of intrapsychic discovery and process will inform clinical technique in working with diverse populations that come from low-income and minority groups. It brings to light the convergence of theories of intersectionality with the lived experiences and the reality of the environments from which clients come.

Disclosure statement

No potential conflict of interest was reported by the author.

References

Abram, J. (2008). Donald Woods Winnicott (1896-1971): A brief introduction. *International Journal of Psychoanalysis, 89*, 1189-1217. doi:10.1111/j.1745-8315.2008.00088.x

Adams, P. L. (1990). Prejudice and exclusion as social traumata. In J. D. Noshpitz & R. D. Coddington (Eds.), *Stressors and the adjustment disorders* (pp. 362-391). New York, NY: John Wiley.

Ainsworth, M. D., Blehar, M. C., Waters, E., & Wall, S. (1978). *Patterns of attachment: A psychological study of the strange situation*. Hillsdale, NJ: Erlbaum.

Avan, B. I., & Kirkwood, B. I. (2010). Theory and methods: Review of the theoretical frameworks for the study of child development within public health and epidemiology. *Journal of Epidemiology and Community Health, 64*(5), 388-393. doi:10.1136/jech.2008.084046

Banyard, V. L. (1995). "Taking another route": Daily survival narratives from mothers who are homeless. *American Journal of Community Psychology, 23*(6), 871-891. doi:10.1007/BF02507019

Bassuk, E. L., Buckner, J. C., Perloff, J. N., & Bassuk, S. S. (1998). Prevalence of mental health and substance use disorders among homeless and low-income housed mothers. *American Journal of Psychiatry, 155*(11), 1561-1564. doi:10.1176/ajp.155.11.1561

Bausman, K., & Goe, W. R. (2004). An examination of the link between employment volatility and the spatial distribution of property crime rates. *American Journal of Economics and Sociology, 63*(3), 665-696. doi:10.1111/j.1536-7150.2004.00309.x

Belle, D., Doucet, J., Harris, J., Miller, J., & Tan, E. (2000). Who is rich? Who is happy?. *American Psychologist, 55*, 1160-1161. doi:10.1037/0003-066X.55.10.1160

Berman, G., & Paradies, Y. (2010). Racism, disadvantage and multiculturalism: Towards effective anti-racist praxis. *Ethnic & Racial Studies, 33*(2), 214-232. doi:10.1080/01419870802302272

Bowers, M. E., & Yehuda, R. (2016). Intergenerational transmission of stress in humans. *Neuropsychopharmacology, 41*(1), 232-244. doi:10.1038/npp.2015.247

Bowlby, J. (1982). *Attachment and loss: Vol. 1. Attachment* (2nd ed.). New York, NY: Basic Books. (Original work published 1969).

Bronfenbrenner, U. (1999). Environments in developmental perspective: Theoretical and operational models. In S. L. Friedman & T. D. Wachs (Eds.), *Measuring environment across the life span: Emerging methods and concepts*. Washington, DC: American Psychological Association.

Brown, D. R., Keith, V. M., Jackson, J. S., & Gary, L. E. (2013). (Dis)respected and (dis)regarded: Experiences of racism and psychological distress. In D. R. Brown & V. M. Keith (Eds.), *In and out of our right minds: The mental health of African American women*. (pp. 3-28) New York, NY: Columbia University Press.

Brown, G. W., & Moran, P. M. (1997). Single mothers, poverty and depression. *Psychological Medicine, 27*(1), 21-33. doi:10.1017/S0033291796004060

Bruce, M. L., Takeuchi, D. T., & Leaf, P. J. (1991). Poverty and psychiatric status: Longitudinal evidence from the new haven epidemiologic catchment area study. *Archives of General Psychiatry, 48*(5), 470-474. doi:10.1001/archpsyc.1991.01810290082015

Caruth, C. (2010). *Unclaimed experience: Trauma, narrative and history*. Baltimore, MD: Johns Hopkins University Press

Costello, E. J., Farmer, M. Z., Angold, A., Burns, B. J., & Erkanli, A. (1997). Psychiatric disorders among American Indian and White youth in Appalachia: The great smoky mountains study. *American Journal of Public Health, 87*, 827-832. doi:10.2105/AJPH.87.5.827

Cunradi, C., Caetano, R., & Schafer, J. (2002). Socioeconomic predictors of intimate partner violence among White, Black, and Hispanic couples in the United States. *Journal of Family Violence, 17*, 377-389. doi:10.1023/A:1020374617328

Davis, K. (2008). Intersectionality as buzzword: A sociology of science perspective on what makes a feminist theory successful. *Feminist Theory, 9*(1), 67-85. doi:10.1177/1464700108086364

DeNavas-Walt, C., Proctor, B. D., & Smith, J. C. (2014). *Income and poverty in the United States: 2013*. United States Census Bureau. https://www.census.gov/content/dam/Census/library/publications/2014/demo/p60-249.pdf

Egeland, B., Jacobvitz, D., & Sroufe, L. (1988). Breaking the cycle of abuse. *Child Development, 59*, 1080-1088. doi:10.2307/1130274

Evans, G. W., & English, K. (2002). The environment of poverty: Multiple stressor exposure, psychophysiological stress, and socioemotional adjustment. *Child Development, 73*, 1238-1248. doi:10.1111/1467-8624.00469

Feinberg, C. (2015). The Science of Scarcity: A behavioral economist's fresh perspective on poverty. *Harvard Magazine*. Retrieved from http://harvardmagazine.com/2015/09/

Fryers, T., Melzer, D., & Jenkins, R. (2003). Social inequalities and the common mental disorders. *Social Psychiatry and Psychiatric Epidemiology, 38*(5), 229-237. doi:10.1007/s00127-003-0599-2

Gallo, L. C., & Matthews, K. A. (2003). Understanding the association between socioeconomic status and physical health: Do negative emotions play a role? *Psychological Bulletin, 129*(1), 10. doi:10.1037/0033-2909.129.1.10

Geronimus, A. T., Bound, J., Waidmann, T. A., Hillemeier, M. M., & Burns, P. B. (1996). Excess mortality among blacks and whites in the United States. *New England Journal of Medicine, 335*, 1552-1558. doi:10.1056/NEJM199611213352102

Gould, E., & Dastrup, S. (2012). *Housing and the great recession.* Stanford, CA: Stanford Center on Poverty and Inequality.

Grote, N. K., Zuckoff, A., Swartz, H., Bledsoe, S. E., & Geibel, S. (2007). Engaging women who are depressed and economically disadvantaged in mental health treatment. *Social Work, 52*(4), 295-308. doi:10.1093/sw/52.4.295

Gump, J. (2010). Reality matters: The shadow of trauma on African-American subjectivity. *Psychoanalytic Psychology, 27*(1), 42-54. doi:10.1037/a0018639

Haan, M. N., Kaplan, G. A., & Syme, S. L. (1989). Socioeconomic status and health: Old observations and new thoughts. In J. P. Bunker, D. S. Gomby, & B. H. Kehrer (Eds.), *Pathways to health: The role of social factors* (pp. 76-135). Menlo Park, CA: Henry J. Kaiser Family Foundation.

Hamilton, C., & Carmichael, S. (1967). *Black power.* New York, NY: Random House.

Harrell, S. P. (2000). A multidimensional conceptualization of racism-related stress: Implications for the well-being of people of color. *American Journal of Orthopsychiatry, 70*(1), 42-57. doi:10.1037/h0087722

James, S. A., LaCroix, A. Z., Kleinbaum, D. G., & Strogatz, D. S. (1984). John Henryism and blood pressure differences among black men. II. The role of occupational stressors. *Journal of Behavioral Medicine, 7*(3), 259-275. doi:10.1007/BF00845359

Kessler, R. C., & Neighbors, H. W. (1986). A new perspective on the relationships among race, social class, and psychological distress. *Journal of Health and Social Behavior, 27*, 107-115. doi:10.2307/2136310

Kochhar, R., & Fry, R. (2014). *Wealth inequality has widened along racial, ethnic lines since the end of the Great Recession.* Washington, DC: Pew Research Center.

Krieger, N. (1990). Racial and gender discrimination: Risk factors for high blood pressure? *Social Science & Medicine, 30*(12), 1273-1281. doi:10.1016/0277-9536(90)90307-E

Lago, C. (2011). Diversity, oppression, and society: Implications for person-centered therapists. *Person-Centered & Experiential Psychotherapies, 10*(4), 235-247. doi:10.1080/14779757.2011.626621

Lazarus, R. S., & Folkman, S. (1984). *Stress, appraisal, and coping.* New York, NY: Springer.

Lempers, J., Clarke-Lempers, D., & Simons, R. (1989). Economic hardship, parenting, and distress in adolescence. *Child Development, 60*, 25-49. doi:10.2307/1131068

Link, B. G., & Phelan, J. C. (1996). Understanding sociodemographic differences in health—The role of fundamental social causes. *American Journal of Public Health, 86*(4), 471-473. doi:10.2105/AJPH.86.4.471

Lynch, J. W. (1996). Social position and health. *Annals of Epidemiology, 6*, 21-23.

Lynch, J. W., Kaplan, G. A., & Salonen, J. T. (1997). Why do poor people behave poorly? Variation in adult health behaviours and psychosocial characteristics by stages of the socioeconomic lifecourse. *Social Science and Medicine, 44*, 809-819. doi:10.1016/S0277-9536(96)00191-8

Maclay, C., & Marsden, H. (2013). Responding to the psychological context of extreme poverty: Using cash transfers to stimulate productive investment decisions in Bangladesh. *Social Indicators Research, 113*, 691-710. doi:10.1007/s11205-013-0296-9

McAdoo, H. P. (1988). *Black families* (2nd ed.). Newbury Park, CA: Sage.

McCall, L. (2005). The complexity of intersectionality. *Journal of Women in Culture and Society, 30*(3), 1771-1800. http://www.journals.uchicago.edu/doi/pdf/10.1086/426800

McLeod, J. D., & Nonnemaker, J. M. (2000). Poverty and child emotional and behavioral problems: Racial/ethnic differences in processes and effects. *Journal of Health and Social Behavior, 41*, 137-161. doi:10.2307/2676302

McLoyd, V. C. (1990). The impact of economic hardship on black families and children: Psychological distress, parenting and socioemotional development. *Child Development, 61*, 311-346. doi:10.2307/1131096

Mickelson, K. D., & Kubzansky, L. D. (2003). Social distribution of social support: The mediating role of life events. *American Journal of Community Psychology, 32*(3/4), 265-281. doi:10.1023/B:AJCP.0000004747.99099.7e

Miller, J. E., & Korenman, S. (1994). *Poverty dynamics and cognitive development among young children.* New Brunswick, NJ: Rutgers University, Institute for Health, Health Care Policy and Aging Research.

Milner, H. R. (2013). Analyzing poverty, learning, and teaching through a critical race theory lens. *Review of Research in Education, 37*(1), 1-53. doi:10.3102/0091732X12459720

Miranda, J., & Green, B. L. (1999). The need for mental health services research focusing on poor young women. *The Journal of Mental Health Policy and Economics, 2*(2), 73-80. doi:10.1002/(ISSN)1099-176X

Munin, A. (2012). *Color by number: Understanding racism through facts and stats on children.* Sterling, VA: Stylus.

Paradies, Y. (2006). Defining, conceptualizing and characterizing racism in health research. *Critical Public Health, 16*, (2), 143-157. doi:10.1080/09581590600828881

Paradies, Y., Ben, J., Denson, N., Elias, A., Priest, N., Pieterse, A., & … Gee, G. (2015). Racism as a determinant of health: A systematic review and meta-analysis. *Plos ONE, 10*(9), 1-48. doi:10.1371/journal.pone.0138511

Pierce, C. M. (1995). Stress analogs of racism and sexism: Terrorism, torture, and disaster. In C. V. Willie, P. P. Reiker, B. M. Kramer, & B. S. Brown (Eds.), *Mental health, racism and sexism* (pp. 277-293). Pittsburgh, PA: University of Pittsburgh Press.

Poole, R., Higgo, R., & Robinson, C. A. (2013). *Mental health and poverty*. Cambridge, UK: Cambridge University Press.

Sareen, J., Afifi, T. O., McMillan, K. A., & Asmundson, G. J. (2011). Relationship between household income and mental disorders: Findings from a population-based longitudinal study. *Archives of General Psychiatry, 68*(4), 419–427. doi:10.1001/archgenpsychiatry.2011.15

Scholle, S. H., Haskett, R. F., Hanusa, B. H., Pincus, H. A., & Kupfer, D. J. (2003). Addressing depression in obstetrics/gynecology practice. *General Hospital Psychiatry, 25*, 83–90.

Shah, A. K., Shafir, E., & Mullainathan, S. (2015). Scarcity frames value. *Psychological Science, 26*, 402–412. doi:10.1177/0956797614563958

Siefert, K., Bowman, P. J., Heflin, C. M., Danziger, S., & Williams, D. R. (2000). Social and environmental predictors of maternal depression in current and recent welfare recipients. *American Journal of Orthopsychiatry, 70*(4), 510–522. doi:10.1037/h0087688

Siefert, K., Heflin, C. M., Corcoran, M. E., & Williams, D. R. (2001). Food insufficiency and the physical and mental health of low-income women. *Women & Health, 32*(1/2), 159–177. doi:10.1300/J013v32n01_08

Stiehm, W. (2001). Poverty law: Access to healthcare and barriers to the poor. *Quinnipiac Health Law Journal, 4*, 279–310.

Substance Abuse and Mental Health Services Administration. (2011). *National survey on drug use and health: Summary of national findings*. Retrieved from http://www.samhsa.gov/data/sites/default/files/NSDUHNationalFindingsResults2010-web/2k10ResultsRev/NSDUHresultsRev2010.htm

Sutherland, M. E., & Harrell, J. P. (1986). Individual differences in physiological responses to fearful, racially noxious, and neutral imagery. *Imagination, Cognition and Personality, 6*(2), 133–150. doi:10.2190/BJVV-1KK5-ATGW-RUY8

Taylor, J., Henderson, D., & Jackson, B. B. (1991). A holistic model for understanding and predicting depressive symptoms in African-American women. *Journal of Community Psychology, 19*(4), 306–320. doi:10.1002/(ISSN)1520-6629

Vest, J., Catlin, T., Chen, J., & Brownson, R. (2002). Multistate analysis of factors associated with intimate partner violence. *American Journal of Preventive Medicine, 22*, 156–164. doi:10.1016/S0749-3797(01)00431-7

Vogel, L., & Marshall, L. L. (2001). PTSD symptoms and partner abuse: Low income women at risk. *Journal of Traumatic Stress, 14*(3), 569–584. doi:10.1023/A:1011116824613

Walker, C. (2004). Modernity in black: Dubois and the (re)construction of black identity in the souls of black folk. *Philosophia Africana, 7*(1), 83–93. doi:10.5840/philafricana20047114

Wan, K. W. (2008). Mental health and poverty. *Perspectives in Public Health, 128*(3), 108.

Williams, D. R., Yu, Y., Jackson, J. S., & Anderson, N. B. (1997). Racial differences in physical and mental health socio-economic status, stress and discrimination. *Journal of Health Psychology, 2*(3), 335–351. doi:10.1177/135910539700200305

Williams, K. U. (2008). *Exploring internalized racism: A critical review of the literature and implications for clinical social work* (Doctoral dissertation). scholarworks.smith.edu.

Wilson, W. (2009). *More than just race: Being black and poor in the inner city*. New York, NY: W.W. Norton.

Winnicott, D. W. (1971). *Playing and reality*. London, England: Routledge.

Winnicott, D. W. (2013). The use of an object in the context of Moses and Monotheism. In J. Abram (Ed.), *Donald Winnicott today* (pp. 293–301). London, England: Routledge.

Yehuda, R., Daskalakis, N. P., Bierer, L. M., Bader, H. N., Klengel, T., Holsboer, F., & Binder, E. B. (2015). Holocaust exposure induced intergenerational effects on FKBP5 methylation. *Biological Psychiatry*. [Online]. Retrieved from http://www.biologicalpsychiatryjournal.com/article/S0006-3223(15)00652-6/abstract

Zilberman, M. L., Tavares, H., Blume, S. B., & El-Guebaly, N. (2003). Substance use disorders: Sex differences and psychiatric comorbidities. *Canadian Journal of Psychiatry, 48*(1), 5–13. doi:10.1177/070674370304800103

Banging on a Locked Door: The Persistent Role of Racial Discrimination in the Workplace

Tracy R. Whitaker

ABSTRACT
Workplace discrimination continues to limit both the workforce participation and satisfaction of many Americans. Whereas many minority groups experience discrimination in the workplace, African Americans often experience the cumulative effects of multiple forms of discrimination. The levels of discrimination that African Americans face not only impede their ability to gain employment, but also negatively affect their career mobility. From traditional forms of discrimination based on race, gender, age and ability, to new forms of discrimination based on credit scores, appearance, criminal records and employment status, African Americans continue to disproportionately encounter structural barriers that restrict their participation in the workforce.

Racial discrimination continues to play a role in not only decreasing the enjoyment associated with the workplace, but also in decreasing the likelihood that some people will be able to enter the workforce at all. The prevalence and consequences of discrimination in the workplace are well documented; yet, there is also discrimination that is experienced prior to joining the workplace, referred to as preinterview discrimination, or preemployment discrimination (Ford, Gambino, Lee, Mayo, & Ferguson, 2004). Every stage of the employment process, including applying, interviewing, hiring, compensation, promotion, and termination, can be polluted by discrimination (Whitaker, Herbison, Rich, & Seiler, 2015). The employment application process itself is often marred by processes, stereotypes, prejudices, and biases that disadvantage minority populations in general, and specifically, African Americans (Bertrand & Mullainathan, 2004; Gaddis, 2015; Purnell, 2013). When compared to workplace discrimination, preemployment discrimination may have even more adverse consequences in that it can effectively restrict workforce participation. This article will examine some of the current preemployment discrimination practices that are being used to impede the participation of African Americans in the workforce.

The persistence of workplace discrimination

In 2015, the Equal Employment Opportunity Commission (EEOC) received 89,385 charges of employment-based discrimination (U.S. EEOC, n.d.). At a minimum, these statistics demonstrate that almost two decades into a new millennium almost 100,000 Americans are still confronted by unfair practices that limit their abilities to participate in the workforce at levels to which they aspire and deserve. The levels of discrimination that African Americans face not only impede their ability to gain employment, but also negatively affect their career mobility. When compared to Whites, African Americans earn significantly less money, tend to be unemployed at higher rates, and are more likely to work in occupations with lower status and pay (Bertrand & Mullainathan, 2004; Jones,

2009). They are also likely to report higher levels of employment discrimination in hiring and promotion and to assert that they did not receive the same opportunities that were available to other employees. (Khosrovani & Ward, 2011; Ortiz & Roscigno, 2009).

Gaddis (2015) found that "although a credential from an elite university results in more employer responses for all candidates, black candidates from elite universities only do as well as white candidates from less selective universities" (p. 1). In addition, Black graduates from elite universities are more likely to be offered jobs with less pay and status than their White counterparts (Gaddis, 2015). Again race proves to be the factor that cannot be equalized by education, skills, experience, ambition, or class.

Discrimination can impede career mobility, opportunities for organizational leadership, and workforce satisfaction and enjoyment (Whitaker et al., 2015). Discrimination can also undermine the stability of the employment experience, threatening much more than an individual's personal level of comfort for an 8-hour shift. In fact, families, communities, and the larger society are negatively affected when discrimination compromises the ability of African Americans to participate fairly and fully in the institution of work. However, African Americans are even more disadvantaged when they cannot enter the workforce due to biases that arrest their participation at the point of application. From historical forms of discrimination based on race, gender, age, and ability, to new forms of discrimination based on first names, criminal records, employment status, and employer bias, African Americans continue to disproportionately encounter barriers that effectively restrict their access to jobs.

First names

African Americans are frequently ridiculed and lambasted for the names they give their children (Nittle, 2015). Although within the sports and entertainment worlds, Black names with complex spellings and pronunciations are mastered by announcers and merchandisers alike, within the employment world, they can serve as a proxy to identify those who "need not apply." Uniquely African American names have been studied to test their relationships to crime and microaggressions in elementary school (Kalist & Lee, 2009; Kohli & Solórzano, 2012). Brown and Lively (2012) describe how "Black names" are closely linked to deficit-based perceptions of Black people and serve to create "academic, professional, social and cultural disadvantages for African Americans" (p. 668). The economic sphere can also be included in the list of consequences. It might be difficult for people to successfully argue that they did not receive fair consideration for a position based on their name, yet research and experience support these claims (Appiah, Bloom, & Yoshino, 2015; Bertrand & Mullainathan, 2004). Bertrand and Mullainathan (2004) found that applicants whose names were more readily identified with African Americans than applicants with White-sounding names consistently received less favorable responses to their resumes, despite having identical credentials and similar addresses.

A recent study found a pattern that when "Black names" were searched online, advertisements suggesting an arrest record were more likely to appear, as opposed to those ads not appearing when "White names" are searched. This pattern occurred whether there was an actual arrest associated with the name (Sweeney, 2013). The implication of a criminal record appearing for an African American applicant, though not appearing for potential competitors, presents a clear disadvantage that is hard to dispute.

This documented bias has led some African Americans to question whether they should use their real names, if those names could present an insurmountable barrier to the application process (Appiah et al., 2015). However, there is also a risk with a person using a pseudonym to apply for a job. If the application is successfully vetted and offered a position, at what point can the applicants safely "come clean" and reveal their true identity? Whether the revelation of the real name comes during the job interview or when completing the final paperwork for human resources, the applicant faces potential repercussions from having deceived his new employer.

Criminal records

High rates of arrest and incarceration, and subsequent criminal records, for African American men result in their disproportionate exclusion from the workforce (Paul-Emile, 2014; Purnell, 2013). Although Title VII of the Civil Rights Act of 1964 prohibits blanket discrimination based solely on a criminal record, many African American men cite their histories of conviction as major obstacles to finding employment (Wozniak, 2011). However, criminal records did not pose the same barriers for White men. In fact, White men with criminal histories were as likely to find jobs as Black men who did not have criminal records (Porter, 2006). According to Paul-Emile (2014), "the combination of a criminal record and minority status creates a distinctive and powerful social stigma that studies show is significantly more detrimental that minority or criminal record status alone" (p. 898). The lack of consideration for employment that African American men receive when they have arrest or criminal histories suggests that their punishment is ongoing and that their "debt" to society is essentially unpayable. Sometimes, an ex-offender's best option is to make his case personally with an employer. This option allows him to put a human face on a particular set of circumstances and to provide a rationale for past events and optimistic projections for present and future events. However, if ex-offenders are denied even the option to interview, they cannot begin to build a relationship with the employer, a circumstance that is particularly detrimental to African Americans with criminal histories (Purnell, 2013). For those who have been incarcerated, avoiding recidivism is a persistent challenge; one that is made more difficult by a lack of employment.

Employment status

Employment gaps and periods of unemployment can also damage African Americans' competitiveness in the labor market (Bias against hiring, 2011; Chen & Berman, 2011; Frauenheim, 2011). During the economic downturn of the last decade, many employers identified the best candidates as those who were already employed, neglecting to even consider those who were unemployed. The EEOC has expressed concern that this type of discrimination has a disparate impact on protected groups of people, especially African Americans (Bias against hiring, 2011; Frauenheim, 2011). When the lack of a job is a barrier to being considered for a job, that scenario leaves people with few options for entering the labor market.

Discrimination based on employment status causes particular hardships for women who are receiving Temporary Assistance to Needy Families (TANF) subsidies and for whom work is a requirement (Meara & Frank, 2006). Many of these women face multiple barriers to employment such as physical and mental health conditions, low levels of education, substance abuse, and domestic violence (Goldberg, 2002; Meara & Frank, 2006). In addition, TANF recipients are also likely to have been out of the workforce and to have limited work experience (Pilkinton, 2010). TANF recipients who are African American are also subject to the same discrimination facing other members of their racial communities (Danziger et al., 1999). However, TANF recipients with barriers to employment are more likely to lose their benefits because of sanctions related to program noncompliance (Goldberg, 2002; Meara & Frank, 2006). In this case, discrimination adds another barrier that can result in serious consequences for these women and their children.

Employer bias

Despite efforts to build workplaces that are diverse, the biases of those tasked with hiring decisions frequently stymie these good intentions. Too often, the limited life experiences of these gatekeepers inform their judgments about job applicants who are then included or excluded based on those judgments (Burrell, 2016). Employers may unconsciously want to surround themselves with people with whom they believe there is shared commonality and reject those who may make them feel uncomfortable (Turnbull, 2015). These unconscious biases lead people to assess applicants' qualifications differently, even when it is the same attribute (Burrell, 2016). For example, "nonwhites were rejected for being unassertive, but in whites, modesty was seen as a virtue" (Burrell, 2016, p. 72).

Rather than isolating one characteristic, complex bias results from several intersecting demographic characteristics, such as race, class, gender, and ability (Kotkin, 2009; Shaw, Chan, & McMahon, 2012; Weissinger, 2009). Many believe that these layered forms of discrimination rebut the notion of unconscious bias, contending instead that this form of discrimination is neither subtle nor unconscious (Graves, 2016; Kotkin, 2009). This type of bias, resulting from the accumulation of historical negative characterizations about some groups, is the growing basis of discrimination claims, but difficult to prove (Best, Edelman, Krieger, & Eliason, 2011; Kotkin, 2009).

Impact of preemployment discrimination

Discrimination has been associated with a range of disorders in African Americans, including hypertension, depression, anxious, sleep disturbances, fatigue, and bodily pain (Birzer & Smith-Mahdi, 2006; Burgess et al., 2009). Although the true impact of preemployment discrimination is not well known, it is likely to be more devastating than workplace discrimination. Preemployment discrimination is more difficult to recognize, and applicants who are repeatedly denied consideration are likely to identify the problem within themselves. Unlike workplace discrimination, where there are other people with whom the aggrieved worker can compare experiences, preemployment discrimination is experienced in isolation. Victims of preemployment discrimination do not know the basis of their denials for interviews and therefore are unable to make adjustments in either their resumes or their skills to become more competitive. The problem is simply that their help is unwanted. Additionally, unless they can identify a pattern with other applicants, targets of preemployment discrimination are not likely to be successful in seeking redress. With the flood of resumes that employers receive, it is no longer unusual for applicants to not receive a response at all when they are denied consideration. Many people wait for weeks or months before accepting that they are not going to get a call. People may experience this silent rejection again and again until they are no longer actively seeking employment. It may appear that they have dropped out of the labor market; when in fact, they were locked out.

Conclusion

Racial discrimination in the workplace is not new. However, outright discrimination practices based on a person's ethnic and racial identity have been joined by other, more insidious practices that are more difficult to identify and address, yet achieve the same result as their predecessors—the maintenance of workplaces that are segregated and stratified by race. The concern with preemployment racial discrimination is not that people who are unqualified are denied jobs. Rather, it is that African Americans, who deserve equal opportunities to be considered for and to compete fairly for employment, are too frequently denied these opportunities. Of particular concern is the powerlessness of African Americans affected by this discrimination to remediate their situations, or at least to remediate these situations honestly. Until there is widespread recognition that discrimination results in organizations that are less productive, desirable, and competitive, too many African Americans will continue to bang on the invisibly locked doors of the labor market.

Disclosure statement

No potential conflict of interest was reported by the author.

References

Appiah, K. W., Bloom, A., & Yoshino, K. (2015). Can I change my name to avoid discrimination? *New York Times Magazine*, pp. 17. Retrieved from https://www.nytimes.com/2015/05/17/magazine/can-i-change-my-name-to-avoid-discrimination.html

Bertrand, M., & Mullainathan, S. (2004). Are Emily and Greg more employable than Lakisha and Jamal? A field experiment on labor market discrimination. *American Economic Review*, *94*(4), 991–1013. doi:10.1257/0002828042002561

Best, R. K., Edelman, L. B., Krieger, L. H., & Eliason, S. R. (2011). Multiple disadvantages: An empirical test of intersectionality theory in EEO litigation. *Law & Society Review, 45*(4), 991–1025. doi:10.1111/j.1540-5893.2011.00463.x

Bias against hiring the unemployed is legally risky, counterproductive. (cover story). (2011). *HR Focus, 88*(10), 1–4. Retrieved from http://proxyhu.wrlc.org/login?url=http://search.ebscohost.com/login.aspx?direct=true&db=bth&AN=66179836&site=ehost-live

Birzer, M. L., & Smith-Mahdi, J. (2006). Does race matter? The phenomenology of discrimination experienced among African Americans. *Journal of African American Studies, 10*(2), 22–37. doi:10.1007/s12111-006-1001-8

Brown, A. F., & Lively, J. T. (2012). "Selling the farm to buy the cow": The narrativized consequences of "Black names" from within the African American community. *Journal of Black Studies, 43*(6), 667–692. doi:10.1177/0021934712441204

Burgess, D. J., Grill, J., Noorbaloochi, S., Griffin, J. M., Ricards, J., van Ryn, M., & Partin, M. R. (2009). The effect of perceived racial discrimination on bodily pain among older African American men. *Pain Medicine, 10*(8), 1341–1352. doi:10.1111/j.1526-4637.2009.00742.x

Burrell, L. (2016). We just can't handle diversity (cover story). *Harvard Business Review, 94*(7), 70–74. Retrieved from https://hbr.org/2016/07/we-just-cant-handle-diversity

Chen, V. L., & Berman, J. (2011). Companies are hiring. Just not you. *Bloomberg Businessweek* (4242), pp. 10–11. Retrieved from https://www.bloomberg.com/news/articles/2011-08-11/companies-are-hiring-dot-just-not-you

Danziger, S., Corcoran, M., Danziger, S., Heflin, C., Kalil, A., Levine, J., … Tolman, R. (1999). *Barriers to the employment of welfare recipients.* National Poverty Center. Institute for Research on Poverty. Ann Arbor, MI: University of Michigan.

Ford, T. E., Gambino, F., Lee, H., Mayo, E., & Ferguson, M. A. (2004). The role of accountability in suppressing managers' preinterview bias against African-American sales job applicants. *Journal of Personal Selling & Sales Management, 24*(2), 113–124. Retrieved from https://www.tandfonline.com/doi/abs/10.1080/08853134.2004.10749023

Frauenheim, E. D. (2011). Is there a bias against hiring the jobless? *Workforce Management, 90*(4), 10–11. Retrieved from http://proxyhu.wrlc.org/login?url=http://search.ebscohost.com/login.aspx?direct=true&db=bth&AN=59906027&site=ehost-live

Gaddis, S. M. (2015). Discrimination in the credential society: An audit study of race and college selectivity in the labor market. *Social Forces, 93*(4), 1451–1479. doi:10.1093/sf/sou111

Goldberg, H. (2002). *Improving TANF program outcomes for families with barriers to employment.* Center on Budget and Policy Priorities. Washington, DC: Center for Budget and Policy Priorities. doi:10.1044/1059-0889(2002/er01)

Graves, E. G. J. (2016). Unconscious bias or conscious bias? *Black Enterprise, 46*(9), 10. Retrieved from http://proxyhu.wrlc.org/login?url=http://search.ebscohost.com/login.aspx?direct=true&db=bth&AN=115708982&site=ehost-live

Jones, T. (2009). Race, economic class, and employment opportunity. *Law & Contemporary Problems, 72*(4), 57–87. Retrieved from https://scholarship.law.duke.edu/faculty_scholarship/2194/

Kalist, D. E., & Lee, D. Y. (2009). First names and crime: Does unpopularity spell trouble? *Social Science Quarterly (Wiley-Blackwell), 90*(1), 39–49. doi:10.1111/j.1540-6237.2009.00601.x

Khosrovani, M., & Ward, J. W. (2011). African Americans' perceptions of access to workplace opportunities: A survey of employees in Houston, Texas. *Journal of Cultural Diversity, 18*(4), 134–141. Retrieved from https://www.ncbi.nlm.nih.gov/pubmed/22288211

Kohli, R., & Solórzano, D. G. (2012). Teachers, please learn our names!: Racial microagressions and the K-12 classroom. *Race, Ethnicity & Education, 15*(4), 441–462. doi:10.1080/13613324.2012.674026

Kotkin, M. J. (2009). Diversity and discrimination: A look at complex bias. *William & Mary Law Review, 50*(5), 1439–1500. Retrieved from https://papers.ssrn.com/sol3/papers.cfm?abstract_id=1099327

Meara, E., & Frank, R. G. (2006). *Welfare reform, work requirements and employment barriers* (Working Paper 12480). Cambridge, MA: NBER (National Bureau of Economic Research).

Nittle, N. (2015, October 15). *Why people with black names face social bias.* Retrieved from about.com: acerelations.about.com/od/diversitymatters/fl/The-Controversy-Over-Black-Names.htm

Ortiz, S. Y., & Roscigno, V. J. (2009). Discrimination, women, and work: Processes and variations by race and class. *Sociological Quarterly, 50*(2), 336–359. doi:10.1111/j.1533-8525.2009.01143.x

Paul-Emile, K. (2014). Beyond Title IV: Rethinking race, ex-offender status, and employment discrimination in the information age. *Virginia Law Review, 100*(5), 893–952. Retrieved from http://www.virginialawreview.org/volumes/content/beyond-title-vii-rethinking-race-ex-offender-status-and-employment-discrimination

Pilkinton, M. (2010). TANF recipients' barriers to employability: Substance abuse and domestic violence. *Journal of Human Behavior in the Social Environment, 20*, 1011–1023. doi:10.1080/10911359.2010.494940

Porter, B. (2006). Black males locked out of jobs. *Black Enterprise, 36*(7), 44. Retrieved from http://proxyhu.wrlc.org/login?url=http://search.ebscohost.com/login.aspx?direct=true&db=aph&AN=19498057&site=ehost-live

Purnell, D. (2013). Examining disparate impact discrimination on ex-offenders of color across voting, government policy and aid receipt, employment, and housing. *Harvard Journal of African American Public Policy*, 1–15. Retrieved from https://www.questia.com/library/journal/1P3-3726794861/examining-disparate-impact-discrimination-on-ex-offenders

Shaw, L. R., Chan, F., & McMahon, B. T. (2012). Intersectionality and disability harassment: The interactive effects of disability, race, age, and gender. *Rehabilitation Counseling Bulletin, 55*(2), 82–91. doi:10.1177/0034355211431167

Sweeney, L. (2013). Discrimination in online ad delivery. *Communications of the ACM, 56*(5), 44–54. doi:10.1145/2447976.2447990

Turnbull, H. (2015). The affinity bias conundrum: The illusion of inclusion part III. *Profiles in Diversity Journal.* Retrieved from http://www.diversityjournal.com/13763-affinity-biasconundrum-illusion-inclusion-part-iii/

U.S. Equal Employment Opportunity Commission. (n.d.). *Charge statistics (National FY 1197 through FY 2015).* Washington, DC: Author. Retrieved from https://www.eeoc.gov/eeoc/statistics/enforcement/charges.cfm

Weissinger, S. E. (2009). Gender matters. So do race and class: Experiences of gendered racism on the Wal-Mart shop floor. *Humanity & Society, 33*(4), 341–362. doi:10.1177/016059760903300405

Whitaker, T., Herbison, B., Rich, K., & Seiler, R. (2015). Workplace discrimination. In *Social works speaks: National Association of Social Workers policy statements, 2015–2017* (10th ed.). Washington, DC: NASW Press.

Wozniak, A. (2011). Field perspectives on the causes of low employment among less skilled black men. *American Journal of Economics & Sociology, 70*(3), 811–844. doi:10.1111/j.1536-7150.2011.00791.x

Tilted Images: Media Coverage and the Use of Critical Race Theory to Examine Social Equity Disparities for Blacks and Other People of Color

Gracie Lawson-Borders

ABSTRACT
In the second decade of the 21st century societal advancements continue to fall short in closing the gap in social policies for Blacks and other people of color. From health to housing and education, people of color and low-income groups continue to struggle at a greater rate to receive services and support. Media coverage often reflects these disparities, particularly in urban communities. This analysis uses Critical Race Theory (CRT) as a theoretical tool to analyze the 2016 report Racism's Toll: Report on Illinois Poverty to illustrate the challenges faced in addressing social issues and how they are covered in the media. CRT provides a prism through which to examine coverage of health, housing, and education disparities and provides a context for understanding and seeking ways to change disparities in social policies and programs.

Introduction

In the second decade of the 21st century there are certain elements of social, cultural, and political changes that have a familiar sound. Many African Americans, other people of color, and low-income groups often struggle to receive basic or comparable housing, education, employment, and other needs. This trend dates historically to laws and policies that institutionalized inequities that negatively affect people of color. For example, during Reconstruction, power brokers in the South pushed back against the hard-fought battles of the Civil War. We saw the rise of a de facto separation of people that resulted in institutionalized Jim Crow laws in the former Confederate states of the South. Jim Crow by another name—overt and covert discrimination—such as housing covenants also creeped into the social milieu in Northern states that often held discriminatory practices in housing and education (Orfield, Ee, Frankenberg, & Siegel-Hawley, 2016). The nation's capital is also illustrative of these practices with Black Codes in the 1840s that prohibited free Black people from "operating eating establishments and taverns … " and denied them "licenses for any trade other than driving carts or carriages" (Kijakazi et al., 2016, p. viii). Free Blacks in that period started societal movement barred by legal and systemic processed that constructed barriers to success. Their public voice was silenced by poll taxes in many Southern states that sought to suppress the Black vote, and similar behavior spilled over into communities in the North. The 1964 Civil Rights Act fell short, even though it should have leveled the playing field. It was designed to make discrimination illegal in the use of public facilities and in employment practices in the labor force. Additionally, the 1965 Voting Rights Act, which removed barriers for Blacks to vote, did not curtail entrenched behavior in many places across the country. These two pieces of federal legislation came on the heels of the 1955

Brown v. Board of Education case, which ended the separate but equal fallacy in education institutions across the country. However, the results of these historical legal actions were not completely realized or were often dependent on the geographic location, the school district, the state, and even at certain periods of time in history. As recently as 2016, schools in Cleveland, Mississippi, were ordered by a federal court to end segregation more than 60 years after *Brown* (Bendix, 2017). Historical practices have set the tone for where many people of color find their lives situated today. This article analyzed the 2016 report, *Racism's Toll: Report on Illinois Poverty*, which posits four key premises that impact people of color:

> First, public policies often legalized racist practices. Other times they were less overt, serving to encourage, tolerate, or ignore racist practices. The result, though, is the same: great opportunity for whites to get ahead and great barriers for people of color.
>
> Second, this isn't merely a reflection on government policies of the past; recent public and private policies and practices carry the legacies of their predecessors, if not in overt intent then in impact, leading to that same end result: great opportunity for whites to get ahead and great barriers for people of color.
>
> Third, hundreds of years of institutionalized opportunities for white Americans and hundreds of years of institutionalized barriers for people of color have compounding effects over many generations. The average person in America today is not self-made, no matter how ingrained that national narrative is. We are all products of our family trees, and our family trees were (and continue to be) either fertilized or poisoned by policy... .
>
> Fourth, the scars from the sanctioned practice of redlining in the mid-20th century—refusing to make mortgage loans in non-white communities—are clearly still visible today in communities all across the country. Combined with ongoing housing discrimination and lack of investment in lower income neighborhoods, the result is that place matters greatly for life outcomes... . (Terpstra & Rynell, 2016, p. 13)

Figure 1 illustrates how economic changes in one area, such as rent increases, does not meet the needs of all residents when the cost is not affordable.

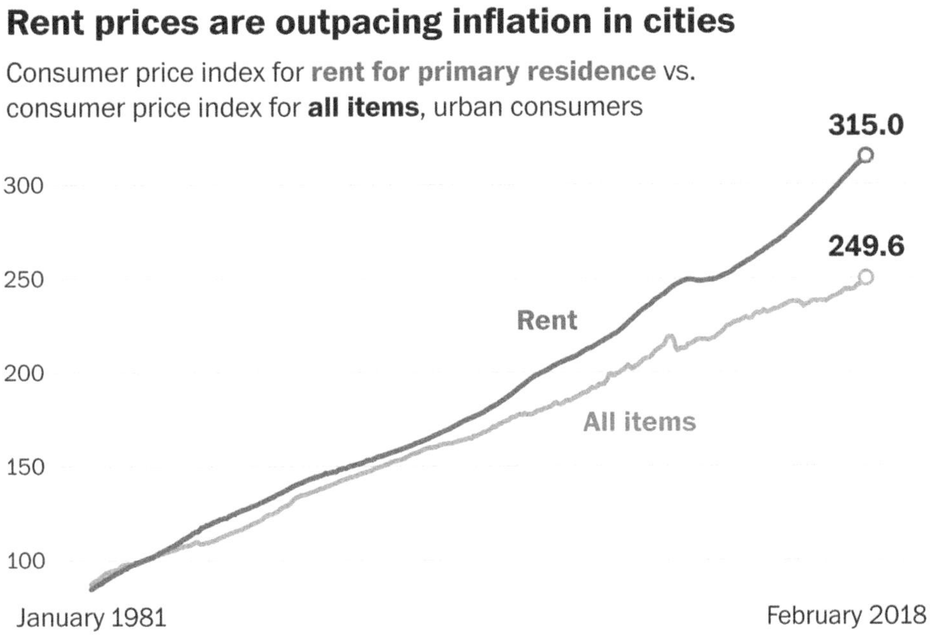

Figure 1. Rent prices are outplcing inflation in cities across the country.
Retrieved from https://www.washingtonpost.com/news/wonk/wp/2018/04/06/how-12-experts-would-end-inequality-if-they-ran-america/?utm_term=.f95ff581e65c#section1

This analysis uses Critical Race Theory (CRT) as a theoretical tool to analyze the 2016 report *Racism's Toll* to illustrate the challenges found in addressing disparities in social issues and the tilted depictions in media coverage. Through a combination of historical exigencies and current practices that marginalize people by race, ethnicity, and socioeconomic status, many people are stunted before they have an opportunity to develop. If you are not privy to the right schools, neighborhoods, and economic support, some challenges are magnified when efforts are made to progress to college, good jobs, home ownership, and other social enhancements:

> On average, a child born in a community of color and a child born in a white community on the very same day will have vastly different community resources at their disposal to help them reach their potential. From the quality of the schools, to the safety of the parks, to the availability of good jobs, to the accessibility of transportation options, the ongoing legacy of housing segregation even today gives more advantages to white children while throwing more roadblocks in the path of children of color. (Terpstra & Rynell, 2016, p. 13)

Nature or nurture and everything in between matters for the health and success of individuals in society. Critical Race Theory (CRT) is used to contextualize the continued role that race plays in the lives of African Americans and other people of color who are not often privileged by mainstream educational, cultural, political, and economic opportunities. CRT provides a prism through which to examine issues of health, housing, and education disparities. The 2016 report *Racism's Toll* is analyzed to provide context on the consequences of certain laws, policies, and programs and what alternatives can be presented to help improve lives and the human condition. The research on media coverage of poverty and race, as well as analysis of the 2016 study, reflect the ongoing challenges of disparities in society's economic echo system.

Media Coverage

Research and scholarship over the past decades reflect varying perspectives on the impact of social disparities for African Americans and people of color. The research and reports on media representations of poverty, race, and other social issues run the gamut, often with distorted depictions at different points in time for Blacks and other people of color. In 1996 when former President Bill Clinton signed sweeping welfare reform policy in the country, "Welfare reform was high on the nation's agenda," and African Americans were often depicted as abusers of the system (Clawson & Trice, 2000, p. 53). Media coverage of race, class, and poverty are not mutually exclusive. News reports are often intertwined with a mixture of findings that conflate causes of poverty and the impact of race, class, and poverty on people in society (Clawson & Trice, 2000; Gilens, 1996; Golding & Middleton, 1982; Martindale, 1996; Rose & Baumgartner, 2013).

When media coverage portrays titled images of poverty, it can have the potential to influence or change support for people in need. If coverage of race and poverty casts African Americans as the majority of the nation's poor and benefactors of welfare and other social programs, it can create a negative public reaction (Gilens, 1996). However, U.S. Census data continue to show as recently as 2018 that African Americans are only 13.4% of the U.S. population and cannot statistically be the largest poverty group in the country: White, non-Hispanic is 60.7%, Hispanic 18.1%, Asian 5.8%, and American Indian/Alaska Native 1.3% (U.S. Census.gov Quick Facts, 2018). Media portrayals of poverty can influence public policy if news coverage characterizes stories with a need to support the less fortunate versus distorted reports of abuse of social and government policies (Rose & Baumgartner, 2013). Rose and Baumgartner conducted a study on how media framed poverty from 1960 to 2008. They found changes in public policy and support from President's Lyndon Johnson's War on Poverty to current times. The report found that media coverage shifted from addressing causes of poverty to complaints about welfare programs and representations of the poor as less than favorable, which impacted public policy and support for government programs (Rose & Baumgartner, 2013).

A study in 2000 that examined photos in news magazine stories for five years from 1993 to 1998 found that Blacks were disproportionately portrayed as the face of poverty (Clawson & Trice, 2000). The study built off the work in an earlier study by Martin Gilens in 1996 with similar results of photos specifically showing Blacks in various negative portraits of poverty—for example, crime, welfare, and poor neighborhoods. Clawson and Trice found that the five magazines examined— *Business Week, Newsweek, New York Times Magazine, Time,* and *U.S. News & World Report*— exaggerated the role of Blacks and poverty. The images made it appear that "Blacks were 49% of the poor" in contrast to the 1996 Current Population Survey that showed "African Americans making up 27 percent of the poor" (Clawson & Trice, 2000, p. 56). They found that the five magazines surveyed showed:

> ... blacks were disproportionately portrayed among magazine portrayals of the poor between 1993 and 1998. Blacks were especially overrepresented in negative stories on poverty and in those instances when the poor were presented with stereotypical traits. In addition, the "deserving," poor were underrepresented in the magazines. Overall, the photographic images of poor people in these five magazines do not capture the reality of poverty; instead, they provide a stereotypical and inaccurate picture of poverty which results in negative beliefs about the poor, antipathy toward blacks, and a lack of support for welfare programs. (2000, p. 62)

A contemporary example of policy changes is media coverage that President Donald Trump's administration is reviewing changes to the social welfare netthat would shift social support programs such as the SNAP program for food supplement to the poor and working class to merging departments such as the U.S. Education and the Labor Departments (Thrush & Green, 2018). The reaction, both supportive and nonsupportive, is reflected in the diametrically opposed responses to poverty and public policy:

> Supportive—The core of Mr. Trump's safety net policy is an expansion of work requirements to foster self-sufficiency among recipients of food assistance, Medicaid and housing subsidies to reduce dependence on the government. "Our goal is to get people on the path to self-sufficiency," according to Andrew Bremberg, director of the Domestic Policy Council.
>
> Non-supportive—It's a war on the poor, pure and simple, according to president of the NAACP Legal Defense Fund... . (Thrush & Green, 2018, par 33 and par. 36)

The picture for economic, health, education, and other disparities continues to receive media coverage focused on challenges with some coverage on solutions (Stein, 2018):

> It is no small task: The 100 richest Americans control more wealth than the poorest 80 million households, and as the richest citizens continue to capture the lion's share of new wealth—the top 5 percent has captured 74 percent of the wealth created in this country since 1982—the situation is only growing more extreme. (p. G1)

If the rich keep getting richer and the poor get poorer, the United States will not readily close the disparity gaps for many of its citizens. Reports on seven policy expert opinions to address economic inequality suggest everything from the fact that housing costs are too high for the poor to increasing spending on early childhood education and care; to shipping the one percent wealthiest to other countries; to the expansion of Social Security suggested by the director of the program on race, ethnicity, and the economy at the Economic Policy Institute (Stein, 2018).

Critical Race Theory

Critical Race Theory (CRT) origins are in legal studies in which it examines race and racism's continued impact on society, particularly after the Civil Rights Movement (Harris, 2012). Legal scholars Derrick Bell, a former Harvard Law professor, and Alan Freeman were foundational in the start of CRT studies (Delgado, 2005; Delgado & Stefancic, 1993). Criticism of CRT often centers on Bell's assertions that race is a central discussion in the United States from law to politics and social concerns (Delgado, 2005). Ensuing research by numerous scholars have focused a lens on racism and its impact through laws and the court, where racism can sometimes be perpetuated by the legal process in which justice is arguably supposed to be blind. "Critical race theorists attempt to show how contemporary law—including contemporary antidiscrimination law—paradoxically accommodates and even facilitates racism" (Harris, 2012, p. 2). This is a recurring theme in CRT research. Harris's (2012) work on CRT points to themes and issues that legal studies sought to elucidate on whether implicit bias; unconscious or unintentional racism; or structural racism in which structures are in place through laws, policies, and programs continue to limit improvements for Blacks and others in different aspects of society. CRT research has traversed disciplines and areas such as epistemological questions and structural issues in the legal system such as mass incarceration addressed by legal scholar Michelle Alexander. The research also looks at the Black and White paradigm; personal narratives; implicit bias theory, LatCrit, or Latina/o Critical Theory; and racism's connection to oppression of other groups by class, gender or sexuality, language, and cultural issues (Harris, 2012; Patton, 2016; Sonn & Quayle, 2013; Yosso, 2005). Ladson-Billings and Tate (1995) used CRT to examine racial issues in education followed by several education scholars such as the work of Howard and Navarro (2016), which examined 20 years of CRT scholarship in education.

CRT's grounding in legal scholarship identified some important elements of the research that are still operationalized in the use of prominent themes in CRT research found in an annotated bibliography in the *Virginia Law Review* (Delgado & Stefancic, 1993). Their work identified 10 prominent themes in CRT research that continue to resonate in contemporary CRT scholarship across disciplines from education to media studies. Table 1 lists the research themes identified by (Delgado & Stefancic, 1993) that were a part of CRT research for more than 20 years that are applicable to analysis in this article.

The thematic approaches relevant to this article include Themes 1, 2, 3, 4, 5, and 7, with deference to research that focuses on Theme 1: Critique of Liberalism; Theme 3: Revisionist Interpretation of American Civil Rights Law and Progress; Theme 4: A Greater Understanding of the Underpinnings of Race and Racism; and Theme 5: Structural Determinism. The inequities that many Blacks, Latinos, and other groups encounter often result from different views on the way civil rights laws would benefit all or from negating the impact of race and racism on so many lives in the past and present.

Racism's Toll: Report on Illinois Poverty

Laws and Policies That Create a Legacy of Inequities

The 2016 Illinois report can be viewed as a road map to many of the social issues faced on a national scale. The critical report, sponsored by the Social Impact Research Center part of the Heartland Alliance, focused on some of the profound issues faced in the state of Illinois, from poverty to a legacy of inequities on state and national levels and quality of life issues. Terpstra and Rynell (2016) anchor the report on structural racism's toll with a historical synopsis of laws and policies that have contributed to inequities in education, housing, health, and employment, among other social issues. They argue that the legacy of inequities are imbedded and real:

> The long arc of our nation's history shows how the people in power at any given time—white Americans—crafted policies that were routinely designed to advance their own wealth and well-being. From land ownership to education to housing to transportation policy and everything in between, white Americans handed themselves the tools to realize their potential and get ahead.

> At best, these policy-induced advantages excluded people of color, but at worst they catalyzed a vicious cycle of deprivation, stripping them of their freedom, lands, safety, cultural practices, and dignity, and ensuring they were worse off than before. (p. 13)

Such laws and policies have occurred for centuries, and a few are used here to illustrate arguments central to Critical Race Theory (CRT) that racism is more often normalized in contemporary society

Table 1. Critical Race Theory (CRT) Research Themes.

Theme 1: Critique of liberalism	Most, if not all, CRT writers are discontent with liberalism as a means of addressing the American race problem. Sometimes this discontent is only implicit in an article's structure or focus. At other times, the author takes as his or her target a mainstay of liberal jurisprudence such as affirmative action, neutrality, color blindness, role modeling, or the merit principle.
Theme 2: Storytelling and counterstorytelling and "naming one's own reality"	Many Critical Race theorists consider that a principal obstacle to racial reform is majoritarian mind-set—the bundle of presuppositions, received wisdoms, and shared cultural understandings persons in the dominant group bring to discussions of race.
Theme 3: Revisionist interpretation of American civil rights law and progress	One recurring source of concern for Critical scholars is why American antidiscrimination law has proven so ineffective in redressing racial inequality—or why progress has been cyclical, consisting of alternating periods of advance followed by ones of retrenchment. Some Critical scholars address this question, seeking answers in the psychology of race, White self-interest, the politics of colonialism and anticolonialism, or other sources.
Theme 4: A greater understanding of the underpinnings of race and racism	A number of Critical writers seek to apply insights from social science writing on race and racism to legal problems. For example: understanding how majoritarian society sees Black sexuality helps explain law's treatment of interracial sex, marriage, and adoption; knowing how different settings encourage or discourage discrimination helps us decide whether the movement toward Alternative Dispute Resolution is likely to help or hurt disempowered disputants.
Theme 5: Structural determinism	A number of CRT writers focus on ways in which the structure of legal thought or culture influences its content, frequently in a status quo-maintaining direction. Once these constraints are understood, we may free ourselves to work more effectively for racial and other types of reform.
Theme 6: Race, sex, class, and their intersections	Other scholars explore the intersections of race, sex, and class, pursuing such questions as whether race and class are separate disadvantaging factors, or the extent to which Black women's interest is or is not adequately represented in the contemporary women's movement.
Theme 7: Essentialism and anti-essentialism	Scholars who write about these issues are concerned with the appropriate unit for analysis: Is the Black community one, or many, communities? Do middle- and working-class African Americans have different interests and needs? Do all oppressed peoples have something in common?
Theme 8: Cultural nationalism/separatism	An emerging strain within CRT holds that people of color can best promote their interest through separation from the American mainstream. Some believe that preserving diversity and separateness will benefit all, not just groups of color. We include here, as well, articles encouraging Black nationalism, power, or insurrection.
Theme 9: Legal institutions, Critical pedagogy, and the bar	Women and scholars of color have long been concerned about representation in law school and the bar. Recently, a number of authors have begun to search for new approaches to these questions and to develop an alternative, Critical pedagogy.
Theme 10: Criticism and self-criticisms; response	Under this heading we include works of significant criticism addressed at CRT, either by outsiders or persons within the movement, together with responses to such criticism.

Source: Delgado and Stefancic (1993).

(Harris, 2012). Despite advances after *Brown* in 1955, the 1964 Civil Right Acts, and the 1965 Voting Rights Act, the laws did not curtail some of the social inequities embedded in the fabric of American society.

Terpstra and Rynell argue that many of the nation's laws and policies are "rooted in land or housing policy," which influences so many issues impacting the well-being of individuals in their communities (2016, p. 14.) The disparities date to 1619 when the first 20 Africans arrived in Jamestown, Virginia, in those early trappings of indentured life. This was followed by the institution of slavery in the United States, which lasted until 1865. The outcry against human bondage centuries ago was the foundation of the modern civil rights movement of the mid-20th century. Little contemporary discussion centers on the 1790 Naturalization Act, but it is this law that established the following policy:

"Free white persons" of "good character" living in the U.S. for 2 years were eligible for citizenship, while also stating that all Native Americans, Free Blacks, and any woman whose father had not been a citizen were ineligible for citizenship. (Terpstra & Rynell, 2016, p. 14)

Citizenship translated into the ability to buy property and protection through the laws of the land. Table 1 illustrates 10 themes in CRT research, and two of the research themes—Themes 3 and 4, revisionist interpretations of civil rights law and an understanding of race and racism—are pertinent to what might have been possible if the 1938 Fair Labors Standard Act, 1934 National Housing Act, and the 1944 Serviceman's Readjustment Act (the GI Bill) had not fallen to racial bias and discrimination. More people of color should have been allowed to take full advantage of these laws, and perhaps the lives and legacies of some Blacks and others would have been different. The Fair Labor Act set the tone for workplace laws that exist today, such as minimum wage, work hours, child labor laws, and benefits. However, then as now, many people were not protected under the law:

… Generations of mostly immigrant farm workers and black Americans have been unable to receive the same benefits and protections others get, are at risk of myriad exploitations, and continue to be at a disadvantage in building financial security and securing assets. (Terpstra & Rynell, 2016, p. 15)

Housing

Discussions on housing disparities are influenced by the underpinnings of the 1934 National Housing Act and GI Bill, even if they are not identified as linked to contemporary housing issues. For example, the Housing Act was designed to assist in homeownership, home loans, and insurance. The Federal Housing Administration (FHA) created so-called residential security maps to identify areas at risk for investment. "Black neighborhoods were marked red on maps to indicate they were unsafe and thus ineligible for financing. Many private lenders also adopted the practice of redlining in an effort to comply with FHA underwriting rules," (Terpstra & Rynell, 2016, p. 15). Redlining created discriminatory home loan practices by financial institutions that resulted in everything from class-action lawsuits to Pulitzer Prizes won by journalists who produced news stories that identified redlining practices for home loans. These practices left Blacks, Latinos, and others with the inability to obtain financing, or they were faced with exorbitant interest rates, which affected the ability to realize part of the American dream—home ownership. The practice of redlining was outlawed in 1968, but its vestiges continue in some places today:

Redlining is considered one of the most substantial contributors to today's vast racial wealth differences, because it resulted in the denial of fair home mortgages to millions of families of color and thus denied these families the opportunity to accumulate equity to pass down as wealth to future generations. (Terpstra & Rynell, 2016, p. 15)

The GI Bill offered hope after WWII of a better opportunity for servicemen through education and housing support. Again, few Blacks and other people of color who served in the world's most wrenching war could not benefit from the opportunities provided by the federal policy. "On paper, the GI Bill was for all veterans; in practice, with redlining and Jim Crow laws in full effect, veterans of color were systematically prevented from taking advantage of the GI Bill programs," (Terpstra & Rynell, 2016, p. 15). Education opportunities were thwarted because "while white universities benefited from the influx of funding that the GI Bill provided, they were not required to adopt a policy of desegregation" (Terpstra & Rynell, 2016, p. 15). CRT research addresses racism and inequities that appear in education, housing, and health that, whether advertent or inadvertent, occurred through federal laws and policies that impact the success of people of color today (Patton, 2016; Stovall, 2016).

Terpstra and Rynell (2016) examine how laws in the 20th and 21st centuries have also had an adverse effect on the lives of Blacks and people of color. One stands out significantly: the 1986 Anti-

Drug Act, which set minimum sentencing for drug offenses. Its requirements have led to mass incarceration of Blacks and Latinos for minor drug infractions compared to Whites:

> Because of its relatively low cost, crack cocaine was more available to lower-income people who are disproportionately people of color. Conversely, powder cocaine is more expensive, and therefore tended to be used by those who are wealthy—and who are predominately white... . Congress continued to pass harsh mandatory minimum sentences for crack cocaine, making crack cocaine the only drug with a mandatory minimum penalty for a first offense of simple possession. As a result, the prison population boomed, with people of color disproportionately represented in dramatic numbers. (2016, p. 16)

Legal scholar Michelle Alexander's 2012 seminal book, *The New Jim Crow: Mass Incarceration in the Age of Colorblindness*, discussed in depth the insidiousness of the Anti-Drug Act on the lives of Blacks and other people of color. The people impacted were incarcerated with long sentences often for minor drug infractions such as possession, affecting their families and ability to fully participate in society.

Quality of Life Across a Spectrum

The 2016 Illinois report describes how racism's toll impacts the social welfare of citizens in the state. Issued faced in Illinois with 12.5 million citizens can be viewed as a sample of what occurs in other states in the United States. The 2016 poverty rate in Illinois

> "white 9.3%, black 30.6% and Latino 19.9%" reflect glaring differences across racial and ethnic groups (Terpstra & Rynell, 2016, p. 26). Other state data points to similar discrepancies in areas such as the unemployment rate at "5.9% white, 14.4% black, 8.1% Latino" and food insecurity has similar dismal numbers at "10.5% white, 26.1% black, 22.4% Latino," and rent burden rates are just as troublesome with "20% white, 35% black, 24% Latino." (Terpstra & Rynell, 2016, p. 26)

The number of Blacks and Latinos are often double that of Whites in poverty levels, lack of food security, and carrying the burden of paying a large percentage of their income on rental costs for housing. Delgado and Stefancic's (1993) findings on CRT research in Table 1 on Themes 2, 3, and 4 from storytelling narratives to revisionist interpretations and an understanding of the underpinnings of race and racism are pertinent to the quality of life issues Illinoisans face in the 2016 report. Arguments from scholars around these themes point to racism's continued influence on inequities across a spectrum of life needs.

Housing inequities identified in the Illinois report are often indicative of a similar impact across the country. In Illinois college graduation rates for students of color in state public universities are "18 percentage points lower than the rate for white students," and it starts early with state school districts in which "most students of color receive 16% less in funding per student than districts serving the fewest students of color" (Terpstra & Rynell, 2016, p. 28). The housing challenges do not fare well for Blacks and Latinos compared to Whites in Illinois. The data point to ongoing challenges for Blacks and others in housing:

> Homeownership rates in Illinois [are] 74% white, 38% black, 51% Latino... . The share of poor population living within 1 mile of a hazardous chemical facility in Illinois [is] 13% white, 16% black, 22% Latino... . Mortgage loan application denial rates in the Chicago region [are] 15% white, 34% black, 27% Latino... . In Illinois distressed housing neighborhoods, 51% of residents are of color. In neighborhoods that are not distressed, only 33% of residents are of color. (Terpstra & Rynell, 2016, p. 29)

Such examples from the list of disparities illuminates the myriad of issues people of color face in Illinois. CRT research points to the persistence of these inequities despite progress in laws and policies. Support for Blacks and other people of color continues to fall short in more instances than not, whether in housing, education, or health (Alemán & Alemán, 2016; Chapman, 2013).

Employment and Health

Similar patterns of disparities are apparent in employment and health areas in Illinois. "Financial security is essential to human dignity and is the backbone of a strong state and nation" (Terpstra & Rynell, 2016, p. 27). Racial disparities across income and employment such as lack of or poor education, criminal justice policies such as the Anti-Drug Act of 1986, and economic development hinder progress for people of color. In Illinois unemployment by education level shows "unemployment with no high school, 9% white and 31% black; unemployment with a high school diploma, 6.1% white, 15.3% black; unemployment with some college, 5.5% white and 7.7% black; and unemployment with a bachelor's or higher, 3.1% white and 7.3% black," (Terpsta & Rynell, 2016, p. 27). In May 2016, the national unemployment rate was 4.7%, according to the U.S. Department of Labor, Bureau of Labor Statistics ("Database, Tables", 2016). In Illinois in 2016 the unemployment for Blacks on all educational levels was higher than the national rate.

Racial disparities in healthcare have long-term effects on the well-being of individuals. The life expectancy from birth in Illinois is "white 79.3 years and black 73.7 years," and infant mortality rates reflect similar differences with "4.2% White, 13.1% Black, and 5.3% Latino" (Terpstra & Rynell, 2016, p. 31). The data point to early infant death rates and shorter life expectancy for Blacks and Latinos compared to Whites. The national data used to identify food sources is also reflective of racial disparities in access to food: "Households of color with children in the U.S. are twice as likely as white households to be food insecure, 14% white, 32% black, 27% Latino" (Terpstra & Rynell, 2016, p. 31). Food insecurities might include food deserts such as some urban areas lacking grocery stores or access to fresh produce or limited to fast foods and small grocery marts. Health issues from food to healthcare, insurance, and general well-being affect the life span. Again, national data in the 2016 Illinois report point to the disparities:

> Health conditions and causes of death, U.S.: Blacks and Latinos are about 2 times as likely to have poor or fair health as whites. Blacks and Latinos experience 7 to 9 times the rate of tuberculosis and HIV infection than whites. Blacks are 1.2 times as likely to die from coronary heart disease and 1.5 times as likely to die from strokes as whites. (Terpstra & Rynell, 2016, p. 31)

Limitations

The limitations in this article include an analysis based on one state: *Racism's Toll: Report on Illinois Poverty*. Illinois is one of the top 10 most populated states at number five, with 12.5 million residents, according to the U.S. Census Bureau. It can be viewed as a microcosm of the country; however, the specific details of the report would be strengthened by similar studies of the 10 most populated states, as well as large urban areas, and the small to medium-sized rural areas. The 2016 presidential election revealed that people have a broad range of perspectives relative to social disparities on everything from race to ethnicity, rural and large states, as well as immigration status. Critical Race Theory is a robust theoretical foundation that could be merged with theories from sociology and psychology to explain societal behavior and response to laws and policies that have impacted Blacks, immigrants, and other people of color. Media coverage of social images continues to be a rich area for examination, arguably since the Kerner Commission report in 1968.

Conclusion

Critical Race Theory (CRT) is useful as a theoretical foundation to examine racial inequities that occur in housing, education, and health as part of a host of social issues. For example, covenants that were put in place to exclude people of color from home ownership in some communities hampered housing stability and wealth accumulation. Even with hard work and having the requisite funds to purchase a home, hidden barriers such as redlining practices often prevent home ownership. CRT scholarship identifies ways in which such occurrences hamper the ability to fulfill part of the American dream of homeownership. Public education has a troubled past because of funding inequities and debunking the myth of "separate but equal," which *Brown v. Board of Education* in 1955 decreed. However, lack of implementation by local government officials persisted for decades, including the resegregation in Cleveland, Mississippi, schools cited earlier in this article. Local school funding models have been based on tax formulas that apply across a state or within county and local school districts. State and federal legal challenges keep education disparities at the forefront, but CRT research Themes 1 and 3, which critique liberalism and revisionist interpretations of American civil rights laws, ponder the question of why there are persistent shortfalls if legal precedents are supposed to end such problems (Delgado & Stefancic, 1993). The Centers for Disease Control and Prevention (CDC) continues to provide national data on health disparities from public health concerns to diseases and life expectancy; however, challenges persist in attempting to fulfill the needs for people of color and low-income and other marginalized groups. The 2010 Affordable Healthcare Act sought to open the door to healthcare for millions of Americans. The Act has faced constant challenges politically and legally since its inception.

The 2016 Illinois report on Racism's Toll in the state suggests ways to move toward equity in society for all groups. The report calls for action on all levels—national, state, and local, and groups and individuals—to persist in efforts to lower racial disparities in this country for basic human rights. The report identifies the historical legacy of laws and policies that undermine equity that must be removed or reformed to address centuries of structural racism that has disproportionately impacted people of color in society.

> Regardless of whose ancestors bear principal liability for our inequitable social evolution to this point, we are now all so invested in the norms and procedures of the status quo that it will not change without the dedicated efforts of everyone—both its beneficiaries and victims. (Terpstra & Rynell, 2016, p. 35)

From education to housing and health, efforts are needed to improve the lived experiences of people of color so that all Americans advance.

CRT research was used to contextualize the analysis of education, housing, and health disparities issues that continue to hamper progress for many people of color. Examination of laws and polices across decades in this country illustrate that making laws and policies are not enough if implementation denies or limits rights for everyone. CRT's beginnings in legal studies was a natural formation that spread across research in numerous disciplines. It is the human condition that must advance from the foundations of this work.

> For our nation to achieve its goal of shared prosperity, all of its people must be able to participate fully in the nation's economic, political, and civic life. In an equitable society, a person's race, ethnicity, gender, religion, sexual orientation, or ZIP code would not determine their health, income, wealth, or access to opportunity. Equity is a moral imperative aligned with American values of equal opportunity. (Terpstra & Rynell, 2016, p. 33)

The ability to change health, housing, education, and other social disparities rests with everyone.

Disclosure Statement

No potential conflict of interest was reported by the author.

References

Alemán, S., & Alemán, E. (2016). Critical race media projects: Counterstories and Praxis (Re)Claim Chicana/o Experiences. *Urban Education, 51*(3), 287–314. doi:10.1177/0042085915626212

Alexander, M. (2012). *The new jim crow: Mass incarceration in the age of colorblindness*. New York, NY: The New Press.

Bendix, A. (2017, March 14). *A Mississippi school district is finally getting desegregated*. The Atlantic. Retrieved from http://www.theatlantic.com/education/archive/2017/03/a-mississippi-school-district-is-finally-getting-desegregated/519573/

Chapman, T. K. (2013). You can't erase race! Using CRT to explain the presence of race and racism in majority white suburban schools. *Discourse: Studies in the Cultural Politics of Education, 34*(4), 611–627.

Clawson, R. A., & Trice, R. (2000). Poverty as we know it: Media portrayals of the poor. *Public Opinion Quarterly, 64*, 53–64.

Database, Tables and Calculators by Subject. (2016). *United States department of labor, bureau of labor statistics*. Retrieved from http://data.bls.gov/timeseries/LNS14000000

Delgado. (2005). *Critical race theory. New dictionary of the history of ideas international encyclopedia*. Retrieved from http://www.encyclopedia.com/topic/Critical_Rce_Theory.aspx

Delgado, R., & Stefancic, J. (1993). Critical race theory: An annotated bibliography. *Virginia Law Review, 79*(2), 461–516. doi:10.2307/1073418

Gilens, M. (1996). Race and poverty in America. *Public Opinion Quarterly, 60*(4), 515–541. doi:10.1086/297771

Golding, P., & Middleton, S. (1982). *Images of welfare: Press and public attitude to poverty (aspects of social policy)*. Hoboken, NJ: Blackwell Publishing (Wiley-Blackwell Company).

Harris, A. P. (2012). *Critical race theory. From the selected work of Angela P Harris*. Retrieve from http://works.bepress.com/angela_harris/17/

Howard, T. C., & Navarro, O. (2016). Critical race theory 20 years later: Where do we go from here. *Urban Education, 51*(3), 253–273. doi:10.1177/0042085915622541

Kijakazi, K., Atkins, R. M., Paul, M., Price, A., Hamilton, D., & Darity, W. A., Jr. (2016, November). *The color wealth in the nation's capital, a research report*. A joint publication of the Urban Institute, Duke University, The New School, and the Insight Center for Community Economic Development. Retrieved from http://www.urban.org./research/publication/color-wealth-nations-capital/view/full_report

Ladson-Billings, G., & Tate, W., IV. (1995). Toward a critical race theory of education. *Teachers College Record, 97*(1), 47–68.

Martindale, C. (1996). *Newspaper stereotypes of African Americans, in images that injure, ed. Paul Martin Lester*. Westport, CT: Praeger.

Orfield, G., Ee, J., Frankenberg, E., & Siegel-Hawley, G. (2016). *Brown at 62: School segregation by race, poverty and state*. Civil Rights Project, UCLA. Retrieved from https//civilrightsproject.ucla.edu/

Patton, L. D. (2016, March). Disrupting postsecondary prose. *Urban Education, 51*(3), 315–342. doi:10.1177/0042085915602542

Rose, M., & Baumgartner, F. R. (2013, February). Framing the poor: Media coverage and U.S. poverty policy, 1960–2008. *Policy Studies Journal, 41*(1), 22–53. doi:10.1111/psj.12001

Sonn, C. C., & Quayle, A. F. (2013). Developing Praxis: Mobilising critical race theory in community cultural development. *Journal of Community & Applied Psychology, 23*, 435–448. doi:10.1002/casp.2145

Stein, J. (2018, April 6). How 12 experts would end inequality if they ran America. *The Washington Post*, pp. G1 and G4.

Stovall, D. (2016). Out of adolescence and into adulthood: Critical race theory, retrenchment, and the imperative of praxis. *Urban Education, 51*(3), 274–286.

Terpstra, A., & Rynell, A. (2016). *Racisim's toll: Report on illinois poverty*. Social Impact Research Center. Retrieved from ILPovertyReport.org

Thrush, G., & Green, E. L. (2018, June 22). Behind Trump's plan to overhaul the government: Scaling back the safety net. *The New York Times*. Retrieved from https://www.nytimes.com/2018/06/21/us/politics/trump-government-overhaul-safety-net.html?hp&action=click&pgtype=Homepage&clickSource=story-heading&module=second-column-region&region=top-news&WT.nav=top-news

U.S. Census.gov Quick Facts. (2018, June 22). Retrieved from https://www.census.gov/quickfacts/fact/table/US/PST045217

Yosso, T. J. (2005). Whose culture has capital/? A critical race theory discussion of community cultural wealth. *Race Ethnicity and Education, 8*(1), 69–91. doi:10.1080/1361332052000341006

The Last Stages of Gentrification: Washington, DC, Mayoral Elections and Housing Advocacy

Lorenzo Morris

ABSTRACT

For seven decades from the establishment of home rule and largely independent local government in Washington, DC, mayoral politics, as well as socioeconomic change in city life, have been substantially defined by efforts to protect housing access and to protect vulnerable African American communities against the loss of their homes. Housing policy and racial sensitivity have been intertwined in a on-again off-again struggle against persistent gentrification. The mayoral politics seem to be successful only when factors of racial/economic inequality are integrated with housing policy. Ironically, the more narrow the emphasis on low income housing, the more sensitive has been the decline of black residential retention in the city. To some extent, low-income housing policy has become a public warning against the rising tide of gentrification.

Introduction

The Washington, DC, Democratic Party mayoral primary in April 2014 was completely unspectacular in terms of the city's approximately 40 years of officially open mayoral electoral competition or in terms of urban political rivalries generally. The competition among candidates was marked by the usual levels of issue ambiguity, tainted with the usual racial and economic lines of division, marred by a slightly elevated but unremarkable level of scandal, and ending with a very low but unsurprising level of voter mobilization. Although the politically astute may well have sensed it, there was very little concrete evidence of the fact that this election in all probability marked the end of an era, an indelible turning point in the history of the interracial rapport of forces in city politics.

As so often happens in socioeconomically diverse urban elections, an incumbent mayor was running for reelection while under threat of indictment and encumbered by multiple accusations of financial impropriety. As frequently happens in DC, the incumbent faced a collection of relative unknowns or well-known habitual losers. As usual, the incumbent would rely on the heavily Black wards of the city in his effort to overcome the normally hostile voters in the wealthier White wards of the city. Then came the only real surprise of the election series: The previously little-known opponent would defeat the sitting mayor in a stunning tide of voter abstention. The disenchanted Black voters stayed away from the polls secure, perhaps, in the hope that the expected winner, Muriel Bowser, a Black woman, would have a link to them. Yet, as shown in Table 1, these enthusiasm gap surrounding the Muriel Bowser vote is large. Voter turnout was nearly on the floor in the heavily black wards, 7 and 8. These were also the center of Gary's base. Still, no one in the media could say with certainty where her constituent strength was lodged or from where the strongest influence on

Table 1. A and B DC Mayoral Democratic Primary Election Results and Turnout by Ward, 2006.

(A) November 2006 Mayoral Election—Primary Election

CANDIDATE	WARD 1	WARD 2	WARD 3	WARD 4	WARD 5	WARD 6	WARD 7	WARD 8	Overall
Vincent Orange	1.66%	0.89%	0.79%	1.645	7.99%	1.69%	3.87%	3.92%	2.90%
Adrian Fenty	61.49%	53.91%	54.86%	68.83%	51.94%	52.46%	53.67%	55.58%	57.20%
Michael Brown	0.49%	0.49%	0.35%	0.41%	0.61%	0.78%	0.83%	1.16%	0.61%
Linda Cropp	26.70%	32.79%	27.74%	23.89%	33.75%	34.19%	37.43%	35.48%	30.98%
Artee Milligan	0.06%	0.07%	0.05%	0.14%	0.11%	0.16%	0.07%	0.11%	0.10%
Marie Johns	9.35%	11.71%	15.93%	4.91%	5.43%	10.45%	4.02%	3.53%	8.01%
Nestor Djonkam	0.12%	0.0%	0.03%	0.06%	0.08%	0.12%	0.07%	0.06%	0.07%

(B) Voter Turnout, 2006 Mayoral Primary Election

Ward	Registered Voters	Turnout	%
1	35,164	10,315	29.3
2	34,260	9,515	27.8
3	38,569	14,491	37.6
4	42,124	15,029	35.7
5	41,219	12,572	30.5
6	39,738	12,032	30.3
7	38,996	11,333	29.1
8	28,195	5,398	19.1

Source: District of Columbia Board of Elections.

her campaign or administration might have come. The general election in November only added to this uncertainty when she defeated two well-known White independent candidates of Republican extraction. Perhaps all that was certain about her campaign to critical observers is that she was retracing most of the steps of her mentor, the mayor that preceded the current one. He had gone down in electoral flames stoked by the ire of a Black electorate that felt neglected and betrayed. As the atypically sympathetic *Washington Post* article described the racial balance in the 2014 election:

> A surge of young, mostly white voters living in newly affluent neighborhoods emerged as a powerful force in last November's elections in the District, a seismic shift that mirrors the evolution of the city's population and could reshape its politics in years to come.
>
> For the first time in 40 years, voters between the ages of 25 and 34 outnumbered senior citizens, an analysis of election data shows. Also, for the first time, African Americans, who historically have exerted the greatest influence over District politics, lost their majority among voters.
>
> The young voters cast ballots in gentrifying neighborhoods ... while turnout declined in working and middle-class African American precincts... . (Schwartzman and Mellnick, 2015, p. A1)

In this research, we follow up on the increasingly popular impression that gentrification has laid the groundwork for the decline in Washington's Black electoral influence by considering whether previous declines in that electoral influence, in fact, had laid the groundwork for a reciprocal surge gentrification. In particular, we focus on the largely economic linkage of the racial political power distribution question by examining the extent to which race-conscious voting behavior in the city may be singularly tied to economic inequality and housing questions in mayoral campaigning and policy. Unlike the national political arena, where calls for "Black Power" heralded the future mayor Marion Barry's 1970s arrival in DC politics, race-conscious politics at the local level could never again be delivered separately from class-conscious politics (Gillette, 2001). While the link between racial and economic inequality may be readily discernible across the country, in Washington that linkage is visibly reinforced by spatial and housing distribution patterns—patterns that split it easily and physically into political controversies that, at first glance, may look simply Black and White.

Accordingly, we argue that a persistent decline in the influence of African American voters over the campaigning for and administration of the Washington office of the mayor is reflected both in the declining proportion of their vote in elections and in a persistent emphasis by successful mayors and candidates in promoting low-income support policies, particularly housing policy, that would serve to retain Black voters in the city.

It should also be recognized that racial issues are consistently evident among the dominant themes for Black voters in motivating turnout (Walters & Travis, 2010, p. 23). Turnout levels by race and ward over the past two decades reinforce this point (McClain & Tauber, 2001, 2010). Second, racially motivated Black voter turnout is directly linked to the prominence of economic issue positions in the competition among the candidates. Third, the candidate preferences of Black voters, based on ward differences, appear to be directly related to the candidate's issue positions on economic issues, particularly housing and, to a lesser extent, employment. It is as if the by-gone ideals of Black Power among DC voters have reincarnated and restructured under the banner of "affordable housing power"—an effort to retain a dissipating Black voter influence in the capitol city.

Class- and Race-Focused DC Electoral Map

Washington, DC, is divided into eight residential/voting wards that spatially reflect the indelible division of race and class that both feed and starve its still maturing experience with home rule. Some wards, especially Ward 3, reflect a near-perfect harmony of traditional race and class superordination in which a White population enjoys a median household income of about $250,000 a year (DeNavas-Walt, Proctor, & Smith, 2014). Other wards, especially Ward 8, clearly demonstrate the persistence of historical socioeconomic subordination with a nearly all-Black population whose household income fails to approximate 20% of the income of Ward 3 residents at $43,000 in 2009 (DeNavas-Walt et al., 2014; U.S. Census, 2010). From west to east, these two wards add maximum territorial distance to the socioeconomic and racial distances they embody.

Somewhere on the financially comfortable side of the space between these wards is Ward 4, which actually borders on Ward 3. There the wealthiest Black residents are disproportionately found in single family homes. Having evaded the plight of their fellow Black DC residents, the uninitiated Washington newcomer might well be inclined to assume, on the basis of national urban patterns, that these residents were largely the upwardly mobile products of the post-civil rights success stories. These residents may look like African Americans across the county who through grit, hard work, or educational advantage moved upward to the good side of America's "moving on up" obsession. Yet, unlike most cities, Washington houses a Black upper-middle-class population of independent professionals, high-level government employees, and civic leaders representing intergenerational class segmentation (Frazier, 1957). While the term *class* might exaggerate its composition, the Washington professional class helps to define an intraracial fissure that gives new meaning to its race-conscious politics without breaking the economically inclusive unity of that racial identity (Figure 1).

In any spectrum of race, class, and residential distribution, Ward 3 would be located at one extreme and Ward 8 at the other with Ward 4 somewhere in between. As a consequence, the voting patterns of residents across the city have historically been marked by a general voting distribution that racially and economically divides the city by ward. In fact, the racial division lines across the city are fairly visible in the geographical layout of the city (see Figure 2). The overwhelmingly white ward, Ward 3, is located on the far west; the overwhelmingly black ward, Ward 8, is in far southeast and Ward 4, a racially balanced ward in the north. While the more integrated wards appear to be primed for less disruptive development, the extreme imbalance (see Figure 3) between wards 3 and 8, among others, pose greater housing policy problems. While the racial divisions in voting have been fairly clear, however, the economic ones have not been so clear. It has often been assumed that upper-income Black voters like those in Ward 4 would make voting choices tilted by their income toward those of the White ward voters while retaining a diluted race-conscious voting pattern. Some have argued that a kind of "postracial" breakthrough was embodied in 2006 by the mayoral election of Black Ward 4 representative, Adrian Fenty (Yon, 2010, p. 95). His distinctly middle-class

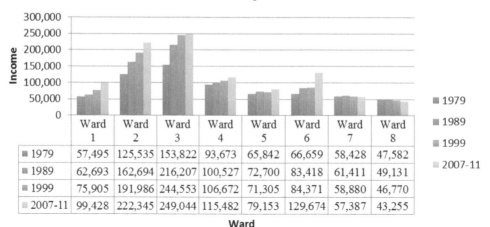

Figure 1. DC household income by ward.

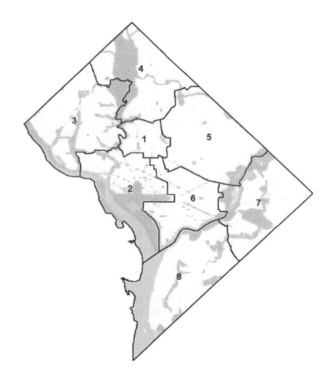

Figure 2. DC wards.

associations and his biracial background were seen as indicative of a "deracializing" neighborhood electorate. Of course, when he was resoundingly defeated in the subsequent election, assumptions of deracialization began to dissipate.

Still, from a different perspective on race consciousness, analysts have frequently suggested that class demarcations in any Black political spectrum would broadly distinguish patterns of

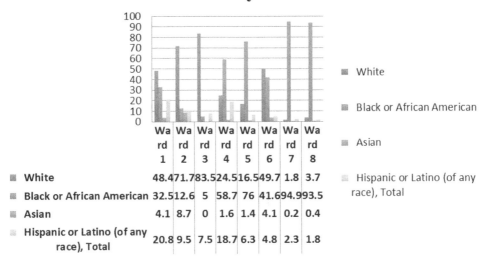

Figure 3. DC racial/ethnic populations by ward, 2010.

participation (Walton, 1994). Focusing more on movement politics than on electoral politics, Manning Marable argues forcefully that Black Nationalism is fundamentally tied to the "lower-class" and, by extension, race consciousness takes roots more firmly among those who have the weakest links to the established economy (Marable, 1993). Wealthier African Americans, in contrast, are presumed to have existed on the margins of some sort of "deracialized" opening to the dominant majority even before such a possibility had a label. In more material terms, the preponderant economic conditions of African Americans have become an essential component of racial identity for those seeking racial group "cohesion" and assertion (Marable, 1995, p. 210). He also argues, as others have, that class issues are submerged or ignored as a potential basis for intraracial division in deference to activists' demands for cohesion (Price, 2009, p. 12).

When Marable argues that the lower class is the source of all Black nationalism, he presents a compelling historical image of Black nationalist organizations committed to politically separate nonelectoral politics—a dismissal of electoral politics that dates back at least to the 1920s. In contrast to the civil rights groups like the NAACP, which pushed for electoral participation, the surging nationalist activists who would form the race consciousness inherited by the 1970s nationalists not only differed in orientation but also in their socioeconomic characteristics. For example, the Universal Negro Improvement Association members of the 1920s, led by Marcus Garvey, were clearly more lower/working class and central city in origin (Vincent, 1989). By extension, the more race-conscious approach to electoral politics should have a low-income group base in national and, particularly, in urban settings. In DC politics, at first impression, that does not seem to have been the case even where a substantial race-class linkage is most evident. Perhaps that is because the linkage, wherever present, is not a causal one; the low-income group leadership on race consciousness may be more of an inspiration than an impetus. The political goal post and group identity for the larger community may have been set by the immediate past experiences of inequality that have characterized the Black community. Accordingly, Melanye Price concludes of class and race in urban politics:

> Class became a huge factor in the maintenance of black residential communities and individual ability to succeed. Class served as a latent influence on the larger argument made ... about racialized ideologies; dialogue about class was framed as the choice between cross-class incorporation and class isolation within a black framework. (Price, 2009, p. 55)

Race consciousness in DC, it may be argued, is tied more to lower-class awareness than to lower-class status or origin. Black voters from the poorest to the richest wards in Washington are more likely to vote for candidates whose campaigns emphasize low-income groups and issues than those with other themes. In some sense, Black opinions may reflect the spatial proximity of the low-income and well-off Black residents to each other even when separated in different wards, especially where social networks from churches to family backgrounds may transcend these boundaries. As Michael Dawson indicates, beliefs in the Black community are reinforced by organizational networks and direct contact, much as other factors in social structure may lead to shared perspectives (Dawson, 2001, pp. 68–69). The signal of concern for the Black voting community has been concern for the poorest constituents, a signal that moves the upper-income voters as well as the lower-income ones. The voting patterns of Ward 4 African Americans ultimately reflect this orientation.

Racial and Economic Issues in DC Mayoral Elections

In fact, if not in grand theory, DC set the stage for the voting power of African Americans in the urban systems. DC was the first major American city with a majority Black population (Gillette, 2001, p. 202). In 1968 at the equilibrium point between the decline of the civil rights movement and the rise of the Black Power movement, DC was joined by Cleveland, Ohio, and Gary, Indiana, as the first three major cities with a Black mayor (though DC's was a presidentially appointed position designated the previous year).

For decades, the electoral struggle for mayoral control in DC appeared to take form in Black and White terms. Given the more than 65% Black majority in the city in which the mayoral elections were contested, the candidates at every level of city governance were overwhelmingly African American. Although White candidates often succeeded in the citywide at-large council elections, as well as in ward-based ones, they never came close in mayoral elections. By the turn of this new century, however, the new and ineluctable dimensions of racial balance in the voting population were evident. Still, it was not until the election of Muriel Bowser in 2014 that the voting power of the emerging White majority was broadly recognized. Mayor Bowser, like her political mentor, Major Adrian Fenty, was seen in the major media as straddling a persistent racial divide—one that is most easily managed in Ward 4, her political base. That is where gentrification appears to retain the greatest interracial balance. To determine whether these changing economic neighborhood characteristics may have diluted the racial sensitivity of the Black mayoral vote, some historical comparison of current voting with ward voting behavior when race and class distributions were more stable and consistent is needed.

Racial Factors in Mayoral Campaigns Overtime

Washington's Washington

The first mayor of DC under home rule came into office in a climate of relative tranquility in race relations compared to the heated "Black Power" conflicts disrupting other heavily Black metropolitan centers. After all, the city was granted home rule by a fairly conservative Congress against strong Southern senatorial opposition in 1973 (Fauntroy, 2010, pp. 26–27). Walter Washington had first been appointed by President Lyndon Johnson to lead the city in the installation of its near independence from the federal government (Fauntroy, 2010, p. 23). Mayor Washington represented the most socially assimilated segment of Black voters. They were the politically dominant, professional, government-linked, and business sectors, Black and White. He lived in a comfortable historic middle-class section of Ward 1 adjacent to Howard University, his alma mater.

When he narrowly won the first open election against two prominent Black professionals, he promised, as much through his reputation as through his campaign, more continuity than change. He had been appointed, close observers claim, because "President Johnson needed someone who would be respected on Capitol Hill and simultaneously be acceptable to residents of Washington, DC" (Travis, 2010, p. 49). His election in 1974 scarcely altered that balance. What new direction Mayor Washington's election could most clearly have symbolized came from his background in housing administration. As head of the New York Housing Authority in 1966, he had managed to bring striking public housing employees under control (Travis, 2010, p. 49). While living in DC, he had worked on providing housing for poor residents under the National Capitol Housing Authority. This very issue, housing the poor, would become a critical issue in mayoral competition for the Black vote in virtually every election to come, even in Washington's subsequent defeat at the polls.

The Marion Barry Insurgency

Most mayoral elections involve "conciliatory" politics where competing interests and partisan forces seek a compromise in the ideological and programmatic middle. First-time-ever Black candidate elections are virtually never like that. They are disruptive and confrontational, ideologically and racially intense. They are what Georgia Persons calls "insurgent elections" (Persons, 1993). Though he was not the first DC Black mayor, Marion Barry might as well have been, judging from the way he structured his 1978 campaign. In fact, the way he structured all four of his successful campaigns, it is as if no Black man had ever been there before him. He was engaged in a permanent insurgency.

Unlike his predecessor and his successors, Marion Barry came to Washington as a would-be incarnation or expression of Black Power. However preoccupied with or proud of their racial identities others may have been, none came to the city from outside with the expressed purpose of raising the electoral profile of African Americans. Barry came to the city as a representative of SNCC, the Student Nonviolent Coordinating Committee, at a point when the SNCC leadership was embroiled in a fascination with and reaction to popular calls for Black Power. Having stepped down as head of SNCC, his former role had just been taken up by the fiery Stokely Carmichael, who rose to national prominence pushing Black Power as the new mantra for activist Black leaders. Carmichael, observers say, fell out with Barry over Black Power advocacy in 1966 just as Barry was opening the SNCC Washington office (Gillette, 2001, p. 202). Barry's openness to mainstream politics was apparently too moderate for the Black Power SNCC wing.

Yet Barry moved to transform the youth-focused activism of his SNCC background to more systemic work with Black youth. Presaging his eventual adaptation of the race-conscious demands that he sought to modify, Barry initially sought and won a U.S. Labor Department grant to deal with youth unemployment. The grant to train "hardcore unemployed youth" led to Pride, Inc., a community service association with similar goals (Gillette, 2001, p. 203).

A decade later, while serving on the school board and the city council, Barry showed that he had not lost touch with the nationalistic side of his experience when he joined with another council member in inviting Minister Louis Farrakhan to the District to celebrate a Nation of Islam event (Barry & Tyree, 2014, p. 93). The next year, in a nearly incredible set of circumstances, Barry found himself the victim in a nationally televised assault by another more militant Black Nationalist group, the Hanafi Muslims. Barry earned enormous popular credit as a hero when he was shot seemingly trying to break up a hostage situation. He claims, on the other hand, that his presence in the city building was a coincidence (Barry & Tyree, 2014, p. 96). Yet his ability to reach across the ideological divide between these extreme nationalist activists and the established civic activists was clearly a function of his own exposure to Black Power activism.

The next year Barry would launch his successful campaign for mayor, propelled in part by this last encounter and his community work with Pride, Inc., but also by winning the endorsement of the establishmentarian *Washington Post* (Barry & Tyree, 2014, p. 112; *Washington Post*, 1978). His campaign was far removed from the popular antiestablishment protest cries of Black Power and explicitly focused on community and economic development. In an additional twist, he would win the White vote over his two systemic-tailored opponents, businessman Sterling Tucker and the incumbent Mayor Washington. On the surface, his first election would appear to be a precocious version of what's called postracial politics. Yet he would never win the White vote again. By his fourth successful campaign, he was down to single digits among White DC voters. It is reasonable to assume that that first campaign was not what it appeared to be on the surface. Short of a dramatic transformation of his character or the electorate, the sharp transition from interracial consensus to segmentation indicates that critical factors may have been hidden just below the surface of the election. The era had begun with the mayoral election of Marion Barry when, as a relative new comer, he broke through a wall of well established and respected local leaders on a wave of "black power" colored campaigning. As evident in Table 2, he easily defeated the incumbent Mayor Washington.

Barry ran four highly race-conscious campaigns for mayor, but they were all conducted under the same explicitly nonracial banners. First, like other insurgent campaigns and novel campaigns more generally, Barry's first campaign was very populist, seeking to mobilize nonvoters in atypical ways. Barry's campaign structure drew as much or more on movement structures than it may have drawn on typical electoral campaign structures. He sought in his speeches to impose emotive oratory along with visionary statements in ways that characterized the charismatic presence of major civil rights leaders (Barry & Tyree, 2014, p. 106). He blended his charismatic style with the substantive mobilization of Black community organizations, from churches and social groups to youth groups, in ways that electoral politics had not generally seen before. The campaign structure closely reflects what Aldon Morris describes in his analysis of the civil rights mobilization as the critical components of a movement structure (Morris, 1984, pp. 278–80). As Barry put it in describing his first campaign: "Washington, DC had never seen my style of politics. I would walk right up, knock on peoples' doors and tell them what they needed to do." He added: "Whenever I gave public speeches, I always made sure to mix in pieces of famous poems and spirituals to add charisma and give people things to remember me by" (Barry & Tyree, 2014, pp. 101 and 106).

His populism included diverse modes of outreach that were completely uncommon in the admittedly new politics of DC. It was notably defined, however, by its peculiar economic and geographical roots. Unlike all his major competition and predecessors, he launched his campaign from the poorest ward and most heavily Black ward in the city with a visible, if not strident, focus on their economic condition.

Table 2. A and B Mayoral Primary and General Elections, 1978.

CANDIDATE	VOTES	PERCENTAGE
(A) September 1978 Mayoral Election—Democratic Primary		
Marion S. Barry, Jr.	32,841	34.65%
Sterling Tucker	31,277	33.00%
Walter E. Washington	29,881	31.52%
Dorothy Maultsby	391	.41%
John Ray	184	.19%
(B) November 1978 Mayoral Election—General Election		
Marion S. Barry, Jr. (D)	68,354	70.16%
Arthur Fletcher (R)	27,366	28.09%
Susan Pennington (U.S. Labor)	1,066	1.09%
Glova Scott (I)	638	0.66%

Source: OurCampaigns.com.

Economic Issues and Race in Barry's Campaigning: Housing and Employment

Significantly, Barry's economic campaign themes were reinforced by Mayor Washington's own background in housing administration. Barry forcefully took up the theme of protecting displaced and low-income Black households. Ownership protection and tenant rights themes seemed to resonant well, if not intentionally, with the new sense of empowerment that the recent acquisition of home rule brought to a self-conscious majority Black city encircled by nationwide echoes of Black Power.

Barry came into citywide prominence by 1970 with his leadership of Pride, Inc., a community service organization focused on youth unemployment. In a large sense, this was a systemic cousin of the protest initiatives that encircled this city, like many larger cities, often in the guise of Black Power. Barry's adaption of the theme, however, was more pragmatic and system sensitive than elsewhere. With a federal grant, awarded by Nixon Labor Secretary Willard Wirty to provide youth job training, he could open a door to the established city leadership (Gillette, 2001, p. 203). When he ran successfully for School Board Chair in 1971, his connection to movement activism was probably no less important than his connection to youth services. That activist link was often reinforced by militant symbols and by the dashikis he sometimes wore (Barry and Tyree, 2014, pp. 83 and 86).

When Barry set his sights on the mayor's office seven years later, the images of Black Power activism had to form an indelible background to his campaign—one that he scarcely needed to articulate for a Black electorate that had watched his occasionally dramatic encounters with the racial complexities of local politics in the mass media. By this time, he had been elected to the City Council, and he may have seemed a little more like a standard fixture in local politics. If, after his persistent media exposure, some voters had come to see him in the more urbane light of an established elected official, that would have been starkly shaken by his televised and bloody encounter with Black nationalist Hanafi Muslim extremists in March 1977 not long before he began his election campaign (Barry & Tyree, 2014, pp. 96–97). In addition, he seemed, in the sensationalizing glare of the media attention, to have stood up to violent hostage takers that held the city government building for days.

On the eve of his first campaign for mayor, therefore, the mixed image of his background as a community development leader struggling through Pride against the economic inopportunity that afflicted the city youth may have been trumped the warrior image in the struggle for racial justice. In this context, his campaign had an obviously strong hold on the Black voters who could scarcely escape the mix of class and race consciousness in his appeals. From a different angle, he may have appeared as the warrior for most voters in the city as a counterweight against the militant excesses of racial and religious extremists. For upper-income voters, who were largely White, his economic orientation on the City Council was highlighted by his support for pro-business tax policies (Gillette, 2001, p. 203; Leon, 2010, p. 75). In fact, an understated aspect of his rather "class-conscious" politics on behalf of the Black community may not have been an effort to destabilize the political foundations of class inequality but instead to equilibrate and moderate that inequality on a more tolerable and less "racialized" basis.

One of his first policy initiatives in the mayoral office, about which he brags in his biography, were the large-scale employment projects for the new Black middle class and the expansion of this group into more expensive DC housing. As soon as he stepped into office, Barry recalls:

> The opportunities in government and all of the contracting that we began to provide in my first term as mayor of the District began to make a phenomenal impact on the wealth of Washington, DC and surrounding Maryland and Virginia areas for black families for years to come. These opportunities for better jobs and incomes allowed black professionals and families to move into housing and neighborhoods in the District where they weren't allowed or couldn't afford to live in before in the "Gold Coast" on Sixteenth Street, Northwest. (Barry & Tyree, 2014, p. 121)

The Gold Coast he mentions is part of what has become a highly integrated, upper-middle-class neighborhood in Ward 4 that soon would be seen as the interracial swing voting district. In flaunting his use of public contracts and resources with the goal of subsidizing business and professional opportunities for African Americans, he apparently measures his success by the number of new households. Although he brags that Black families throughout the metropolitan area benefited from his contracting practices, he focuses on the in-town territory to which he helped them lay claim.

In his litany of first-term program initiatives, housing policy takes a prominent place alongside business development and employment. He brought Robert Moore, a Texas housing expert, into his administration to lead his housing programs. "Bob, we need about a million dollars for this new housing program," Barry recalls saying generally and often, "and (Robert Moore) he'd say 'Let's go get it.' Providing fair and affordable housing was at the top of my agenda of things to get done" (Barry & Tyree, 2014, p. 125).

Affordable housing stands out as one of the most critical economic issues for Mayor Barry because it was so intimately tied to the retention and growth of his most supportive constituents. Yet what seems to distinguish him from his last-term successor, Mayor Williams, was his inclusion of the broader middle-class population in rhetoric and advocacy for protecting DC residents. As popular fears of gentrification leading to massive dislocation of Black residents gave way to increasingly hard evidence of a declining Black population, mayoral candidates would face increasing pressure to demonstrate concern for keeping low-income Black residents in their home(land). For Barry the targeting of low-income housing did not diminish his promotion of middle-class housing for his primary constituency.

In comparison with housing policy, public employment policies are much less free from intervention by the federal government. To some extent, that is because the plurality of employment opportunity in the city is attributable to public sector employment in federal or local agencies. Beyond direct federal government employment, however, Congress has historically bypassed home rule to restrict the city government efforts to require public employees to be DC residents. At the end of Barry's first term, the city passed the Comprehensive Merit Personnel Act (1978), which required that all new city government employees be residents of the District or move into it (Flowers, 2010, p. 217). Congress hastily overturned the law and has since resisted all but the weakest subsequent efforts to give preference to residents. Particularly in the context of the Barry administration, this preference had strong racial overtones. The surrounding suburbs were overwhelmingly White, and the commuters who staffed the government were disproportionately White. It was hard to separate the struggle to keep jobs in the city from the inevitable benefit its success would bring to Black residents. In turn, the politics of advocating for keeping jobs in the city resonated strongly with the civil rights community.

Nevertheless, the civil rights community, especially its African American base, was a community of interests nurtured and enveloped in the perspective of a moral dilemma—a policy perspective that challenges government and centers of economic power for their moral inconsistencies (Myrdal, 1944; Walton & Smith, 2015). Once Mayor Barry's personal transgressions were publicly exposed and began to permeate city politics, it was difficult, if not impossible, for the city's traditional Black leaders to stand by him. Nevertheless, much of his constituency base in Wards 7 and 8 would not abandon him, as evidenced by their massive return to his voter column four years after scandal led to his loss of the mayor's mantle.

His immediate successor, the daughter of a judge and a respected lawyer/businesswoman, Sharon Pratt-Dixon, offered a sharp contrast of substance and image. Perhaps one of the most significant contrasts, that of social class background, was frequently discussed as a matter of image when it may as well have been one of substance. It made a substantial difference in the electoral mobilization of low-income Black voters.

Mayor Sharon Pratt-Kelly: Seeking A Restoration

In 1990 Sharon Pratt-Dixon made history when she supplanted the scandal-laden Mayor Barry and won election as the first female mayor of the District. A brand-new star on the urban electoral scene, she had never held elected office before. Four years later, Sharon Pratt-Kelly (with a new name) would make history again, but with no fanfare, by becoming the first candidate for reelection to mayor to lose virtually every single precinct. The luster of her political star had been so thoroughly tarnished that she disappeared completely from political life. Frequent accusations that she was, as Toni-Michele Travis reports, "out of touch with the common people, especially low-income residents" did not really stick in the first campaign (Travis, 2010, p. 91). In the second one, when she could no longer run as an outsider, the accusations would be more tenacious.

The first time around, she ran largely on the promise of restoring the image of city leadership, assuring sound business management, and bridging gaps between diverse segments of the city. She promised to "clean house with a shovel, not a broom" while skimming the waste from city government (Travis, 2010, p. 90). As a novice, her claims of managerial prowess had to rest largely on her business background in which she had been a vice president of the local electric power company. Still, that claim surely added to the popular impression of an upper-class distance between her and the city's typical representatives, not to mention its typical Black residents. Her marriage to the chair of the City Council, Arrington Dixon, probably helped with her rapport among Black voters and her contact with local political activists.

Her business background and her detachment from Mayor Barry surely added to her success among White voters. Those same voters, however, were not committed to her, and they largely abandoned her four years later in favor of a well-worn mayoral candidate, John Ray (Yon, 2010, p. 203). At same time, Black voters reaffirmed their commitment to the tarnished but undaunted "mayor for life," as Barry came to be labeled.

Mayor Anthony Williams: The Campaigning Accountant

Anthony Williams began his political career under Mayor Barry's leadership of the city, but this city, it must be emphasized, is still the nation's capital, and Congress had imposed itself again on the city administration. Williams was brought into the administration in the guise of a distinctly apolitical bureaucratic player working for the city on a mandate that effectively came from outside the city's voting population at the hands of the Congress. He was brought in to manage the city's business through the Control Board created by the federal government in 1996. The city's new manager, like the Control Board itself, was explicitly put in place to bring greater efficiency and transparency to city administration (Public Law 104–8). Yet the Board and the Williams position were conspicuously established by a congressional leadership generally hostile to the local politicians and repulsed by the personal background and image of Marion Barry. Still, Mayor Barry seemed to embrace Williams and to work well with him. That image doubtlessly helped Williams with his campaign's appeal to Black voters while his urban "cleanup" performance preserved his appeal to the rest of the city.

Given his substantial range of authority as city manager, his first term in the mayor's office was, in a large sense, his second shot at controlling the administration of the city's public sector. He opened his 1999 inaugural with the somewhat politically disembodied title of "Bodies and Souls in Motion," showing a willingness, if not the ability, to harness the movement rhetoric of the past civil rights leaders. At the same time, he affirmed his political inexperience, if not innocence, by bragging, among other things, that he was "a proud, card-carrying member of the Government Finance Officers Association" (Williams, 1999). While he would follow his predecessor in making reference to "affordable housing," he would drown its potential rhetorical or populist value by equating it with "clean communities …, and reliable transportation" (Williams, 1999). If anything defines his first term as mayor, it is more likely administrative efficiency and political insensitivity.

In his first term, Mayor Williams introduced the Housing Preservation Act (2001) intended to protect affordable housing and limit dislocation, but it had little immediate impact on housing affordability. In 2003, the beginning of his second term in office, he proclaimed his goal of bringing "one hundred thousand new residents" to the city. The mayor maintained that he was trying to attract residents from the black middle-class residents that had left for the suburbs. "However," according to William G. Jones, "by 2003 an escalating trend of gentrification was already established. The majority of residents moving into the District were white middle-class individuals and families" (Jones, 2010, p. 167). "Housing values in many communities—even some dominated by barred or boarded-up windows," Jones added, "soared to the point where political debate dwelled not on urban blight but on the perils of gentrification" (Jones, 2010, p. 167).

Mayor Adrien Fenty: Losing The Race

In a news analysis of "How D.C. Mayor Fenty Lost the Black Vote," the authors explain his onetime success in a mayoral election by describing his subtle but intense appeals to black voters:

> Fenty ... drew attention during his 2006 campaign by knocking on thousands of doors across the city. His message was not overtly racial, but he connected with many black voters by emphasizing his roots as a lifelong Washingtonian and son of a prominent small businessman—and by leaving no doubt that he was hungry for the job and would devote superhuman energy to it. (Schwartzman & Jenkins, 2010; see also Demessie & Gillespie, 2013, p. 275).

Much as his successful predecessors on the mayoral campaign trail had done, Councilman Fenty emphasized "affordable housing" and confronting the growing income gap across then city (Yon, 2010, p. 206). He followed up in 2009 with an administrative requirement that builders set aside a proportion of their units for low- and moderate-income residents. This "inclusionary zoning" program may eventually have effects that have not yet been visible. With the average cost of a house in DC close to $500,000 at that time, only a very small percentage of units would be within reach a median-income Black family. Clearly, poorer residents did not recognize any substantial benefits in the requirement.

Unlike his most popular predecessors, Fenty launched his campaign from the wealthiest majority Black ward where residents were least likely to depend on subsidized housing. Moreover, he had introduced himself to the city's larger electorate by taking popular positions on development regulations and the protection of low-income residential areas. At the same time, his solidly middle-class background in a comfortable racially mixed community reinforced the impression that he was a committed advocate for the disadvantaged communities. Unfortunately, it's an impression that would not long survive his postelection administration (Table 2).

From the start, however, Fenty's exceptional campaign strategy contrasted so sharply with that of his predecessor Anthony Williams—the accountant turned efficiency expert turned city manager and half-hearted politician—that he revived thoughts of Barry's grassroots style. Fenty's relentless door-to-door campaigning was certainly unmatched and far beyond that of any other candidate in the post-Barry years. The mere fact that he was regularly seen in the Black community allowed him to acquire the image of being closer to that community than any other. Unfortunately for his Black community credentials, however, almost the minute he began to govern that image began to crumble.

Unlike other city leaders whose disaffection from the Black community was most immediately felt by its poorest residents, Fenty had the absence of mind to offend the Black middle class in a kind of early onset ineptitude. He went on the offensive in public education by picking a fight with the teachers. In particular, he presided over a sweeping assault on the teachers' union control over job security and teacher evaluation, leading to threats of massive teacher firings (Pitzer, 2010, p. 9). Local resentment was aggravated by the undertones of unprofessionalism and racism. Major school reforms were initiated by his newly appointed school chancellor, Michele Rhee, whose only substantial experience in public schooling was as a consultant. Yet she seemed to focus her appeals more toward the general public and the media than toward the teachers. Secondly, her lack of rapport with the established local education community was not compensated by any strong ties to the Black community—a disjuncture that some thought she, as a non-African American, would make more of an effort to overcome (Pitzer, 2010, p. 9). Still, Fenty stood behind her like the captain of a ship sinking in popularity.

Fenty and his education administrator may well have missed an old lesson from W.E.B. DuBois in the "Talented Tenth." DuBois links the salvation of the mass of African Americans to the leadership of the then-emerging Black middle class at the beginning of the 20th century (DuBois, 1903). Aside from preachers, that talented middle class would be heavily composed of teachers. Teachers, he argued, would provide the social guidance for the community by helping the community at large to establish viable social goals, to distinguish "means of living from the object of living" (Du Bois, 1932). Decades later, the influence of teachers and teachers' associations over the political preferences and opinions of local Black communities, though difficult to measure, is surely substantial. If nothing else, indelible evidence of their influence emerges from the fact that all DC mayors have sought to avoid conflict with them—and all reelected ones have successfully avoided it.

In some sense, the public and vocal opposition from teachers to the Fenty-Rhee administration's education policy may have become the rallying cry of a reinforced link between race and class in the city's division over mayoral leadership. A postprimary election poll found that about half of all Black respondents thought Mayor Fenty "cared more about white residents" (Demessie & Gillespie, 2013, p. 285; *Washington Post*, 2010). In contrast, White residents overwhelmingly saw his behavior as racially neutral. Similarly, 80% of the voters who supported Vincent Gray, the winner, over Fenty felt that Fenty "cared more about upper income residents" (*Washington Post*, 2010). That number is just slightly less than the proportion of Gray voters who thought Fenty favored White residents, and yet the same proportions of the small number of respondents who thought he favored Black residents were evenly distributed between his supporters and his opponents' supporters (*Washington Post*, 2010). This suggests that the racial divide in terms of attitudes and perceptions was less predictive of voter behavior than attitudes toward class. Still, the outcome can only be explained by the racially definable voter behavior that led to Fenty's stunning rejection by Black voters. When they said he cared more about the upper class, their concept of class was apparently colored by shades of race.

While the city's economy had experienced no special decline in the four-year period, voter criticism of Fenty corresponded with economic discontent (Gillespie, 2014). Along with the substantive importance of economic issues in voter rejection of Mayor Fenty, the symbolic racial aspects of voter preferences surface in the link between voter economic policy dissatisfaction with Fenty and their opposition to Chancellor Rhee.

Accordingly, Demessie and Gillespie observed that those "who thought the economy was the most important issue were about 83% less likely to vote for Fenty. Voters who disapproved of Michele Rhee's performance as schools chancellor were 93% less likely to vote for Fenty" (Demessie & Gillespie, 2013, pp. 288–289). The racial dimension here is reinforced by the clear evidence that attitudes toward Rhee divided sharply along with racial lines (Gibson, 2015; Costello, 2011). It is not surprising, therefore, that the man who would easily unseat him had strong ties to the low-income Black community and to its "mayor for life."

Mayor Vincent Gray: An Unconscious Heritage

Although the "mayor for life," Marion Barry, was not really stingy with his blessings on his successors, none could be viewed as the chosen one other than Vincent Gray; none was praised and promoted by him like Gray. Gray had come into city politics from Ward 7, the ward closest to that of Barry in terms of geography as well as socioeconomic and racial characteristics. Gray inherited much of the devoted Barry constituency in his first mayoral campaign, and that electorate largely carried him over the top. These were the Black voters, particularly in Wards 7 and 8 but still visible in the other wards where there was a substantial Black vote adding to his support. As clearly reflected in a pre-election 2010 poll published by the *Washington Post*, the popularity of Gray's opponent, Mayor Fenty, had plummeted in the space of two years with Africa Americans across the city while declining much more moderately among White residents. As Figure 4 illustrates, the intensity of Fenty's disapproval visibly corresponds to the density of the Black population.

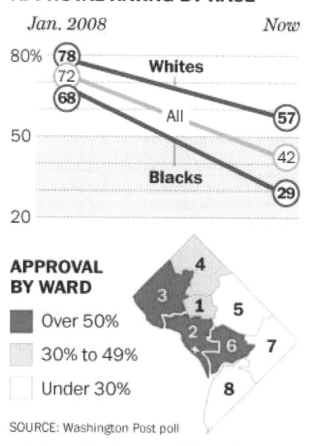

Figure 4. Race and the preelection decline of Mayor Fenty.yh

Source: Washington Post (2010); http://www.washingtonpost.com/wpdyn/content/article/2010/01/30/AR2010013002452.html.

In his unsuccessful reelection campaign, while largely abandoned by other sectors of the electorate, the voters in the heavily White wards remained on his side. These wards, Wards 2, 3, and 6, the wealthiest and the mostly White, gave Mayor Fenty positive job approval ratings as the election contest with then-Council Chair Vincent Gray approached. Even with that support, these voters apparently shared some of the city's overall drop in support for the mayor. He went from a 78% job approval rating among White residents in 2008 to 57% approval in 2013. Still, that was nothing like the crash landing he suffered among Black residents. His approval in this group, slightly lower to start, tumbled in the same period from 68% to 29%, a steep decline of 39% (Stewart & Cohen, 2011). That change is reflected in the three most heavily Black wards—5, 7, and particularly 8—where ratings were all below 30%. The more racially mixed wards, Wards 1 and 4, ended with approval ratings in the 30% to 49% range. As a consequence, it is difficult to image that any candidate who had recently won the city's Black votes, as had Council Chair Gray, could have lost the Black vote to Fenty.

With something of a late start in the 2010 Democratic mayoral primary, it was reasonable to believe that Gray would have a hard time raising substantial funding for his campaign. Nevertheless, he was relatively successful, so successful that that fact might have attracted suspicion. In any event, he soon became the target of an investigation for campaign finance corruption by U.S. Attorney Ronald Machen and the frequent object of news media suspicion. By early 2014, five close associates of the mayor confessed their guilt in campaign-related crimes including a wealthy financier who implicated the mayor. As a consequence, Mayor Gray went into the last weeks of the reelection campaign with a heavily damaged public image and the cloud of a perspective indictment hanging over his head. Ironically, a year later no indictment had materialized, when the U. S. federal attorney, who had shepherded the investigation, left office. Whatever chance at reelection the mayor may have had early on was apparently lost in the investigative scandal. His successor would then emerge from a large field with no apparent front-runner initially to fill the void left by the hobbling of his campaign.

Mayor Muriel Bowser: Answering the Call of Voter Abstention

What would happen if the city organized an election for mayor and virtually no one showed up to vote? Presumably we will never know for sure, but the 2014 mayoral election had such poor voter participation that we came fairly close to finding out. With merely 26% of the eligible electorate participating in the all-important primary and a smaller percentage in the general election, turnout was lower than usual, but among Black voters it was abysmal. Judging from the distribution of turnout by ward, the Whitest ward, Ward 3, had a turnout of 33.5%, and the wards with highest Black proportions, Wards 7 and 8, had turnout rates of 21.5% and 15.5% respectively.

Given that Ward 7 is former Mayor Gray's home ward, the low participation was particularly disappointing for many. Contrast these turnout rates with turnout in the 1994, the last time Marion Barry ran for mayor: Turnout was 50% in Ward 7 and 45% in Ward 8. Surrounded by scandal with

Table 3. A and B DC Mayoral Primary Election Results and Turnout by Ward, 2014.

(A) April 2014 Mayoral Election—Democratic Primary									
CANDIDATE	WARD 1	WARD 2	WARD 3	WARD 4	WARD 5	WARD 6	WARD 7	WARD 8	Overall
Jack Evans	4.97%	17.58%	8.97%	2.72%	2.30%	3.28%	2.02%	2.35%	4,877, 5.03%
Andy Shallal	5.62%	4.23%	3.88%	3.23%	3.15%	2.73%	1.44%	1.66%	3,196, 3.30%
Reta Lewis	0.42%	0.34%	0.36%	0.42%	0.49%	0.48%	0.81%	0.97%	490, 0.51%
Vincent Orange	1.21%	0.51%	0.46%	1.82%	4.40%	1.05%	3.78%	3.66%	1,946, 2.01%
Muriel Bowser	45.53%	50.19%	63.49%	49.62%	34.02%	37.26%	28.80%	31.18%	42,045, 43.38%
Vincent Gray	23.35%	14/01%	11.45%	36.15%	47.26%	23.12%	59.48%	57.92%	31,613, 32.62%
Carlos Allen	0.16	0.04%	0.04%	0.10%	0.14%	0.19%	0.17%	0.14%	120, 0.12%
Tommy Wells	18.57%	12.96%	11.13%	5.67%	8.00%	31.70%	3.16%	2.60%	12,393, 12.79%

(B) Voter Turnout, 2014 Mayoral Primary Election		
Ward	Registered Voters	Turnout, %
1	44,202	12,320, 27.87%
2	33,904	8,171, 24.10%
3	42,251	14,161, 33.52%
4	47,996	16,920, 35.25%
5	50,094	13,344, 26.64
6	54,566	16,605, 30.43%
7	49,347	10,621, 21.52%
8	46,677	7,252, 15.54%

Note. Total registered voters: 369,937. Total turnout: 99,394 (26.93%).
Source: District of Columbia Board of Elections.

memories of his imprisonment fresh in voters' memories, a politically diluted Mayor Barry could still more than double the motivation to participate among Black voters in the Bowser-led election. It is fair to say that Muriel Bowser rode into the mayor's office on a tidal wave of voter indifference or disaffection (Table 3).

Like her predecessors, Mayor Bowser won the highest percentage of her vote, 74.8%, in Ward 8 with its overwhelmingly Black population and the lowest percentage, 39.2%, in Ward 3 with its virtually all White and high-income population. At 63.4% of her vote, the tally for Ward 4, the relatively racially balanced area, falls in place almost dead center between the least racially balanced areas. It's perhaps a little surprising that she did not do much better in Ward 4, her home district.

In this context it should be noted that the third-place candidate, a White Republican, Carol Schwartz, also won her highest votes, 10% and 8%, from Wards 7 and 8 respectively, where Bowser won the most. Relative to her winning predecessors, Bowser's Black vote, though favorable, was weak by comparison. Moreover, the very low primary voter turnout of 15.5% in Ward 8 symbolizes the Black vote weakness and highlights a flaw in her appeal.

In the May following her inauguration, Mayor Bowser promoted her housing proposal while touring the rapidly gentrifying Shaw neighborhood with HUD Secretary Julián Castro. She faced lower-middle-income African American residents who were clinging on to fleeting parcels of homeownership in a traditionally Black and mixed-income center of local culture. Seemingly protected on its northern flank by Howard University, residential association activists, including their minority White members, were consistently raising alarms against the deluge of upper-income "colonizers" from the suburbs. Mayor Bowser had claimed that "access to affordable housing was a main tenet" of 2014 campaign (Stein, 2015, p. B2). She touted her 2016 budget proposal that included $100 for housing programs. Yet a *Washington Post* report, among others, raised serious questions about the adequacy and tardiness of city hall intervention when it warned that:

> ... if Shaw wants to keep its remaining longtime residents, affordable housing must come quickly. The Shaw and Logan Circle neighborhoods, according to data from the Urban Institute, were 25 percent white in 2000. In 2010, they were 48 percent white, a share of the population that has only increased in the past five years. (Stein, 2015, p. B2)

As the first Washington major elected with a majority White population, though not necessarily the first such majority among voters, Mayor Bowser is perhaps more heavily exposed to speculation about her approaches to retaining and sustaining the city's established population. At the same time, any pressure on her to focus on the older residents at the expense of the wave of newcomers must confront the more forceful financial incentives that a welcoming approach to the wealthier newcomers would entail. That leaves reinforced subsidized housing policy, and to a lesser extent employment policy, as the most likely mayoral initiatives to appeal to Black voters and retain them in their home neighborhoods.

Almost from the start of her administration, Mayor Bowser found her city in the middle of a national wave of local- and state-level initiatives to raise the minimum wage. She also had such a platform indirectly bequeathed to her by her predecessor, Mayor Gray, who, after long deliberation, had rejected a minimum wage increase. His decision turned into a media sensationalized rejection and finally reached its conclusion amid ongoing organized labor protests. These were vigorous protests against the megacorporations, particularly Wal-Mart, widely viewed as aggravating the nation's growing race/class income gap (Debonis, 2013). Barely a year into her administration, Mayor Bowser was faced with another major initiative to raise the minimum wage. This time it involved a ballot initiative to increase the wage floor to 15 dollars an hour, a proposal inspired by a broader national movement (DePillis, 2015, p. A1). Fortunately, perhaps for her, that proposal was largely swept up in the broader national debate over minimum wage, giving way to center stage once again for housing policy.

The House Key: The Racial Symbolism of Housing Policy Advocacy

As a saying often set to music implies, "a house is not a home" unless it houses a sense of belonging that binds its inhabitants together. Similarly, publicly supported housing does not make a kind of homeland reminiscent of the racially constructed enclaves in segmented societies, but the promotion of affordable housing resonates so strongly and so directly with the decades-long struggle of Black voters to protect their place in mayoral politics that housing policy seems like the urban equivalent of homeland defense policy. While it is not possible to attribute clear weights or measures to the degrees or types of such policy advocacy, it is possible to identify a substantial and consistent relationship between successful mayoral leadership and affordable housing advocacy. Accordingly, this section broadly examines visibility of housing policy advocacy in the campaign promises and inaugurations of Washington to see if it is reflected in the popularity and/or longevity of their mayoral leadership.

Every popular mayor, particularly every mayor who was reelected, has been a visible advocate for affordable housing since the first one. Every mayor whose first term ended on a negative electoral vote was comparatively invisible on affordable housing in the face the mayoral successor. Of course, since the first mayor of the city, Walter Washington, entered office coming out of a career directing public housing in DC and elsewhere, the theme was easily prominent in the establishment of the office. Coming at a time, the early 1970s, when the dissolution of the city's solid Black majority was unforeseen, if not unforeseeable, and when the word *gentrification* was largely unknown, housing policy did not seem to have the racial overtones that it would later take on.

Still, Washington's strongest policy legacy is probably tied to housing, since his administration could not make a great many steps away from the intrusive and often disrespectful congressional oversight. When Washington sent his first budget to Congress in 1967, for example, Congressman John McMillan (D), chair of the House Committee on DC, "responded by having a truckload of watermelons delivered to Washington's office" (see Jaffe & Sherwood, 1994, p. 64).

That kind of Congressional interference and the demeaning attitude that accompanied it, apparently facilitated, if not enabled, the link between the restrictions on home rule for the District and racially discriminatory Congressional behavior, particularly that of Southern Congress members. Coming out of the civil rights movement and entering mayoral politics in heat of the Black Power period, Marion Barry scarcely needed to campaign as he did to capitalize on that impression among the city's Black voters (Barry & Tyree, 2014, pp. 86, 94). Still, Barry could tie it to the national level, as he did in 1988 when he was the first one to put DC statehood on the Democratic National Convention platform. He reinforced the movement link in his speech by arguing:

> And this year, the 25th anniversary of the historic march on Washington, 23rd anniversary of the Voting Rights Act, 20 years after the assassination of Martin Luther King and Robert Kennedy, I call on you, fellow Democrats and freedom-loving people, to help us get full voting rights and statehood now. (Freed, 2012)

FOR other voters, home rule with its racial overtones seems to have coincided with a kind of "homeland" economic development. Accordingly, Barry linked business development with expanding local empowerment. At the same time that Barry advocated expanded low-income housing, he uniquely pushed for expanded middle-class housing, a policy perspective that highlighted the middle-class Black households moving to the suburbs but could benefit the incoming White middle class as well. In transitioning from Mayor Barry's administration to the mayoralty, Anthony Williams took up the policy of middle-class housing with the diminished assumption that it would help retain Black residents while the record of its impact would confirm its benefits for largely White gentrifying newcomers (Jones, 2010, p. 167; Williams, 1999).

Given his administrative and technocratic background, it is especially likely that Williams could foresee the unintended racial impact of housing policy. Nevertheless, the goals for the Black community may have been reinforced by his numerous references to civil rights and "empowering" communities in his inaugural address; an inaugural designed to elevate such a goal (Williams, 1999).

In contrast, Barry's first successor, Mayor Kelly, mentioned housing in her inaugural address but only as a problem of "the shortage of affordable housing" (Kelly, 1991). She made no promise to propose a solution at that time, and she subsequently delivered on that absence of promise in the course of her one term in office.

Like Mayor Kelly, Mayor Fenty came into city politics from the comfortable homes of Ward 4, and like Kelly's inaugural speech, housing was scarcely given any attention in his inaugural. A passing reference to "more inclusive" housing was slipped between allusions to the historical evolution of cities (Washington Post, 2007). In contrast, he started his door-to-door campaign early in the pre-election year with his kickoff speech that envisioned "a mix of housing options, including affordable housing, and housing for our poor and homeless" (The Boind Buyer, 2006). More important for Black voters, his previously unparalleled campaigning on virtually every block in the city's Black neighborhoods gave him an image that appealed to Mayor Barry's voters. His first year in office, however, like the remaining three, was marked by several prominent initiatives in education, policing, and economic development but nothing major on housing. Absent the community interaction and prominent housing policy initiatives sensitive to the increasing fear of dislocation, Fenty lost the Black vote and all the largely Black wards, including his home ward, Ward 4.

The challenge for Mayor Gray, as Fenty's successor, in appealing to Black voters across the city was largely to demonstrate his distance from Fenty on racially sensitive issues. That meant, first of all, undoing Fenty's signature initiatives in education.

Secondly, it meant recognizing the territorial background of the city's racial segmentation. In line with that perspective, he activated the Comprehensive Housing Strategy Task Force in 2012 with the unrealized goal of providing $100 million for subsidized housing.

As such, his inaugural speech with a refrain of "one city" as the chorus for listing the socioeconomic and racial differences is understandable (Washington Post, 2011). Perhaps as a consequence, he had less reason than others to address housing policy. Nevertheless, his failure to do so and his subsequent demise are consistent with the prognosis for mayoral candidates for election or reelection who depend heavily on the Black vote.

By the end of Gray's term in office, if not long before, dependence on the Black vote was not the automatic assumption for campaigns that it historically had been. DC vote numbers had succumbed to the racial imbalance of gentrification. The relative growth in the White electorate, along with the indictment scandal handicapping Gray's reelection bid, would seem to be enough to explain his loss to Muriel Bowser in the primary election, especially since she did much better with White voters. Still, changes in the electorate would not explain Bowser's comparative success with Black voters outside of Gray's home ward. Of course, scandal would dampen the Black vote but, as Marion Barry's reelections indicate, it is not a sufficient excuse for losing the vote.

Given Bowser public association with Mayor Fenty's unpopular politics, Bowser surprised most observers with the support she received from Black voters. What may have elevated candidate Bowser is the housing issue and her relationship to it. In part, her position on current housing issues contributed to her support, but in large part the circumstances surrounding housing issues during the election put her in a favorable position. For almost a year before the election, the housing problem in heavily Black and poor neighborhoods had been, in varying ways, at the center public discussion and news media attention (Fisher & Hendrix, 2014).

First, homelessness and housing for low-income families had been an issue for the previous mayor. In addition, city council members, particularly Councilwoman Bowser, came under pressure to replace problematic homeless shelters and to find long-term housing for displaced families (Davis, 2016). As a consequence, she was compelled to address the affordable housing issue more broadly in the course of her campaign. Yet, given the inability of Mayor Gray or other councilmembers to put forward popular proposals, she was under no great pressure to offer a policy solution.

Still, by the time of her inauguration, the impact of public pressure was evident. In a speech that offered about 13 policy-related promises, two relate to housing. A promise to "fight homelessness head-on" was sensitive but vague. On affordable housing, however, she was probably more specific than on any other concern. "We'll invest $100 million in affordable housing so that all our residents have a chance at joining the Middle Class" (Bowser, 2015). That promise was given greater substance by the start of her second year when she announced that she was allocating $82 million from the "city's Housing Production Trust Fund for the creation or preservation of more than 800 units of affordable housing" (Hauslohner, 2016, p. B2).

While her housing initiative says very little about how effectively or directly her administration would respond to the racially sensitive concerns of the Black voters who had previously backed her opponent, it illustrates the public pressure for housing in its most affected community. In fact, the increasing prominence of the issue in the years before her election may well have compelled a similar or greater response from any mayor. In the end, however, 800 affordable housing units would barely slow the erosion of the Black population—a voting population that is still self-conscious enough to feel its elusive power slipping away.

In a broad sense, the politics of affordable housing in the city and the public appeals of the city's mayors in campaigning and in starting their administrations reflect the simple demography of the city and electoral power of a racially sensitive Black electorate. With the emergence of home rule for the city, the first mayor inaugurated a focus on housing access in the nationally race-conscious context of "Black Power." That time period, the beginning of the 1970s, basically circumscribes the national movement toward minority group urban voter mobilization. The next mayor, Barry, ultimately defineed and confirmed the power of the Black vote in the city. He was followed by a mayor, Kelly, who sought "restoration" of the city while minimizing race as a basis for mobilization and downgrading the focus on housing. Housing was brought back as a concern under Mayor Williams, the next mayor, but its racial content was largely diluted through a focus on development and economic efficiency. His successor, Fenty, offered, perhaps unintentionally, a largely "deracialized" policy perspective that was weak on affordable housing. The curve moved back toward a more race-conscious electorate under Mayor Gray, but the housing policy emphasis was missing. The issue of housing, however, returned most forcefully under the most recent mayor. It came in a period of fairly subdued racial discourse but at a time when voting patterns of the Black voters demonstrated both their issue concerns and their sense of despair. They were concerned about protecting their housing and, in this regard, their homeland. Yet they apparently had despaired of any possibility of interrupting the tide of dislocation from the city generations have called home since the Emancipation. Their political response seemed to include, at least for some time, their massive abstention from the polls.

Conclusion

From its emergence under home rule as a largely self-governing city, Washington moved out from among the country's small group of cities with a financially sound Black population to become the wealthiest city for African Americans on the basis of income in the country. At the same time, the gap in wealth between Blacks and Whites generally increased, and the number of low-income Black residents grew. All the while, the low-income residents were struggling to maintain their residences in the city as prices increasingly pushed them across the Maryland border. With the turn of the century, the future dissolution of the Black voter majority increasingly seemed to overshadow a broad spectrum of city politics and, along with that image of population redistribution, the city's mayoral campaigns have been haunted by a compelling but politically unmanageable issue, managing housing development. It is an issue that at times has been seen as promising but more often as menacing by the Black majority and most often as inevitable. In its menacing, if not inevitable, incarnation it is called gentrification.

It was not until the 2014 mayoral election that the anticipatory "writing on the wall" was transcribed into a statistical ratio of eligible voters by race. In concert with that change, the structure of mayoral politics, particularly campaigning, also began to change. For the first time two of the three leading general election candidates had Republican Party backgrounds, though campaigning as independents, and they were both White. Yet perhaps more significant structurally were the campaign issues or lack of them. The core of issues affecting the retention and economic stability of low-income African Americans were substantially diminished though still visible. While they were increasingly losing their homes in the District, African Americans turned to public housing policy as a way of affirming, if not protecting, their political presence in the city. In this assessment of their mayoral politics, the point has not been to measure their impact on housing, in part because city leadership would largely agree that the outcome could only be described in degrees of disappointment. The point is to examine the ways in which race consciousness in politics can transcend the boundaries of identity to include a socioeconomic concern—in particular, public support for housing.

The depth and magnitude of the mayoral focus on housing policy may not be clear, but the persistence and sensitivity of affordable housing access has been evident in mayoral campaigning and politics from the beginning of home rule in DC. It has been an issue that intertwines with racial issues and class sensitivities and seemingly passes for a symbol and a measure of race-conscious responsiveness to a declining Black electorate. Where the Black middle class has shown a concern for affordable housing, it has apparently been linked to a larger group identity. When middle-class housing has received special mayoral attention, as it did under mayors Barry and Williams, it has been tied to a relatively greater sense of political security in the Black electorate. When campaign promises and policy prescriptions demonstrated no consistent tie to programmatic or economic outcomes likely to benefit Black residents, as with Mayor Williams, the fears and facts of Black displacement by gentrification were on the rise.

When finally all that is left for mayoral housing policy to gain attention and supporters, as with Mayor Bowser, is the promotion of low-income housing and homeless shelters, then the last stage of gentrification has apparently been reached.

Disclosure Statement

No potential conflict of interest was reported by the author.

References

Barry, M., & Tyree, O. (2014). *Mayor for life: The incredible story of Marion Barry, Jr*. New York: Strebor Books.
Bowser, M. E. (2015). *Mayoral Inaugural Address*. Washington, DC.
Costello, M. T. (2011). *Politics and pupils: How the conflict between the washington teachers' union and the fenty administration impacted education reform in the district of Columbia*. Dissertation. ProQuest Dissertation Publishing. Retrieved from https://wrlc-huprimo.exlibrisgroup.com/discovery/fulldisplay?docid=proquest871114161&context=PC&vid=01WRLC_HOW
Davis, A. C. (2016, February. 9). "*District mayor reveals sites proposed for homeless shelters across city*," Washington Post. Retreived from https://www.washingtonpost.com/local/dc-politics/homeless-shelters-to-bespread-across-capital-under-plan-by-mayor-bowser/2016/02/09/318bc360-cf3111e5-88cd-753e80cd29ad_story.html.
Dawson, M. C. (2001). *Black visions: The roots of contemporary african- american political thought*. Chicago, Illinois: University of Chicago Press.
Debonis, M. (2013 July 10). "*D.C. Council approves 'living wage' bill over Wal-Mart ultimatum*," Washington Post. Retreived from https://www.washingtonpost.com/local/dc-politics/dc-council-approves-livingwage-bill-over-wal-mart-ultimatum/2013/07/10/724aab6e-e96f-11e2-a301ea5a8116d211_story.html
Demessie, M., & Gillespie, A. (2013). From Fenty to Gray: The salience of urban gentrification, black politics, and substantive representation in Washington, DC's 2010 Mayoral Elections. In R. K. Perry (Ed.), *21st century urban race politics: representing minorities as universal interests* (pp. 271–295). Emerald Group Publishing Limited.
DeNavas-Walt, C., Proctor, B. D., & Smith, J. C. (2014). *Income and poverty in the United States: 2013*. Washington, DC: United States Census Bureau.
DePillis, L. (2015, August 17). As pay rises, will restaurants start rolling out the robots? In *Washington post*. (pp. A1).
Du Bois, W. E. B. (1903/1994). *The souls of black folk*. Chicagp, Illinois: Dover Publications.
DuBois, W. B. (1932). Education and work. *Journal of Negro Education*, 60–74. doi:10.2307/2292016
Fauntroy, M. K. (2010). Home rule for the district of Columbia. In R. Walters & T-M.Travis (Eds.), *democratic destiny and the district of Columbia* ((pp. 21–44)). Lanham, MD: Lexington Books.
Fisher, M., & Hendrix, S., (2014, September 13). "Bowser? Catania? Schwartz? D.C. mayoral race rests on an uninspired electorate," Washington Post. Retreived from https://www.washingtonpost.com/local/dc-politics/bowser-catania-dc-mayoralrace-rests-on-an-uninspired-electorate/2014/09/13/285c3f58-387a-11e4-bdfbde4104544a37_story.html.
Flowers, A., Fishman, D., Harris, D., Norton, E. H., Ball, J., Glasper, K. L., ... Jones, W. G. (2010). *Democratic destiny and the District of Columbia: Federal politics and public policy*. Lanham, MD: Lexington Books.

Freed, B. R. (2012, September 7). "Flashback: Marion barry addresses the 1988 democratic national convention." *Mayoral Inaugural Address*. Retreived from http://dcist.com/2012/09/flashback_marion_barry_addresses_th.php

Frazier, E. F. (1957). *Black bourgeoisie: The rise of a new middle class in the United States*. Glencoe, Illinoisa: The Free Press.

Gibson, T. A. (2015). The rise and fall of Adrian Fenty, Mayor-Triathlete: Cycling, gentrification and class politics in Washington DC. *Leisure Studies*, 34(2), 230–249. doi:10.1080/02614367.2013.855940

Gillespie, A. (2014). A modest proposal. what has this got to do with the liberation of black people? The impact of Ronald W. W alters on african american thought and leadership. In *Whose black politics: Cases in post-racial black leadership* (pp. 139). New York: Routledge.

Gillette, H., Jr. (2001). Protest and power in Washington, DC: The troubled legacy of Marion Barry. In J. Adler & D. Colburn (Eds.), *African-American Mayors: Race, politics, and the American city* (pp. 200–226). Urbana, Illinois: University of Illinois Press.

Hauslohner, A. (2016, January). "D.C. to direct $82 million to new and existing affordable housing." Washington Post. B–2. Retrieved from https://www.washingtonpost.com/local/dc-politics/dc-to-direct-82-million-tonew-and-existing-affordable-housing/2016/01/29/3f10d808-c6d1-11e5-9693933a4d31bcc8_story.html.

Jaffe, H. S., & Sherwood, T. (1994). *Dream city: Race, power and the decline of Washington D.C.* New York, NY: Simon & Schuster.

Jones, W. P. (2010). Banished: Housing policy in the district of Colombia and the struggle of working families. In R. Walters & T-M. Travis (Eds.), *Democratic destiny and the district of Columbia: Federal politics and public policy* (pp. 157–181). Lanham, MD: Lexington Books.

Kelly, S. P. (1991). *Finding 'new anchors of hope and promise*. Washington, DC: Mayoral Inaugural Address.

Leon, W. (2010). Marion Barry: A Politician for the Times. In R. Walters & T-M. Travis (Eds.), *Democratic destiny and the District of Columbia: Federal politics and public policy* (pp. 61–87). Lanham, MD: Lexington Books.

Marable, M. (1993). *Blackwater: Historical studies in race, class consciousness, and revolution*. Denver, CO: Univ. Press of Colorado.

Marable, M. (1995). History and black consciousness: The political culture of black America. *Monthly Review*, 47(3), 71. doi:10.14452/MR-047-03-1995-07

McClain, P. D., & Tauber, S. C. (2010). *American Government in Black and White*. Boulder, CO: Paradigm Pub.

Morris, A. (1984). *The origins of the civil rights movement*. New York, NY: The Free Press. .

Myrdal, G. (1944). *An American dilemma, Volume 2: The negro problem and modern democracy* (Vol. 2). New York, NY: Transaction Publishers.

Persons, G. A. (ed.). (1993). *Dilemmas of black politics: Issues of leadership and strategy*. New York, NY: Harper Collins Publishers.

Pitzer, H. K. (2010). What's best for kids" vs. teacher unions: How teach for america blames teacher unions for the problems of urban schools. *Workplace: A Journal for Academic Labor*, 17, 9.

Price, M. J. (2009). *Dreaming blackness: Black nationalism and african american public opinion*. NewYork, NY: New York University Press.

PUBLIC LAW 104-8—APR. 17, 1995. 109 STAT. 99.

Schwartzman and Jenkins. (2010, September 18). "How D.C. Mayor Fenty lost the black how vote," Washington Post. http://www.washingtonpost.com/wpdyn/content/article/2010/09/18/AR2010091804286.html

Schwartzman and Mellnick. (2015, March 7). *A wave of mostly white voters is reshaping the politics of D.C.* Washington, DC: The Washington Post. (p. A1).

Stein, P. (2015, May 22). *Is pricey Shaw a model for retaining affordability amid regentrification?* Washington, DC: The Washington Post. (p. B2).

Stewart, N., & Cohen, J., (2011, January 31). "D.C. Mayor fenty's approval rating plummet," Washington Post, www.washingtonpost.com/wpdyn/content/2010/01/AR2010013002452.html.

The Boind Buyer. (2006, November 10). "Fenty's agenda for DC; Mayor-elect emphasizes housing." Retreived from http://bondbuyer.com; http://sourcemedia.com

Travis, T. M. C. (2010). Sharon Pratt Kelly: The reform mayor. In R. Walters & T-M. Travis (Eds.), *Democratic destiny and the district of Columbia: Federal olitics and public policy* (pp. 87). Lanham, MD: Lexington Books.

U.S. Bureau of the Census, 2010. HOUSEHOLD INCOME IN 2009

Vincent, T. (1989). The garveyite parents of malcolm X. *The Black Scholar*, 20(2), 10–13. doi:10.1080/00064246.1989.11412923

Walters, R., & Travis, T.-M. C. (2010). *Democratic destiny and the district of Columbia: Federal politics and public policy*. Lanham, MD: Lexington Books.

Walton, H. (1994). *Black politics and black political behavior: A linkage analysis*. Westport, Conn.: Praeger Publishers.

Walton, H., & Smith, R. C. (2015). *American politics and the African American quest for universal freedom*. New York: Routledge.

Williams, A. A. (1999, January 2). Bodies and Souls in Motion," *Inaugural Address*. Washington, DC: Mayoral Inaugural Address.

Washington Post. (2011, January 2). "Mayor Vincent C. Gray's inauguration speech." Washington, DC.

Washington Post. 1978. "Marion barry for mayor," Report by Washington Post Editorial http://www.washingtonpost.com/wpsrv/local/longterm/library/dc/barry/78endors.htm

Washington Post. (2010). D. C. Poll. http://www.washingtonpost.com/wpsrv/politics/polls/postpoll_013110.html

Washington Post. (2007). "Mayor Fenty's plans." November 8; and "Fenty, champing at the bit, set to take up city's Reins." January 3. Washington, DC.

Yon, R. (2010). The declining significance of race: Adrian Fenty and the smooth electoral transition. In A. Gillespie (Ed.), *Whose black politics: Cases in post-racial black leadership* (pp. 196–213), New York: Routledge.

Education Policy and Outcomes Within the African American Population

Martell L. Teasley

ABSTRACT
The educational status among African Americans is a story of continuing achievement and continuing disparities in outcomes. On one hand, there are continuing stories of high academic accomplishments among Black Americans who attend and graduate from high-ranking American institutions of higher education. On the other hand, the continuing gap in educational opportunities and outcomes within Black America is shaping present and future education disparities. This essay examines the impact of recent education policy on education reform and outcomes for African Americans. The dynamic characteristics of the Black American educational experience are discussed. Some attention is given to historical factors that helped shape present-day education reform measures and their impact on the African-American educational experience. Education policy as a public health issue is briefly addressed throughout this article. Suggestions are made for future policy initiatives and advocacy, teaching, and for human-service professionals working with Black children and youth in school settings.

There is perhaps no greater barometer of success and opportunities for intergenerational mobility than educational obtainment. While there are outstanding stories of great academic accomplishments among Black Americans graduating from top-tier institutions of higher education in the United States, the widening gap in educational opportunities and outcomes within Black America and among other racial and ethnic groups continues to shape present and future education disparities (The Education Trust, 2014; Ladd, 2002a). This essay examines the general educational landscape of African Americans to include success and shortcomings. The impact of recent education policymaking and its effect on Black America's education opportunities and experience will be discussed. According to *Healthy People 2010* and *Healthy People 2020*, other than families, schools are the most influential institution within the country on the lives of young people. Schools "provide a setting in which friendship networks develop, socialization occurs and behavioral norms are developed and reinforced" (American Public Health Association, 2004, p. 1). Attention is given to public health throughout this article as it relates to educational policy for African-American children and youth.

The author first reviews the demographic characteristics and educational status of African-American children and youth. Recent educational policy measures are discussed for their impact on the educational outcomes of Black American children and youth. This includes an examination of primary, secondary, and postsecondary education, and recent education reform measures. Suggestions are made for future policy initiatives, instruction/teaching, and for human-service professionals participating in educational settings with African-American school-aged children and youth. The terms *African American* and *Black* are interchanged throughout this document.

Head Start

Head Start Programs are important to public health because they help prepare children for school readiness and school success (American Public Health Association, 2004). "Children who do not learn to read in the first grades, who read poorly, or who are retained in grade more than once are more likely than their peers to be drawn into a pattern of risky behaviors" (American Public Health Association, 2004). As an early-education program starting during the War on Poverty in 1965, Head Start continues to demonstrate its worth in preparing preschool children for school success. Findings from a nationally representative sample in a congressionally mandated follow-up study on the impact of Head Start Programs on third graders determined that Black children attending Head Start programs achieved a sustained impact on their language and literacy development, and cognitive and socioemotional development, as reported by teachers, parents, and self-report measures (Puma, 2012). Kim's (2013) review of research literature on Head Start programs reveals a host of positive outcomes for participating African-American children and youth. This includes significant improvements in test scores, particularly in math, in comparison to their nonattending Black peers. Findings from a comparison study of low-income African Americans, using random assignment with four-year-old children placed in a Head Start programs and those on a waitlist, determined that growth rates were significantly higher for the Head Start children in terms of school readiness. Growth rates were determined by a battery of instruments including social, language, and cognitive skills, and health indicators. Simply put, Head Start programs have been a major component of success in early childhood education for African-American children and should continue.

However, given its 45-year expansion, and as African Americans have made socioeconomic and educational gains, Head Starts Programs have witnessed diminishing returns. Today, gains in academic achievement for those attending Head Start programs are associated with children's socioeconomic background, those who identify as needing English language accusation, and geographical location (McCoy, Morris, Connors, & Celia, 2016). Studies have demonstrated that Head Start Programs have their greatest impact in urban dwellings (Morris et al., & Joo, 2010). While African Americans are the majority of children and youth in urban school systems, 65% of Black Americans now live in suburban dwellings. Critics contend that Head Start represents expensive bureaucratic programming for jobs that produce little gain in proportion to the magnitude of funding outlays, while doing little to solve minority children's deficits in school readiness (Ludwig & Phillips, 2008). The political misfortunate of Head Start is that it has become a conservative versus liberal talking point in the battle over U.S. federal education expenditures. These factors have combined to create an era where Head Start programs are starting to experience major financial cuts.

Demographic characteristics

Primary and secondary education

In a review of education demographics, at 14.4% of the U.S. population in 2015, there are 8.1 million African-American children and youth enrolled in public schools, and less than a half-million enrolled in private schools. At 15% of the total U.S. school population, the majority (76%) attend urban schools, with 57% of these students attending schools in the South. For African-American students attending private schools, 75% attend religious schools, with 35% of these students attending Catholic schools (The Education Trust, 2014).

Approximately half of all African-American students attend K–12 public schools where they are the majority of students (The Education Trust, 2014). Surpassing their attendance in private schools, African Americans are now 30% of school-aged children and youth attending charter schools in the U.S. In comparison to Whites at 5.1%, the national dropout rate for Black youth is higher than the national average at 7.4%, but lower than Hispanics at a rate of 15.1% annually. About 15% of African Americans have obtained a GED instead of a high school diploma (U.S. Census Bureau, 2016). In

2015, the percentage of African Americans 25 and older with a high school diploma or higher was 84.7% (U.S. Census Bureau, 2017).

African-American children and youth have made gains in academic achievement in recent decades. For example, under No Child Left Behind from 2003 until 2013, fourth- and eighth-grade math performance scores increased at a higher rate for African-American students than their White counterparts (The Education Trust, 2014). From 2002 to 2012, African-American high school graduate enrollment in college increased from 57% to 62%. SAT scores have risen by 22% since 2008, along with a 12% increase in the number of Black Americans taking the SAT from 2002 until 2012. What is more, there are schools that serve low-income Black American students that have been identified as among the best in the country. For example, Walnut Hills public college-preparatory high school in Cincinnati, Ohio, and Paxon School for Advanced Studies in Duval County, Florida, are long-standing public schools that demonstrate high levels of achievement for African Americans. Other examples are Mastery Charter in Philadelphia and Providence; St. Mel on the Chicago west side; the Urban Prep Academy of Chicago; the Metro Academic and Classical High School in St. Louis, Missouri; Franklin High School in Settle; and the Oakland, California Unified School District's Manhood Development Program. Researchers have demonstrated that the common thread for school success in low-income majority-minority schools is when students gain a sense of identity and purpose through a cultural connection, and when there are caring, competent, and dedicated teachers and school administrators who are free of bias with high expectations for African-American school-aged youth (Carter, 2008; Pitre, 2014).

Colleague attendance and graduation

Access to college and universities is increasingly important in an advancing a high-tech society and the global job market. African-American high school graduates enrolling in college during the fall after high school graduation rose from 52% in 2002 to 62% in 2012. Entering higher education through community colleges lowers the chance of graduation from a four-year institution. Forty percent of Black American students graduated from four-year colleges compared to 63% of White American students (The Education Trust, 2014). Representing 10% of the nation's overall college graduates, 28.3% of Black Americans attended college or graduate school in 2015. For African Americans 25 and older, 33% had some college or an associates degree, 13% obtained a bachelors degree, 20.2% had a bachelors degree or higher, 7.8% obtained a graduate or professional degree in 2015 (U.S. Census Bureau, 2016).

In terms of college and graduate school attendance, Black females (32%) outpace Black males (24%). Black females (23.1%) are more likely to graduate with a bachelors degree or higher when compare to Black males (18.2%; U.S. Census Bureau, 2017). In 2012, for all degrees earned by African Americans, "Black females earned 68% of associates degrees, 66% of bachelors degrees, 71% of masters degrees, and 65% of all doctor's degrees awarded to Black students" (U.S. Department of Education, 2012).

College readiness

College readiness provides a lens into preparation for postsecondary education and students' ability to be successful at the highest-ranking institutions of higher education. There are signs of increasing achievement for Black Americans in this area. One sign of college readiness is that the number of Black students taking Advanced Placement (AP) classes in high school tripled from 2002 until 2012. Nevertheless, it is standardized exams such as the ACT and the SAT—primary indicators for college readiness—that serve as historical barriers to college entry for Black Americans in the nations' top colleges and universities.

One barrier has been the completion of the Free Application for Federal Student Aid (FAFSA). The FAFSA form was a cumbersome undertaking to complete until, in September 2015, President Obama announced a revamping of the process for FAFSA completion. It is estimated that some two million students who are eligible for federal Pell Grant funding fail to complete the FAFSA form annually because of complications in the application process. FAFSA became easier to complete for the 2017–2018 school year, which facilitates more students from low-income families in financing college admissions.

During the past five years, the number of African-American high school graduates taking the ACT rose by 22% (The Education Trust, 2014). As 15% of the overall student population, only 9% of African Americans took the ACT in 2013 and they were only 5% of students who passed. A review of aggregate data from the U.S. Department of Education (2016) from 2004–2014 finds that all ethnic groups scored higher on all sections of the SAT than African Americans. Subsequently, if the vetting for the approximately 50,000 annual admission's slot to the nation's top 25 universities and colleges where to be race neutral and based solely on competitive scoring, African Americans "would be buried by a huge mountain of high-scoring non-black students" (The Journal of Blacks in Higher Education, 2005).

ACT and SAT scores historically correlate with family income, background, gender, and parental education (Karanja & Austin, 2014). On average, children from high-income families produce higher scores on standardized tests. "For instance, on comparing the student from low, medium, and high SES," it was "found that students from low SES, medium SES, and high SES, had a 58%, 63%, and 78%, respectively, chance of enrolling in college" (Karanja & Austin, 2014, p. 532). However, even low-income Whites have higher aggregate SAT scores when compared to upper-middle-income African-American youth. In explaining this disparity, scholars have pointed out, data in this area does not account for family assets as part of overall family wealth, in which African Americans are at a gross disadvantage when compared to their White American counterparts (Karanja & Austin, 2014). According to a recent report from the Jack King Cooke Foundation, "students from families in the bottom economic quartile comprise only 3% of enrollment in the most competitive schools. That's in contrast with 72% of students in those schools who hail from families in the wealthiest quartile" (Camera, 2016).

The well-known "racial scoring gap" on college readiness examinations has actually widened in recent years, and is the source of great interest by education policymakers, researchers, universities, and even the judicial system (Bohrnstedt, Kitmitto, Ogut, Sherman, & Chan, 2015). Perhaps this is partly due to the aggregate economic decline for African Americans that took place during the Great Recession—today, nearly 40% of Black children and youth attending school live below the poverty line. On average, African-American students achieve less than 2% of the top scores on college readiness examinations. "With respect to various measures of quality such as certification, subject matter background/expertise, pedagogical training, selectivity of college attended, test scores, and experience, less-qualified teachers are disproportionately found in schools with greater numbers of ethnic minority, low-income students" (Cowan, 2014, p. 213). As a form of corrective action and given the long history of academic disadvantage experienced by this group, prevailing affirmative action admissions policies allow for the admission of approximately 3,000 Black first-year students into the nations' top 25 high-ranking universities, which amount to "about 6% of all first-year students at these institutions" (The Journal of Blacks in Higher Education, 2005). Affirmative action in higher education provides funding in the form of grants and fellowships through initiatives to help minorities and women gain access, opportunities, and resources for participation in higher education.

As with other sectors of society, there are continuing challenges to affirmative action in post-secondary education, and many have fought and continue to fight to end the practice. A seminal case in the demise of affirmative action programs is the 1994 California Proposition 209, which set the stage in the challenge to end affirmative action in postsecondary education. Proposition 209 amended the state's constitution by banning the use of race, ethnicity, or gender in the consideration in public employment, government contracting, and public education. Legally vetted by a state referendum in 1996, Proposition 209 has withstood legislative overturn and judicial challenges. It has reduced the numbers of African American enrollment in the University of California and its constituent universities. It was Grutter v. Bollinger, in 2003, in which the U.S. Supreme Court upheld the right of the University of Michigan Law School to consider race in its admissions decisions. The state of Texas banned affirmative action in its university system from 1997–2003 with the Supreme Court's decision in Grutter, which overruled Hopwood v. State of Texas (Garces, 2012, p. 6). There are currently seven states that ban affirmative action in postsecondary education: Arizona, California, Florida, Michigan, Nebraska, New Hampshire, and Washington (Garces, 2012). These states have witnessed a "significant drop in the enrollment of black and Hispanic students in their most selective colleges and universities" (Liptak, 2014). Finally, in an effort to weaken or disavow the 2016 U.S. Supreme Court decision in Fisher v. the University of Texas, which upheld affirmative action in higher education, the Trump administration in 2018 rescinded federal Obama-era guidelines for affirmative action in college admissions. At the time of this writing, the impact of this policy shift is yet to be witnessed.

Historically Black colleges and universities

Historically, Black colleges and universities (HBCUs) are essential to postsecondary education for African Americans. "The Higher Education Act of 1965 defined the HBCUs as any historically black college that was both established before 1964 and whose primary purpose was to educate African Americans" (Glaude, 2016). In the 1970s, HBCUs educated over 75% of African Americans. Today, only 9% of African Americans attend HBCUs, but they award 20% of undergraduate degrees to African Americans and produce 50% of African-American professionals (Glaude, 2016). Unfortunately, many of these important institutes for Black communities are under serious financial hardship, hindering their mission. In fact, five HBCUs closed over the past 20 years and others continue to struggle financially.

Given the economic deficits of many African Americans attending college, 74% of students attending HBCUs qualify for Pell Grants (Bidwell, 2014). As such, 80% of revenues for HBCUs comes from student loans (Glaude, 2016). Nevertheless, given the economic downturn experienced during the Great Recession, education policy under the Obama administration witnessed the U.S. Department of Education selecting to tighten credit requirements for Parent PLUS student loans in 2011, causing a reduction in loans of over 200,000 fewer recipients in 2013. As a result, "Between 2011 and 2013, there were 54% fewer [Parent] PLUS loan recipients at for-profit colleges and 45% fewer at HBCUs" (Bidwell, 2014). This practice decimated the financial portfolio of many HBCUs, causing a financial crisis and a loss of up to 20% of the student body at some HBCUs (Glaude, 2016). In late 2013, subsequent political advocacy resulted in the repeal of the stricter requirements for such loans; however, many HBCUs have not recovered from the revenue shortfall experienced during the period.

Education policy

School resegregation

Despite the triumph of the 1954 Brown v. Board of Education Supreme Court decision to eliminate legal school segregation from public schools, segregated school systems have re-emerged after over 60 years of continued education reform throughout the United States. "On average, White students attended schools that were 9% Black while Black students attended schools that were 48% Black, indicating a large difference in average Black student density nationally" (National Assessment of Educational Progress, 2015). Today, in the South, 12% of African-American students attend schools where Whites are only 1% of the student population (Hannah-Jones, 2014). The resegregation of public schools in America is not by happenstance. Hannah-Jones found in her investigation of the resegregation of schools in Tuscaloosa, AL, patterns that are symbolic of a growing trend in southern school districts:

> In the South, once the most segregated in the country, had by the 1970s become the most integrated, typically as a result of federal court orders. But since 2000, judges have released hundreds of school districts, from Mississippi to Virginia, from court-enforced integration, and many of these districts have followed the same path as Tuscaloosa's—back toward segregation. Black children across the South now attend majority-black

schools at levels not seen in four decades. Nationally, the achievement gap between black and white students, which greatly narrowed during the era in which schools grew more integrated, widened as they became less so. (Hannah-Jones, 2014)

In 2000, at the start of the Bush administration, there were 595 school districts nationwide under court order to desegregate, only to plummet to 380 at the end of the second Bush administration in 2008 (Hannah-Jones, 2014). The number was reduced to 340 during the Obama administration. Research demonstrates that school districts are more likely to segregate after the removal of court mandates. For example, in districts released from desegregation orders between 1990 and 2011, 53% of Black students now attend school where minorities are nine out of 10 students enrolled (Hannah-Jones, 2014).

In general, school systems that are predominately Black in population are the product of lower household property tax revenues, and are therefore under-resourced with inadequate facilities, books, labs, special services, and computers. Such school systems, mainly found in urban locations, where most African Americans attend, are more likely to have uncertified teachers and teachers that do not have postsecondary degrees in the individual subjects they are teaching. This makes education reform policy formation critical to academic access and opportunity for African Americans (Hannah-Jones, 2014).

Education reform

The problem with education reform efforts within the U.S. concerning Black America is that policies are crafted based on the economic prowess of state and local market forces instead of a close examination of the education needs of Black communities. Take for example the enactment of No Child Left Behind in 2002 under the Bush administration. This policy "was nearly 40 years in the making" (Greene & Burke, 2016) as a desired method of creating accountability for academic outcomes. In many ways, NCLB was the triumph of conservative education policy as characterized in *A Nation At Risk* (The National Commission on Educational Excellence, 1983), *Losing Ground* (Murray, 1984), and *The Bell Curve* (Herrnstein & Murray, 1994)—all demanding a move away from civil rights–era government funding under Title I provisions to poor communities, based on social welfare needs without accountability, to a system based on funding for measurable, progressive, and sustained achievement (Greene & Burke, 2016).

No Child Left Behind

No Child Left Behind was enacted based on the belief that all children deserve the opportunity to have good teachers in schools that perform to acceptable standards, as measured by reliable and valid standardized testing (Klein, 2015). As a response to the call for school accountability in past education reform measures, NCLB reversed school funding streams and approaches to the question of what to do about failing schools. Instead of providing government funding to poor school districts, which started in 1965 under Title I of the Elementary and Secondary Education Act during President Lyndon B. Johnson's War on Poverty, NCLB gave funding to reward schools that meet Adequate Yearly Progress (AYP) goals. It required states to hold school districts accountable for making AYP for all students in reaching proficiency in reading and math by 2014 (Klein, 2015). If a school failed to meet AYP goals for two consecutive years, "it must be identified for improvement, and there must be sanction" (Klein, 2015).

With many identified schools in urban school districts populated by a majority of African-American school-aged children and youth, by 2008, 28% of these schools failed increasing AYP standards, and by 2011 the number rose to 38% of schools (Klein, 2015). Other than tutoring and "supplemental services" for failing schools, NCLB authorized the restructuring of schools that are identified as continuously failing to meet AYP. Consequently, given the continued problems of urban schools, with their low tax base for funding school systems, many were doomed to fail AYP due to the inadequate infusion of capital needed to change the dynamics of underfunded urban school systems. The public health impact of NCLB was significant in that the policy reversed past trends in removal of federal flow of dollars to poor communities. Although NCLB authorized students to leave failing schools, there was, in general, no place for Black students from failing public schools to matriculate to.

The real challenge with NCLB is that it prescribed a "one-size-fits-all accountability model" that "does not work in all conditions," and sharply limits states policy and hinders the capacity of educators to make needed changes. It punishes schools in one state for achievement levels that are defined as great successes in another (Sunderman & Kim, 2004). Hence, NCLB was just another method of education reform that did not take into consideration the ecology community, socio-economic, neighborhood, and familial needs of African Americans.

Zero tolerance policies

No Child Left Behind helped to usher in a new wave of tough discipline practices in schools throughout the country (Jordan, 2013). As a measure to secure school safety, zero-tolerance policies were enacted. The law requires each state to develop a method for designating certain schools as "persistently dangerous" (Jordan, 2013). Now under mandate for standardized testing outcomes, school teachers and administrators used school suspension and expulsion as a response to problematic behaviors. "As federal policy was translated into state law, district policy, and ultimately school practice, a broad range of student behaviors came under the purview of zero tolerance" (Jordan, 2013, p. 5). This sparked the high and disproportionate use of exclusionary discipline practices and the funneling of young people, particularly African-American youth, into the juvenile justice system, and became the start of the now infamous school-to-prison-pipeline (Skiba, Eckes, & Brown, 2009). As Losen and Skiba (n.d.) note, "the typical ninth grader who went to prison had previously attended school only 58% of the time….Two thirds had been suspended at least once in eighth grade" (p. 3). As such, with one in ten Black males ages 18–24 presently incarcerated, they are more likely to gain a GED than any other group. "For black males, 22% of all GED credentials are produced by the prison system each year compared to 5% and 8% for white and Hispanic males, respectively" (Heckman & Lafontaine, 2010, p. 248).

It is African-American children and youth that bear the brunt of zero-tolerance policies in schools; they lead all racial and ethnic groups as recipients of the harshest disciplinary actions, and they are disproportionately suspended and expelled from schools (Losen & Martinez, 2013). Although the greatest amount of school suspension and expulsion takes place in middle schools, as 16% of children in preschools, African-American preschoolers are 48% of those suspended and expelled from preschools. One out of six (17%) African-American students have been suspended from school at least once from K–12 schools. This compares to 1 in 20 (5%) Whites, 1 in 14 (7%) Latinos, 1 in 13 (8%) Native American, and 1 in 50 (2%) Asian-Americans school-aged children and youth (Losen & Gillespie, 2012, p. 6).

Cultural bias

Coupled with zero-tolerance policies is the long-standing challenge of teacher bias in the classroom for African-American children and youth. Research demonstrates that racial stereotypes still plague public education and hinder the equality of opportunity for African-American children and youth. Undoubtedly more research needs to be conducted; yet, there is evidence of teacher bias in the school settings, and its disproportionate, negative impact on African-American children and youth. Gershenson, Holt, and Papageorge (2015) found that teachers' educational expectations for African-American students were significantly lower among non–African American teachers in comparison to their African-American counterparts. Adams, Kurtz-Costes, and Hoffman's (2016) review of research on the consequences of skin tone for African-American school-aged children and youth reveals that they experience pervasive negative bias against dark skin tones across grade levels from primary to postsecondary education. Moreover, in an examination of teacher bias in judgment of pupils' mathematical ability and reading attainment at age seven, Campbell (2015) found that ethnicity, gender, special education needs, and income levels all factor in forming biases that affect judgments about students' ability.

The reauthorization of the Individuals with Disabilities Act 2004 (IDEA) attempted to strengthened provisions to reduce disproportionate representation of African Americans and students from other diverse cultures in special education. As a preventive measure, IDEA 2004 specifically states that evidence-based methods are to be used prior to attempts to develop an Individual Education Plan and placement of children in a special education programs. Similarly, the American with Disabilities Act calls for antidiscrimination practices in schools for students with disabilities. Nevertheless, African-American children and youth continue to experience patterns of cultural bias, and school suspension are intertwined with a special education diagnosis for African-American children and youth. One out of every four Black school-aged children and youth diagnosed with disabilities is suspended from school. "Students with disabilities and Black students were also more likely to be suspended repeatedly in a given year than to be suspended just once" (Losen & Gillespie, 2012, p. 7).

The reverse is true for students without disabilities and for most other racial/ethnic groups. Even within charters schools there are similar findings: research demonstrates that Black youth are 16 times more likely than White students, per every 100 students enrolled, to be suspended from charters (Losen, Keith, Hudson, & Martinez, 2016). These patterns of disproportionality have been found to be significant in research studies. Yet, research on student behavior, race, and discipline has found no evidence that African-American overrepresentation in school suspension is due to higher rates of misbehavior (Skiba, Shure, Middelberg, & Baker, 2011).

Understanding that schools serve as a primary vehicle for children and youth to gain health access, zero-tolerance policies should be declared a public health hazard, particularly given the relationship between racial bias and the enforcement of zero tolerance (Jurkowski & Keefe, 2013). School suspension and expulsion reduces children's time in school and therefore access to health-related services and referrals in schools. The evidence supports that zero-tolerance policies are not effective in the long run and have numerous negative consequences that further hinder successful academic outcomes (Smith & Harper, 2015). Coupled with the shortcomings of public school funding associated with residential structural barriers, in terms of local taxation based on property value, zero-tolerance policies, cultural bias, and discrimination create the context and conditions that are characteristic of many school systems with majority African-American children and youth (Jurkowski & Keefe, 2013). From a public health perspective, this is an untenable position because it costs society more in the long run through greater use of and dependency on social welfare programs, particularly for those that do not graduate from high school. Thus, educational equity is important to equity in public health. "Increasing the high school completion rate, a major goal of the education system, is also fittingly a health objective for the nation" (American Public Health Association, 2004).

Market-based reform

Another product of NCLB is that the law created spaces for school choice and the privatization of education (Hursh, 2007). The current climate is one of market reform as the solution to continued underachievement by students within the American primary and secondary education system. The most prevalent reform options in school choice are school vouchers, charter schools, tuition tax credits, and the use of educational management organizations (Bracey, 2002; Ladd, 2002b). Bracey explains that some reformers are mere opportunists attempting to gain a share of the $700 billion that the U. S. expends on education. School vouchers are based on state-funded scholarships that provide parents with funding for tuition at private schools that meet minimum standards. Given that the majority of schools that accept vouchers are mostly religiously affiliated, school vouchers have been challenged in state court systems, but have prevailed as a school choice option in most states. At their start, character schools were public schools where community residents petitioned local school boards to secede from traditional public schools to form their own charter. Several types of charter school formations have been tried and continue to flourish. For example, Teasley, Crutchfield, Williams, Clayton, and Okilwa's (2016) study of 23 Afrocentric charter schools, through a systematic review of literature, revealed that only 34% of the schools "achieved or exceeded statewide standards in testing and met their state's AYP goals" (p. 99). Today, there are for-profit charter schools that are based on market competition by education management organizations.

Supporters of market reform contend that it will spark innovation and reduce government bureaucracy (Ladd, 2002a). Ladd's (2002b) work on market reform in urban areas cites three overarching reasons why market-based reform places urban populations at a disadvantage: First, there is "market interest" in that large-scale market reform, particularly in low-preforming school systems, tends to favor individual parents and children while neglecting the "legitimate interest of various stakeholders" (Ladd, 2002a). In other words, it "privileges one set of interest over others" (Ladd, 2002a), leaving little balance to reform efforts. Second, "compulsory attendance" means that failing schools cannot shut down unless there is an alternative school to meet student needs. Thus, the chance for the market to work as planned, where failing schools are shut down and students have viable options, is unlikely to occur. Third, there are also "parental perceptions of school quality" (Ladd, 2002a), through which parents view the quality of a school based on the quality of the student body, teachers, and staff. As such, students from low-income backgrounds are at a disadvantage in the competition for attending the best schools and high-quality staff and teachers. This situation is characteristic of many urban school districts and remains an ongoing problem for many under-resourced African-American families and communities.

Conclusion

The United States has made headway in educational opportunities with each generation, but improved access has thus far not served as an immediate cure for long-standing societal problems. While resources for many public schools remain scarce in the current economic environment, traditionally disadvantaged populations continue to suffer the consequences. For school-based professionals and paraprofessionals working with African-American children and youth in educational settings, it is important to have knowledge of the specific dynamics and impact of education policy on academic opportunities and outcomes for this population. Although school-aged children and youth from all racial and ethnic groups have similar needs, there are unique characteristics and challenges that members of a given group may experience. Therefore, it is important to understand how public policy shapes the educational landscape, and what educational policies mean to particular groups. Macro-, mezzo-, and micro-based issues are all important to understand, and must be critically examined for their implications for African-American school-aged children and youth. A public health approach that engages in the assessment and evaluation of school-based methods to improve community and family well-being must help shape future education policy within African-American communities (Jurkowski & Keefe, 2013). This report concludes with some suggestions for policy advocacy and implications for school-based professionals practicing with African-American children and youth.

Implications for policy consideration

Social welfare and education policies have profound impact on the educational opportunities for African-American children and youth. One factor is that the supply of early-childhood educators and K–12 teachers is diminishing because of low pay and the retirement of teachers that are baby boomers (Allegretto & Mishel, 2016). This factor is twofold in that there is a diminishing and disproportionate supply of early-childhood educators and teachers serving African-American children and youth in schools. In an increasingly diverse student population within American school systems, Whites are overrepresented and Blacks and Latinos are underrepresented among the ranks of teachers, particularly in urban areas. As such, crafting and implementing federal and state policies that address this shortage is desperately needed (Allegretto & Mishel, 2016). Given the retirement of baby boomers and the growing diversification of public schools, there is a need to rekindle past efforts which targeted the recruitment of African Americans and Hispanics/Latinos for teacher education. Coupled with this should be the consideration of monetary incentives such as college forgiveness loans, both full and partial, to African Americans and Hispanics/Latinos who successfully complete college teaching-degree programs and who work in said communities. Minority communities should be targeted for recruitment as school teachers and as school administrators. Recruitment of minority school teachers should start at the high school level and tracked into college education. To avoid recipients from immediately leaving their identified communities or not serving low-income communities, loan forgiveness can be tied to reciprocity in teaching in urban school systems with specific metrics. As a latent accountability measure, teaching evaluations can be tied to greater incentives in order to maintain quality teachers in urban schools.

Another salient challenge within K–12 school settings is the disproportionate suspension and expulsion of African-American children and youth. Research demonstrates that school suspension and expulsion has negative effects on education outcomes and that exclusionary discipline practices are not an effective strategy for classroom and school climate management (Losen & Martinez, 2013; Skiba, 2009; Smith & Harper, 2015). Under NCLB and its federal reporting mechanism, only school districts are held accountable for school discipline rates. Thus, a policy suggestion would be to have individual teachers held accountable for their efforts at classroom management, as well as school principles. This would place accountability at the local level and may facilitate alternative ways of dealing with behavioral challenges in the classroom, as well as help to reduce cultural bias that has been identified as a factor in the overuse of exclusionary discipline practices in schools (Campbell, 2015). Legislators within the federal government, states, and local school systems should consider policy initiatives that addresses this issue. In addition, there is a growing number of evidence-based interventions that have demonstrated a change in school climate and a significant reduction in exclusionary discipline practices in schools (Losen & Martinez, 2013).

Although the movement toward greater usage of market-based reform efforts tends to privilege the individual interest of parents, the reality of reform is that there are various stakeholders to include: teachers, staff, administrators, future employers, and students—meaningful reform needs input from all entities instead of private contractual agreements (Ladd, 2002b). Families and communities with greater economic resources are at an advantage in the pursuit of market-based education reform. As a public health measure, education reform that promotes school success for all is important to the nation. "Adult health status is directly associated with higher education levels, regardless of income" (American Public Health Association, 2004).

Nevertheless, African Americans, both as families and communities, must understand that there is continuing movement toward market-based education reform; they should examine the dynamics of market-based reform to decide what works best for their school-aged children and youth, given individual and communities resources. Privatization of education through vouchers, for-profit charter schools, and public charter schools is a moving target that Black communities must negotiate and craft in their best interest. In the long run, and done strategically with the vested interest of Black communities in mind, market-based reform can be cost beneficial to community well-being and youth academic outcomes. It is important to note that there are examples of success (although few in number) in the use of school vouchers for African-American children and youth. Researchers investigating privately funded vouchers in Dayton, New York City, and Washington, DC found some positive achievement gains for African-American students when families opted to attend private schools using school vouchers (Ladd, 2002b).

The problem with affirmative action policies is that they give the appearance of social justice by allowing limited outreach as a corrective measure to the problem of low minority admissions in higher education, while little to nothing is done to correct the structural and economic challenges that impede academic success for African Americans and other minority groups. Then too, in the age of austerity and with the increasing diversification of America, there is a move to rid the country of affirmative action practices in higher education as competition for slots in the best colleges and universities increases. In the Grutter case upholding affirmative action in college admissions, Justice Sandra Day O'Connor opined that the goal is to eliminate affirmative action over the next 25 years. However, at this moment "there is no evidence that substantial progress toward closing the test scoring gap will occur. Thus, the huge and growing gap in SAT scores, and particularly the scores at the highest levels, becomes one of the nation's most urgent problems" (Garces, 2012, p. 6).

Implications for practice

Despite tangible gains in academic achievement over multiple decades, a disparaging number of Black American students lag behind. At the practice level, school-based professionals must have a full ecological perspective of the African-American education experience in America. Such an understanding should not stop at the doors of schools, but must encompass an understanding of the structural and economic challenges that African-American communities face in attempting to promote academic success for Black children and youth. In gaining such an understanding and from a policy perspective, school-based professionals and paraprofessionals need a greater voice in expressing challenges they face in their attempt to implement evidenced-based practices. Public school administrators should work with educators and legislators to develop greater feedback loops between practitioners and education policy advocates and legislators.

Both majority and minority racial and ethnic practitioners must consider a shift in school climate in order to address factors such as cultural bias, academic underachievement, and college readiness for Black children and youth. Across the nation there are examples of public school settings with majority African-American student populations that are educating these students to high standard of achievement. For example, "At George Hall Elementary School in Mobile, Alabama—where 99% of students are African American—94% of the African-American fifth-graders exceeded state math standards, and 73% did so in reading" (The Education Trust, 2014, p. 14). Similarly, at Arcadia Elementary School in Olympia Fields, Illinois, where 90% of the student body is African American, 79% "of the school's African American third-grade students met or exceeded state reading and math standards." At the same time, only "41% of African American third-graders statewide…met or exceeded state reading standards and just 31%…met or exceeded state math standards" (The Education Trust, 2014, p. 14). There is also the example at Elmont Memorial High School in Elmont, New York, where African American are 75% of students and 94% of these students graduated on time in 2012. What these examples demonstrate is that when communities, school administrators, and teachers come together and are committed, successful educational outcomes for African-American children and youth within urban school systems can emerge.

The bottom line is that Black families and communities will have to take charge of the future of their education outcomes. In this effort, African-American communities must create coalitions and build capacity with other ethnic groups that have an interest in education as a public good and as a public health issue. All parities with vested interests must be part of reform efforts and government officials must be held accountable. Local and state officials must be accountable and major African-American institutions, such as HBCUs, cultural and political organizations, and think tanks must design, strategize, and advocate for quality education settings for African-American children and youth. The movement toward market-based reform is taking hold in America and African Americans cannot afford to engage in passivity or lack of participation. Led by leaders within the conglomeration of America's Black church congregations, and in financial collaboration with Black capitalists, wealthy entertainers, and professional athletes, Black American should move to engage in charter school development before their educational interest is purchased by some private entity with a market-based, profit-driven motive.

If Black lives matter, and they do, then access to a quality education and knowledge development are paramount to the future of vibrant and prosperous African-American families and communities. Finally, Black America must not only earn, but demand, continued entry into the nations' highest-achieving colleges and universities, as well as state-sanctioned colleges and universities. They must demand their share of the financial windfall taking place through market-based reform and the privation of public education systems in America. All of this means greater attention to policy advocacy, community planning, fiscal responsibility and accountability, and the appropriate implementation of culturally relevant practice measures that facilitate healthy socialization and educational outcomes for Black children and youth.

Disclosure statement

No potential conflict of interest was reported by the author.

References

Adams, E. A., Kurtz-Costes, B. E., & Hoffman, A. J. (2016). Skin tone bias among African Americans: Antecedents and consequences across the life span. *Developmental Review, 40*, 93–116. doi:10.1016/j.dr.2016.03.002

Allegretto, S. A., & Mishel, L. (2016). *The teacher pay gap is wider than ever: Teachers' pay continues to fall further behind pay of comparable workers*. Retrieved from http://www.epi.org/publication/the-teacher-pay-gap-is-wider-than-ever-teachers-pay-continues-to-fall-further-behind-pay-of-comparable-workers/

American Public Health Association. (2004). *Promoting public health and educational goals through coordinated school health program*. Retrieved from https://www.apha.org/policies-and-advocacy/public-health-policy-statements/policy-database/2014/07/02/10/30/promoting-public-health-and-education-goals-through-coordinated-school-health-programs

Bidwell, A. (2014). *Change to loan qualifications Hurt students at HBCUs, for-profit colleges*. U.S. News & World Report. News. Retrieved from http://www.usnews.com/news/articles/2014/01/08/change-to-loan-qualifications-hurt-students-at-hbcus-for-profit-colleges

Bohrnstedt, G., Kitmitto, S., Ogut, B., Sherman, D., & Chan, D. (2015). *School composition and the Black–White achievement gap* (NCES 2015-018). U.S. Department of Education. Washington, DC: National Center for Education Statistics. Retrieved September 24, 2015, from http://nces.ed.gov/pubsearch.066x.63.9.852

Bracey, G. W. (2002). The War against America's Public Schools: Privatizing Schools, Commercializing Education ERIC ED464416. Retrieved from http://eric.ed.gov/?id=ED464416

Camera, L. (2016). *Poverty preference admissions: The new affirmative action? There are between 25,000 to 35,000 high-achieving low-income students in the* U.S. News & World Report. News. Retrieved from http://www.usnews.com/news/articles/2016/01/12/poverty-preference-admissions-the-new-affirmative-action

Campbell, T. (2015). Stereotyped at seven? Biases in teacher judgment of pupils' ability and attainment. *Journal of Social Policy, 44*(3), 517–547. doi:10.1017/S0047279415000227

Carter, D. J. (2008). Cultivating a critical race consciousness for African Americans school success. *Educational Foundation*, 11–28. Retrieved from https://files.eric.ed.gov/fulltext/EJ839495.pdf

Cowan, C. P. (2014). Improving african american student outcomes: understanding educational achievement and strategies to close opportunity gaps. *Western Journal of Black Studies, 38*(4), 209–217.

Garces, L. M. (2012). *The impact of affirmative action bans in graduate education*. The Civil Rigths Project. The University of California. Retrieved from https://civilrightsproject.ucla.edu/research/college-access/affirmative-action/the-impact-of-affirmative-action-bans-in-graduate-education

Gershenson, S., Holt, S. B., & Papageorge, N. (2015). *Who believes in me? The effect of student-teacher demographic match on teacher expectations* (Upjohn Institute Working Paper No. 15-231). doi:10.17848/wp15-231

Glaude, E. S., Jr. (2016). *Democracy in black: How race still enslaves the American soul*. New York, NY: Penguin Random House.

Greene, S., & Burke, K. (2016). *No child left behind*. Oxford Bibliographies. doi: 10.1093/obo/9780190280024-0039

Hannah-Jones, K. (2014). Sixty years after Brown v. Board of education, the schools in Tuscaloosa, Alabama, show how separate and unequal education is coming back. *The Atlantic*. Retrieved from http://www.theatlantic.com/magazine/archive/2014/05/segregation-now/359813/

Heckman, J. J., & Lafontaine, P. A. (2010). The American high school graduation rate: Trends and levels. *Review of Economics and Statistics, 92*(2), 244–262. doi:10.1162/rest.2010.12366

Herrnstein, R. J., & Murray, C. (1994). *The bell curve: Intelligence and class structure in American life*. New York, NY: Simon & Schuster.

Hursh, D. (2007). Assessing "no child left behind" and the rise of neoliberal education policies. *American Educational Research Journal, 44*(3), 493–518. doi:10.3102/0002831207306764

Joo, K. (2010). Long-term effects of head start on academic and school outcomes of children in persistent poverty: Girls vs. boys. *Children and Youth Services Review, 32*(6), 807–814. doi:10.1016/j.childyouth.2010.01.018

Jordan, H. (2013, November). *Beyond zero tolerance discipline and policing in Pennsylvania public schools.* American Civil Liberties Union of Pennsylvania. Retrieved from https://www.aclupa.org/files/7713/8435/5077/BZT_Report_11-14-13.pdf

Jurkowski, E. T., & Keefe, R. H. (Eds.). (2013). *Handbook for public health social work.* New York, NY: Springer Publishing Company.

Karanja, E., & Austin, N. (2014). What are African Americans doing in college? A review of the undergraduate degrees awarded by U.S. institutions to African Americans: 2005–2009. *The Journal of Negro Education, 83*(4), 530. doi:10.7709/jnegroeducation.83.4.0530

Kim, Y. J. (2013). Head start, 4 years after completing the program. *Education Economics, 21*(5), 503–519. doi:10.1080/09645292.2011.607556

Klein, A. (2015). *Education week. No child left behind: An overview.* Retrieved from: https://www.edweek.org/ew/section/multimedia/no-child-left-behind-overview-definition-summary-html

Ladd, H. F. (2002a). *Market-based reforms in urban education.* Washington, D.C.: Economic Policy Institute.

Ladd, H. F. (2002b). *Market-based reforms in urban education.* EPI Book. Retrieved from http://www.epi.org/publication/books_ladd-educationreform/

Liptak, A. (2014). Court backs Michigan on affirmative action. *The New York Times.* Retrieved from http://www.nytimes.com/2014/04/23/us/supreme-court-michigan-affirmative-action-ban.html?_r=1

Losen, D. J., & Gillespie, J. (2012). *Opportunities suspended: The disparate impact of disciplinary exclusion from school.* The Civil Rights Project. Retrieved from https://civilrightsproject.ucla.edu/resources/projects/center-for-civil-rights-remedies/school-to-prison-folder/federal-reports/upcoming-ccrr-research

Losen, D. J., Keith, M. A., Hodson, C. L., & Martinez, T. E. (2016). *Charter schools, civil rights and school discipline: A comprehensive review.* The Center for Civil Rights Remedies at The Civil Rights Project. Retrieved from: https://escholarship.org/uc/item/65x5j31h

Losen, D. J., & Martinez, T. E. (2013). Out of school and off track: The overuse of suspensions in American middle and high schools [Report]. University of California, Los Angeles, Civil Rights Project, Center for Civil Rights Remedies Retrieved from http://civilrightsproject.ucla.edu/resources/projects/center-for-civil-rights-remedies/school-to-prison-folder/federal-reports/out-of-school-and-off-track-the-overuse-of-suspensions-in-american-middle-and-high-schools/OutofSchool-OffTrack_UCLA_4-8.pdf

Losen, D. J., & Skiba, R. J. (n.d.). *Suspended education urban middle schools in crisis.* The Civil Rights Project. Retrieved from https://civilrightsproject.ucla.edu/research/k-12-education/school-discipline/suspended-education-urban-middle-schools-in-crisis

Ludwig, J., & Phillips, D. A. (2008). Long-term effects of head start on low-income children. *Annals of the New York Academy of Sciences, 11*(36), 257–268. doi:10.1196/annals.1425.005

McCoy, D. C., Morris, P. A., Connors, M. C., & Celia. (2016). Differential effectiveness of head start in urban and rural communities. *Journal of Applied Developmental Psychology, 43*, 29–42. doi:10.1016/j.appdev.2015.12.007

Murray, C. (1984). *Losing ground: American social policy, 1950-1980.* New York, NY: Basic Books.

National Assessment of Educational Progress. (2015). *School composition and the black-white achievement gap.* Retrieved from http://nces.ed.gov/nationsreportcard/pubs/studies/2015018.aspx

Pitre, C. C. (2014). Improving African American student outcomes: Understanding educational achievement and strategies to close opportunity gaps. *The Western Journal of Black Studies, 38*(4), 209–2017.

Puma, M. (2012). *Third grade follow-up to the head start impact study final report, executive summary* (OPRE Report # 2012-45b). Washington, DC: Office of Planning, Research and Evaluation, Administration for Children and Families, U.S. Department of Health and Human Services.

Simson, D. (2012, May 12). *Restorative justice and its effects on (Racially Disparate) punitive school discipline.* 7th Annual Conference on Empirical Legal Studies Paper. Retrieved from SSRN doi: 10.2139/ssrn.2107240

Skiba, R. J, Eckes, S. E, & Brown, K. (2009). African american disproportionality in school discipline: the divide between best evidence and legal remedy. *New York Law School Law Review, 54*(4), 1071–1112.

Skiba, R. J., Shure, L. A., Middelberg, L. V., & Baker, T. L. (2011). Reforming school discipline and reducing disproportionality in suspension and expulsion. In S. R. Jimerson, A. B. Nickerson, M. J. Mayer, & M. J. Furlong (Eds.), *Handbook of school violence and school safety: International research and practice* (2nd ed., pp. 515–528). New York, NY: Routledge.

Smith, E. J., & Harper, S. R. (2015). Disproportionate Impact of K–12 School Suspension and Expulsion on Black Students in Southern States [Report]. Philadelphia, PA: University of Pennsylvania, Center for the Study of Race and Equity in Education.

Sunderman, G. L., & Kim, J. (2004). *Increasing bureaucracy or increasing opportunities? school district experience with supplemental educational services.* Cambridge, MA: The Civil Rights Project at Harvard University. Retrieved from http://www.civilrightsproject.harvard.edu

Teasley, M., Crutchfield, J., Williams, S. A., Clayton, M. A., & Okilwa, N. S. A. (2016). School choice and afrocentric charter schools: A review and critique of evaluation outcomes. *Journal of African American Studies, 20,* 99–119. doi:10.1007/s12111-015-9322-0

The National Commission on Excellence in Education. (1983). *A nation at risk: The imperative for education reform.* U.S. Department of Education. Retrieved from https://www.edreform.com/wp-content/content/uploads/2013/02/A_At_Risk_1983.pdf.

The Education Trust. (2014). *The state of education for African American students.* Retrieved from https://edtrust.org/resource/the-state-of-education-for-african-american-students/

The Journal of Blacks in Higher Education. (2005). *The widening racial scoring gap on the SAT college admissions test.* Retrieved from http://www.jbhe.com/features/49_college_admissions-test.html

U.S. Census Bureau. (2016). *African Americans by the numbers.* Retrieved from http://www.infoplease.com/spot/bhmcensus1.html

U.S. Census Bureau. (2017). *FFF: National African-American history Month: February 2017.* Retrieved from https://factfinder.census.gov/faces/tableservices/jsf/pages/productview.xhtml?src=bkm

U.S. Department of Education, National Center for Education Statistics. (2012). *The condition of education 2012 (NCES 2012-045), Indicator 47.* Retrieved from https://nces.ed.gov/fastfacts/display.asp?id=72

U.S. Department of Education, National Center for Education Statistics. (2016). *Digest of education statistics, 2014 (NCES 2016-006), Table 226.10.* Retrieved from https://nces.ed.gov/fastfacts/display.asp?id=171

We Treat Everybody the Same: Race Equity in Child Welfare

Ruby M. Gourdine

ABSTRACT
For several decades, child welfare researchers have explored the issue of disproportionality in child welfare. Top-level government reports have confirmed that African-American children are disproportionately represented in the child welfare system. This knowledge led to the concern that equity standards are not being implemented in child welfare systems partially due to implicit bias and insufficient data to track services to this population of children. The lack of data and recognition of the disparate entry of African Americans into care will continue unless systems move to having the child welfare system understand overrepresentation and the need for equity in the provision of services. This article shares findings of a research study and is focused on the use of data as a strategy to improve racial equity in child welfare. It uses critical race theory (CRT) to explain how racism can impact equity in the provision of child welfare services.

Introduction

The entry into child welfare system continues to be a catastrophic situation for children and families. For African-American children, the entry in the child welfare system is calamitous because they typically enter at a higher rate and exit at a slower rate (Billingsley & Giovannoni, 1972; Chibnall et al., 2003; Child Welfare Information Gateway, 2016; Cooper, 2013;; Roberts, 2002; U.S. Government Accountability Office, 2007). When child welfare services first began it was not designed for African American/Black children because many of these families used informal systems to take care of children needing care outside of their natural homes (Roberts, 2002). Billingsley and Giovannoni (1972) chronicled the discriminatory treatment of African American children in the child welfare system during the 1970s and Roberts (2002) confirmed the continued disparate treatment in subsequent decades. This article will share findings of an evaluative research study which focused on the use of data and its connection to inequity in the delivery of child welfare services to African-American children.

This study was concerned with the role race plays in the removal of children from their biological family homes. Does this practice of removal acknowledge the role race plays in defining neglect, specifically as neglect typically involves factors related to poverty and poverty is most noted among African-American families? Further, is there a perception that African American child-rearing practices are culturally different and removal from their homes may be the result of lack of cultural sensitivity among workers who view neglect and abuse differently for African-American children (Cooper, 2013; U.S. Government Accountability Office, 2007)? These questions are ones posed when the Black Administrators in Child Welfare (BACW) initiated their Racial Equity Standards Areas (RESA). BACW launched a project with two agencies, one with two sites, that were identified as having overrepresentation of African-American children in care. The evaluative research team analyzed the data collected for this project.

Critical race theory and disparate rates of African-American children in the child welfare system

To give primacy to examining disparities in child welfare, an understanding and application of critical race theory (CRT) helps explain and place in context the actions of the child welfare system to African Americans who are grossly overrepresented in the child welfare system. CRT operates on several basic principles which include the following:

(1) Racism is ordinary, not aberrational—"normal science," the usual way society does business, the common, everyday experience of most people of color in this country;
(2) Our system of White-over-color ascendancy serves important purposes, both psychic and material;
(3) Race and races are products of social thought and relations. They are not objective, inherent, or fixed, they correspond to no biological or genetic reality; rather, races are categories that society invents, manipulates, or retires when convenient; and
(4) Another, somewhat more recent, development concerns differential racialization and its many consequences. Critical writers in law, as well as social science, have drawn attention to the ways the dominant society racializes different minority groups at different times, in response to shifting needs such as the labor market (Delgado & Stefancic, 2006, p 6).

Based upon these principles of CRT, one might gain an understanding of how and why children of color, especially African American, may fare in the child welfare system. The idea that people of color are viewed as "less than" in terms of intelligence, morality, and worthiness can contribute to a personal or systemic bias when needing, seeking, or providing services (Miller, Cahn, & Orellana, 2012). Typically, in the child welfare literature, these racial biases are labeled unconscious or implicit biases (Gourdine, Smith, & Waites, 2015; Mc Roy, 2008). This basically means that implicit bias is unintentional but can awaken when there are cues such as skin color or accents and the person is unaware of his/her bias (Blair, Steiner, & Havranek, 2011). Some may argue that there may be explicit bias as well based on the long-held perceptions of Black inferiority. Further, if one considers that the child welfare system was not developed specifically for African-American children and families but now they are overrepresented in the system, it might be due to the changes in perceptions society places on people of color. And so, as societal needs change, so do the mechanisms that ascribe status to citizens who have been historically discriminated against, so unfair treatment and limited opportunities are too often defined as personal failures. Critical race theory is a framework in which one understands how race impacts people of color in the United States. The author asserts that one must use applicable theories that place in context how systems may react to and function with different racial and ethnic groups. In this article, the premises of critical race theory as a framework are used to explain the race factor in the child welfare system.

Race studies in child welfare

Disproportionality in child welfare

The Children's Bureau defines overrepresentation as an imbalance in the percentage of a subpopulation compared to that group's representation in the larger population (Wells, Merritt, & Briggs, 2009). Chibnall et al. (2003) conducted a multistate study to address the issue of disproportionality of children of color, specifically focusing on African Americans. These authors found that racism and poverty accounted for the disproportionate rates of African-American children in care. If an African-American family was reported, that account was more likely to be substantiated than if the child was of the majority race. Factors such as poverty, lack of resources in poor communities, discriminatory practices in the larger society, the characteristics of the families entering the system, and the media contribute to the overrepresentation or disproportionality in child welfare (p. 19).

To further indicate the enormity of the problem, it is noted that 46 states have disproportionate numbers of African-American children in care. This breakdown indicates that the population of African-American children in care is two times the proportion of African Americans in the states' total population (Children's Research Center, 2009). The center further documents seven states in which this number climbs to four times the occurrence in general child populations in those states. However, more recent data still notes disparate rates: they indicate that the proportion of the overrepresentation has been reduced to 1.6% (Child Welfare Information Gateway, 2016). The National Incidence Study of Child Abuse and Neglect (NIS) is a systematic process which reports rates of entry into the child welfare system and it has consistently indicated that neglect and abuse occur at the same rates for all races (Drake & Jonson-Reid, 2011). In a recent report, NIS data indicate in its fourth wave that Black children experience maltreatment at higher rates (Child Welfare Information Gateway, 2016).

Effects of poverty

Consistently, poverty is cited as a reason for removal of children from their natural homes (Miller et al., 2012). Families experiencing poverty often have a number of stressors resulting in inadequate responses to their child(ren)'s needs. These stressors can be summarized by the existence of poverty, violence exposure, parental incarceration, substance abuse, mental health problems, and single parenthood (Miller et al., 2012). While poverty alone cannot be used as a reason for removal, poverty can exacerbate the circumstances in which removal can occur, particularly if workers and systems are not sensitive to the circumstances. Poverty can also be considered a personal failure and not a systems failure due to lack of education and suitable employment for unskilled laborers (Miller et al., 2012).

Wilson (2009) tackles the issue of unequal opportunity, which stubbornly exists in the African-American community. He states that the persistence of racial inequality in the Unites States is based both on social structure and culture. He defines structure as social positions, social roles, and networks of social relationships that are arranged in our institutions, such as the economy, polity, education, and organization of the family (p. 4). Culture, Wilson (2009) states, is the sharing of outlooks and models of behavior among individuals who face similar place-based circumstances (poor segregated neighborhoods) or have the same social networks (when members of a certain race or ethnic groups share a particular way of understanding life and it guides their behavior; p. 4).

Based upon his book *More Than Race: Being Black in the Inner City*, Wilson (2009) explains how race inequality persists. It is this premise that permeates society's view of the other, in this case African Americans. He affirms the definition of explicit and implicit bias, as most individuals would reject the direct forces of racism but ignore those forces that industry contribute to racial inequality (Wilson, 2009). In his book, he confirms the tenets of CRT and the framework in which to understand inequality and has explained how disproportionate placement and the inequality of services have impacted African-Americans families in the child welfare system.

Racial bias in child welfare

In explaining how system bias affects child welfare decision making, these authors questioned the professional decision making when working with African-American families and cite research studies which confirm that race is a primary determinant of difference in decision making. Riveaux et al. (2008) found that when factors were controlled for (i.e., home and social environment, caregiver capability, and patterns of maltreatment), African Americans had lower risk factors. These studies cited in this analysis include Ards, Myers, Malis, Sugrue, and Zhou (2003), Chibnall et al. (2003), Detaff and Rycraft (2008), and Riveaux et al. (2008). In fact, the Miller et al. (2012) qualitative study revealed the following as contributing to racial bias: poverty, lack of trust, negative perceptions of client's behavior, raising/differing expectations for families of color, holding on to the past, and lack of family engagement. Another important finding was the lack of racial and ethnic diversity in the child welfare workforce.

Cooper (2013) asserts that scholars question whether we are destroying or protecting children from historically disempowered races (i.e., African-American children). Cooper (2013) supports earlier findings of higher rates of entry and slower rates of exiting the child welfare system and this phenomenon is related to the low socioeconomic lifestyles. She concedes that a low income raises the likelihood of being at risk for neglect or abuse, for poverty alone as a factor can be construed as neglect. However, she connotes that there is also inherent bias because of the common beliefs that the poor have faulty parenting standards and are of unworthy character. Parenting styles are complicated and there are not sure-fire ways of insuring that exposure to parenting classes and intervention from those who are supposed to help will insure success (Brown, Gourdine, Waites, & Owens, 2013). Yet Issurdatt and Whitaker (2013) view social workers as having the opportunity to fortify and strengthen parenting skills. Rather than judging parents, it is the social worker's role to empower them while simultaneously protecting their offspring.

Cooper (2013) adds to the disproportionality argument, noting that "the overrepresentation of African Americans evinces bias and as a result this common history affects personal perceptions about non-whites" (p. 232). Breaking the tenets of bias definitions/insights into explicit and implicit bias is instructive. Explicit bias is bias in which a person is keenly aware of their dislike of a particular group and openly states it, whereas implicit bias is described as unintentional and can be elevated by situational cues such as a person's skin color. This type of bias cannot be controlled in a direct manner (Blair et al., 2011).

Racial equity issues

The racial equity movement resulted from the acknowledgement of the disproportionate number of African-American children who come into child welfare systems more often and exit more slowly.

Miller and Esenstad (2015), in pursuing an examination of how states dealt with racial equity, stated the following:

> One of the earliest stages of every state or local agency's focus on racial disproportionality and disparate outcomes is an analysis of child welfare administrative data organized by race/ethnicity, and sometimes gender. Data allow officials to understand the presence and extent of any racial disproportionality and/or disparate outcomes and to pinpoint where and at what decision points any disparities might exist. (p. 9)

Based upon their scan of states they were able to ascertain strategies used to promote racial equity. They found that training was a major strategy, as well as working with various leaders to help determine and react to racial inequity that can occur in child welfare. Other factors are lack of community engagement and lack of trust, and they conclude that agencies must find time to and space to discuss racism and bias (Miller & Esenstad, 2015).

Racial equity standards evaluation project

Under the aegis of the Black Administrators in Child Welfare (BACW) and the evaluation, researchers focused on racial equity and used the Racial Equity Standards Areas (RESA) as the standard to conduct and to evaluate the project.

The primary goals of the project were to:

(1) To determine if integrating RESA into the Council on Accreditation (COA) standards was effective in the delivery of services in a public and a private child welfare agency; and
(2) To understand the extent the lessons learned from the Racial Equity Strategy Standards Integration Project (RESSIP) could be generalized to other minority groups in the foster care system (Gourdine et al., 2015).

Two agencies participated in the project, one public (with two sites) and one private. They were being reaccredited and had overrepresentation of African-American children in care. The project director spent more than a year meeting with these agencies, reviewing policies, practices, and procedures, and providing training and recommendations to them regarding their practices. At the onset of the project, the RESA standards were integrated in to the COA by developing a crosswalk created by the project manager and a representative from COA. These standards were shared by the staff person at COA with agencies that agreed to participate.

Racial Equity Standards Areas (RESA)	
1. **Data**: Innovative	Data systems that collect critical information for making policy and practice decisions that improve placement and reunification outcomes are essential. Through the use of data, agencies can ensure measurable progress on behalf of children toward improving service outcomes and equity across all systems.
2. **Finance**: Creative and Flexible	Financial systems should focus on opportunities to achieve racial equity through culturally appropriate service contracting, monitoring, and distribution of funding services.
3. **Engagement**: Parent and Community	Engaging parents and community members effectively in the child welfare system is both complex and vital to the success of African-American children and families who come to the attention of abuse and neglect agencies.
4. **Kinship Services**: Effective and Appropriate Use	Kinship care is an important resource for children who are removed from their parents and placed into the child welfare system.
5. **Youth**: Informed Practice	African-American youth need to experience a support system on which they can rely and that enables successful transition to adulthood.
6. **Education**: Collaboration and Partnership	A strong educational foundation for African-American children in the child welfare system is essential to achieve positive outcome as adults leading to an improved quality of life.
7. **Health**: Thriving Children, Youth, and Families	Children, especially those in kinship and foster care, are at risk for chronic and complex illnesses.
8. **Legal Services**: Culturally Informed and Competent	Quality legal services are required for African-American children in the child welfare system to assure permanence.
9. **Leadership**: Culturally Competent	Cultural competence is the integration and transformation of knowledge about individuals and groups of people into specific standards, policies, practices, and attitudes.
10. **Program**: Policies, Practices, Review, and Analysis	A key strategy for governmental agency serving African-American children and families should invest in the development and analysis of child welfare policies, practices, and programs.

Note. Developed by the BACW. For further detail and explanation, please refer to the BACW website for the RESA.

Methodology and findings

This study relied on two procedures. The first set of procedures summarized frequencies and relative proportions of characteristics of participants as well as events that occurred during the life of the project (Gourdine et al., 2015). The other included procedures that relied upon the analysis of persons involved in the project and detailed descriptions of programs evaluated for this project. It is the later that is the focus of the project analysis this article covers. These reports were created by the project manager and were written after meetings with agency personnel and an extensive review of records. Based upon these reviews, each agency received a comprehensive report and a set of recommendations that were to be implemented to improve their work toward equable standards in child welfare. This research used a qualitative design. It should also be noted that the sites that participated in the study voluntarily and therefore there are limits in the generalizability of the data presented. To support the study, secondary data resources were used such as published reports, including RESSIP project reports. For this article the project reports were analyzed as they specifically spoke to the use of data in child welfare settings.

The RESSIP director who produced the final reports stated the following:

> And I think a critical event, which was a positive, was when the state said, "You're right." They looked at the data and then said, "Okay. You go meet with the data folks and see what we can do to change things around." They said that they were not collecting complete data on children of color. They could give you numbers of children of color in care but they weren't looking at it in the sense of comparing the types of treatment services that are being provided to children of color versus other kids or either taking that information and using it to look at why outcomes aren't being achieved. So, I think that was a critical moment when they just said, "Yes, we've got to focus on that." And, the fact that they asked for a list of some other programs around the country

that are doing something to address this issue was important. So, I was able to give them about 10 places that had raised this issue to the cabinet level and had special offices or something like that to review the issue. (Interview Transcript #2, March 23, 2014, lines 131–142)

Originally, we were focused on basically looking at the practices that people were using to work with children of color or just the practices in their systems. What do we do when people come in and how do we provide services to them and what's the continuum of care?

> All of that was good, but later on, maybe about halfway through the project, I realized that there're actually some good practices going on. And I then changed the whole dynamic of what we were doing into a data system review, because halfway through, I had already read manuals, the practice guides, the regulations, the day-to-day operations manual, and they were doing what they were supposed to be doing according to either fed, state, or their own personal practices and guidelines. So, those were in place. But originally, the task was to look at the continuum and to see what could be changed in the continuum, and that didn't need to happen, but what I found halfway through was that no one was doing anything in terms of having data stats on individual sessions that were focused on children and families of color, and they all said they were not. While the sites felt that they "treat everybody equally," the data showed some service disparities. (Interview Transcript #2, March 14, Lines 252–263)

These observations by the project director are the impetus for this article and in essence the director admitted that based upon her review that while the sites felt that they treated everyone the same the data indicated that they did not. This article uses the director's reports and analysis to demonstrate the areas that the agency sites needed to focus on to create a more equable system.

It was after these activities that the team began to assess the project. The RESA is included above to demonstrate the areas that had been identified as helping with equity within the agency sites. The private agency was located in the Midwest and the public agency with two sites was located in the East. It was these standards, along with agency policy and procedures, that were examined during the site visits. Once all the visits were completed and final recommendations made to the participating agencies, the evaluators scheduled their visits. These visits were scheduled over several months and completed in fall 2014.

Using these standards, reports were prepared that focused on what agencies were doing "right" and those areas needing attention. This article specifically focuses on the data report summation for the public and private agencies. The standard "Data Innovative" is the first standard in the RESA and the one on which this article focuses.

Listed below are the data standard and the expected components of data collection. The data collection focused on race (specifically on African Americans) and service delivery. These agencies recorded data on number of races but did not collect data by race for services and could not state whether they were delivered in an equitable manner and/or were culturally sensitive. A common refrain among agency employees was that that type of data reporting was not required and therefore was not collected but they admitted that it would be helpful.

Table 1 is an explanation of what constitutes Data Innovative and the five components that help categorize the components reviewed. The summary policy statements are areas observed on site visit and identify areas that the agency has used in their data collection. The summary of recommendations speaks directly to processes agency can use to improve services to children of color. All agencies had data-collection processes and what varied was how these data were used. Additionally, all agencies responded directly to required federal, state, and local governments reports, but were appreciative of knowing about other uses. They were not sure how to incorporate the data based upon the fact that this wasn't required. Further, they were concerned it may create an additional burden on workers (Gourdine et al., 2015).

Table 1. RESA Standard 1

Data Innovative: Data systems that collect critical information for making policy and practice decisions that improve placement and reunification outcomes are essential. Through the use of data, agencies can ensure measurable progress on behalf of children toward improving service outcomes and equity across all systems.
Data Components
1. Reporting system includes data specific to the race of families and children in all caseloads.
2. Agency database identifies gaps in services and racial and ethnic treatment disparities.
3. Data qualitative measurements are used in program and practice improvements.
4. Data-driven decision-making assessment instruments are available.
5. Focused research and reviews are regularly conducted on services provided to children and families of color.

Site review agency A (public agency site 1)

Summary of Policy and Practices
The department uses a process for flex funds to assist families; a family engagement model, which solicits support from family and community; and a process of internal case reviews during which they monitor case-work practices to ensure that families of color are involved. This approach utilizes fathers as resources. In addition, the department uses the faith-based community as a resource and offers cultural and linguistic services to families of color.

Summary of Recommendations
The department should actively seek culturally diverse support services and contract with them to provide services. It should collect data on cultural practices, beliefs, and behaviors and use this information to locate services in the community. It should add preventive services to the repertoire of services available to families and review the financial system to ensure adequate funding. It should use internal data to determine gaps in services to children of color. The agency should use cultural self-assessments as well as a community resource assessment process. Outreach protocols should be developed that identify family, cultural, and faith-based resources (e.g., environmental scans) in the community, which caseworkers should use. In addition, resources that are close to child's neighborhood should be utilized.

Site review agency B (public agency site 2)

Summary of Policy and Practices
The department follows state policy and practice. This site has the capacity to generate special reports at the local level; and it uses strategic planning processes for program planning, goal setting, and resource development; and it uses a peer-review process. It has the capacity to conduct customer surveys to collect information, and it uses a scorecard to track services and program performance. This department uses continuous quality improvement (CQI), and it is data driven. Data on service and treatment support for children of color are collected and are used by management for planning. The department also uses the state assessment instruments.

Summary of Recommendations
The agency should request data on race from the state system to assist in identifying disparities in services. It should use data mapping to identify culturally competent services and resources. The agency should request that the peer-review process be used to review and obtain race-specific information needed. It should regularly evaluate services provided to children through revising scorecard reports, customer interviews, and surveys. The case record and supervisory reviews should identify services to children and families of color. Local departments should gather information on children and families of color beliefs, behaviors, and practices as a basis for alternative services and treatment.

Site review agency C

Summary of Policy and Practices
The agency has an existing policy that data are maintained for Native American children throughout their stay in foster care. However, currently data are not extracted for all service delivery for foster-care children. This is a private agency that can control its internal management system.

Summary of Recommendations
Use race information to generate reports on African-American foster-care children. Use aggregate data reports to identify any gaps in services for African-American children. Supervisory staff will use data to identify gaps in services. Mission and goals will reflect best practices. Their quality-assurance process summary report from the data collected should be developed and shared with each supervisory unit. These reports should demonstrate cultural diversity, mentoring, and due diligence in searching for relatives and provide reasons for placement failures. These reports should include school-related reports and activities, mental health services, and monitoring services provided.

In the process of evaluating the project, researchers learned that data collection was a major issue because the project manager noticed that data was not available by race and therefore services for African-American families and children could not be determined. Most participants in the study felt that they treated everyone the same and basically they did not see themselves doing anything different for children of color, despite service disparities that were apparent to the project director in her report to the agencies (Gourdine et al., 2015). The importance of data collected in the way the project manager recommended was to recognize that African-American children were placed more often and remained in care for longer periods of time. The data could inform workers about the effectiveness of services and perhaps guide them in finding appropriate services for better outcomes. This research raised the question of whether there should be criteria for workers denoting the statistical impact of disproportionality (Gourdine et al., 2015). Disproportionality as a concept is also overlooked in the provision of services, as it was noted that recruiting culturally congruent services is not done due to maintaining already established contracts and/or lack of diverse service providers.

Gathering data on services and tracking them by race is an added task to workers. Frequently, workers are overwhelmed and experience burnout because of the intensity of work-related tasks and possibly the vicarious trauma which they experience. Managers and supervisors are reluctant to increase tasks for workers because they are well aware of the burnout rate and subsequent turnover of child welfare workers. Perhaps the development of a "tool kit" to address these needs could be helpful in implementing new procedures.

Data analytics and data mining: Its impact and purpose for child welfare

Disproportionality and disparities in the treatment of children of color has been a growing concern in the child welfare system. System stakeholders have begun to recognize the problem through the use of data (Duarte & Summers, 2013). The push toward incorporating the use of data to determine the effectiveness of programs and services, as well as to predict the need for services, is moving forward in the quest for answers for combating the persistent problem of disproportionality and disparate care of African Americans in child welfare (p. 1). Disproportionality and disparate treatment of people of color are not only problems for service agencies but represent broader social problems (Duarte & Summers, 2013, p. 7). These authors further noted that the process of implementing a data-collection system required cultural competency training designed to address institutional bias and its impact on child welfare (p. 11).

Langworthy and Robertson (n.d.) report that child welfare systems have traditionally relied on caseworkers to record data and maintain records, but the new approach has been to have systems in place to facilitate data collection and support case workers in this effort (p. 6). When child welfare and educational professionals lack reliable, real-time information on factors such as academic progress, attendance, child welfare services, and court dates, this makes it especially difficult to adequately support educational stability and achievement (Langworthy & Robertson, n.d.).

With administrative data, programs managers, evaluators. and others may examine who is served by the child welfare system, engage in continuous quality-improvement efforts, and evaluate changes in service delivery outputs and outcomes overtime. In addition, using administrative data to evaluate child welfare programs and practices can help inform program development, policy decisions, and program funding to improve the safety, permanency, and well-being of children involved in the child welfare system (Office of Planning, Research & Evaluation Report 2016–17). The types of data available to child welfare systems are administrative data reports, including the Statewide Automated Child Welfare Information Systems (SACWIS), Adoption and Foster Care Analysis and Reporting System (AFCARS), and the National Child Abuse and Neglect Data System (NCANDS). Due to large data systems, the data is often complex and difficult to analyze and therefore are subject to misinformation or data manipulation that may distort the data that is reported in these systems.

The American Bar Association (2008) "prioritizes its efforts to eliminate discrimination based on race and as such encourages law and policy change that research has shown decreases racial and ethnic minority youth contact with the child welfare system" (p. 1). It cites the Casey-CSSP Alliance for Racial Equity work to track data to shape solutions and improve and expand services to reduce disproportionality (p. 2). It suggests that data can track specific services, length of time to the initiation of services, and resources dedicated to promoting family preservation and reunification. They further indicate that services tracking minority families as a way to combat bias in the child welfare system (p. 3).

Several webinars conducted by the Alliance for Racial Equity in Child Welfare and The Center for the Study of Social Policy are promoting the use of data as predictive analytics in child welfare. They note that the data collected on child welfare can be used to predict which families may be in need of child welfare services. Hussey and Baker (2016) raised the issue that predictive analytics based upon human decision making can be coded into human bias in predictions. Their admonition is a warning that the tools used to better serve a population can also bias service in its delivery.

This author is promoting the use of data as a partial solution to the problem of overrepresentation of children of color in the child welfare system but the authors also advise caution because data can be misused and can cause other problems in offering services to children.

Discussion

This study evaluated the reports given to agencies who were participants in a research study using the RESA standards. These reports were very extensive but were summarized in this article for reporting on the use of data to assist programs in improving their outcomes. This study documents the need for workers to understand the climate in which they are providing services and to be aware that data can confirm whether services are effective for different consumers of services. Additionally, much of the recent research in child welfare has confirmed the existence of implicit bias. This can be seen in such statements as "We treat everyone the same" and indicates that evaluation of clients' needs are not necessarily being conducted. As noted in Table 1, there are ten standards these agencies were evaluated against but for this article the author focused on data collection because it is an important focus in child welfare and the successful use of data is believed to improve the circumstances for African Americans in the child welfare system. A major point in the recommendations for agencies collecting data is to collect data by using race as one of the data fields. It is acknowledged in this article that CRT is critical to understand how our society functions. It states that race is a part of social thought and as result society manipulates and invents its relevance to society. As a man-made concept, the inequalities that are experienced can be retired when convenient and can be reinvented. Wilson (2009) asserts that race as a concept has been created to disadvantage a certain group of people and in this discussion, it is African Americans. Society has the option to do better. Will it?

Implications for policy and practice

There is evidence that collection of data can enhance the delivery of services, particularly for African-American children, because it confirms whether the services provided are commensurate to their needs and if they are culturally competent (Gourdine et al., 2015; Miller & Esenstad, 2015). The byproduct of collecting data as it relates to services is that it benefits all children. A concern of these agency heads was that this type of data collection is not required by the state or federal government and as a result felt that it should be mandated by the state to assure compliance. This assumes a "make us do it" stance. While data collection by different categories may seem to be burdensome, it can help with the overrepresentation of children of color, especially African Americans, in the child welfare system. Yet another issue is that trainings need not only to understand diverse cultures but also to focus on unconscious-bias training. Creative ways of implementing new policies can help address worker burnout (Gourdine et al., 2015). There are a number of data systems in place for child welfare agencies. However, conceptualizing the various uses of data can be instructive and productive for those administrators and policymakers because they can determine level of services, evaluate the effective practices among agencies, and have better outcomes for children and their families. This methodology can be useful in combating the inherent implicit bias found to exist in child welfare systems.

Lee, Bell, and Ackerman-Brimberg (n.d.) investigated racial bias in three systems, child welfare, education, and mental health, and found that racial disparities exist at almost every stage. They indicate that decisions in the child welfare system depend upon a decision maker's perspective because the idea of abuse and neglect encompasses a wide range of experiences (p. 20). It is these concerns that this article addressed. The recommendations contained within can assist in improving services for African Americans, who are over-represented in the child welfare system.

Conclusions

This article explored issues of disproportionality and disparities in service delivery to African-American children in care and how these issues can connect to data collection by race in child welfare agencies. Data collection can only be an answer to the problem if it is used and interpreted based on specific criteria. Implicit bias is well documented, and caution must be applied in data use and interpretation to alleviate the aforementioned causes.

Preserving African-American families is a goal despite the inequity that is often found in the systems that are charged with helping them. Ladner and Gourdine (1995) state that "the resilience of the African American family, in spite of racism and discrimination, is possibly one of history's most profound sociological phenomena" (p. 171). The child welfare system must realize that family preservation while maintaining safety is a goal for all families and being colorblind or treating everybody the same is not effective given the context of racism and implicit and explicit bias.

Acknowledgments

Dr. Jacqueline Smith for her consultation and participation in research and Shayna Waites, Howard University doctoral student. Further acknowledgements go to the Black Administrators in Child Welfare (BACW) organization for their work and committment in assuring that African American children in Child Welfare systems recieve adequate care and are served with equity.

Disclosure statement

No potential conflict of interest was reported by the author.

Funding

The evaluation research was funded by The W.K. Kellogg Foundation [Grant P3022176]. However, the views in this article are author's own.

References

American Bar Association House of Delegates. (2008, August 11). *Reducing racial disparities in the child welfare system*. Washington, DC: Author.
Ards, S., Myers, S., Malis, A., Sugrue, E., & Zhou, L. (2003). Racial disproportionality in reported and substantiated child abuse and neglect: An examination of systemic bias. *Children and Youth Services Review, 25*(5/6), 375–392. doi:10.1016/S0190-7409(03)00027-6
Billingsley, A., & Giovannoni, J. M. (1972). *Children of the storm: Black children in child welfare*. New York, NY: Harcourt, Brace, Jovanovich.
Black Administrators in Child Welfare. (n.d.). *The racial equity standard areas*. Washington, DC: Author.
Blair, I. V., Steiner, J. F., & Havranek, E. P. (2011, Spring). Unconscious (implicit) bias and health disparities: Where do we go from here? *The Permanente Journal, 15*(2), 71–78.
Brown, A. W., Gourdine, R. M., Waites, S., & Owens, A. (2013). Parenting in the twenty first century: An introduction. *Journal of Human Behavior in the Social Environment 23*, 2, 109–117. doi:10.1080/10911359.2013.747410
Center for the Study for Social Policy. (2013, July). *Raising the bar: Child welfare's shift toward well- being*. Washington, DC: Author.

Center for the Study of Social Policy. Permanency Innovations Initiative Evaluation Team. (2016). Using child welfare administrative data in the permanency innovations initiative evaluation (OPRE Report 2016-47). Washington, DC: U. S. Department of Health and Human Services, Administration for Children and Families, Children's Bureau, and Office of Planning, Research and Evaluation

Chibnall, S., Dutch, N. M., Jones-Harden, B., Brown, A., Gourdine, R., Smith, J., Boone, A. Snyder, S. (2003). *Children of color in the child welfare system: Perspectives from the child welfare community*. Washington, DC: U.S. Department Health and Human Services, Children's: Bureau.

Child Welfare Information Gateway. (2016, November). *Addressing racial disproportionality in child welfare* (Issue Brief). Washington, DC: U.S. Department of Health & Human Services, Children's Bureau.

Children's Research Center. (2009). *Disproportionate minority representation in the child welfare system*. National Council on Crime and Delinquency.

Cooper, T. A. (2013, winter). Racial bias in American foster care: The national debate. *Marquette Law Review, 97*(2), 215–277.

Delgado, R., & Stefancic, J. (2006). *Critical race theory: An introduction*. New York, NY: NYU Press.

Detaff, A., & Rycraft, J. R. (2008). Deconstructing disproportionality: Views from multiple stakeholders. *Child Welfare, 87*((2)), 37–58.

Drake, B., & Jonson –Reid, M. (2011). NIS interpretations: Race and national incidence studies of child abuse and neglect. *Children and Youth Services Review, 33*, 16–20. doi:10.1016/j.childyouth.2010.08.006

Duarte, C. S., & Summers, A. (2013). A Three-pronged approach to addressing racial disproportionality and disparities in child welfare: The Santa Clara County example of leadership, collaboration and data driven decisions. *Child Adolescent Social Work Journal, 30*, 1–19. doi:10.1007/s10560-012-0279-8

Gourdine, R. M., Smith, J., & Waites, S. (2015). *Racial equity strategy and standards integration project evaluation*. Washington, DC: Howard University School of Social Work E. Franklin Frazier Research Center.

Hussey, C., & Baker, H. (2016, November 17). *Predictive analytics in child welfare: A broader view from the field. for racial equity in child welfare*. Alliance: The Center for the study of Social Policy.

Issurdatt, S., & Whitaker, T. (2013). Keeping parents in the driver's seat. *Journal of Human Behavior in the Social Environment 23*, 2, 118–125. doi:10.1080/10911359.2012.747403

Ladner, J. A., & Gourdine, R. M. (1995). Transracial adoptions. In C. V. Willie, P. P. Rieker, B. M. Kramer, & B. S. Brown. (Eds.), *Mental health, racism and sexism*. Pittsburgh, PA: University of Pittsburgh Press.

Langworthy, S., & Roberson, L. (2014). *Get the data, share the data, use the data.: Recommendations from the three state child welfare and education learning community (CWELC) project*. University of Minnesota Extension, Center for Family Development.

Lee, B., & Ackerman – Brimberg. (n.d.). Implicit bas in the child welfare, education and mental health systems. In M. Harris & H. Benton. (Eds.), *National center for youth law*. Washington, DC: The Center for the Study of Social Policy.

Mc Roy, R. (2008). Acknowledging disproportionate outcomes and changing service delivery. *Child Welfare League of America. 87*, 2, 205–210.

Miller, K. M., Cahn, C., & Orellana, E. R. (2012). Dynamics that contribute to racial disproportionality and disparity: Perspectives from child welfare professionals, community partners, and families. *Children and Youth Services Review, 34*, 2201–2207. doi:10.1016/j.childyouth.2012.07.022

Miller, O., & Esenstad, A. (2015). Strategies to reduce racially disparate outcomes in child welfare: A national scan. In *The alliance for racial equity in child welfare*.

Riveaux, S. J., James, J., Wittenstrom, K., Bauman, D., Sheets, J., Henry, J., et al. (2008). The interaction between race, poverty, and risk: Understanding the decision to provide services to clients and to remove children. *Child Welfare, 87*(2), 151–168.

Roberts, D. (2002). *Shattered bonds: The color of child welfare*. New York, NY: Civitas Books.

U.S. Government Accountability Office. (2007). *African American children in foster care: Additional HHS assistance needed to help states reduce the proportion in care* (GOA Publications No. GAO-07-816). Washington, DC: Author.

Wells, S. J., Merritt, L. M., & Briggs, H. B. (2009). Bias, racism, and evidenced- based practice: The case for more focused development of the child welfare evidence base. *Children and Youth Services Review, 31*, 1160–1171. doi:10.1016/j.childyouth.2009.09.002

Wilson, W. J. (2009). *More than just race: Being Black and poor in the inner city*. New York, NY: W.W. Norton & Company, Inc.

Wulcyzn, F., Gibbons, R., Snowden, L., & Lery, B. (2013). Poverty, social disadvantage and the black white placement gap. *Children and Youth Services, 35*, 65–74. doi:10.1016/j.childyouth.2012.10.005

Game Changers: A Critical Race Theory Analysis of the Economic, Social, and Political Factors Impacting Black Fatherhood and Family Formation

Brianna P. Lemmons and Waldo E. Johnson

ABSTRACT
Family has always been one of the strongest institutions in the African American community. However, over the past 30 years, massive changes have occurred within the structure of African American families, resulting in many fathers living apart from their children. Applying the basic tenets of Critical Race Theory (CRT) and Michelle Alexander's notion of Racialized "Game Changing," this article examines the social, political, and economic factors that have worked to undermine normative Black fatherhood involvement and family formation patterns over time. Two of the major arguments—the slavery argument and the cultural argument—offered in the empirical research literature in an attempt to explain the shifts that have occurred within Black families historically are also examined, followed by an in-depth discussion and analysis of factors that underlie the changes in Black family structure and formation over time. The article concludes with a set of policy recommendations for strengthening Black fatherhood and family formation in the 21st century.

Family has always been one of the strongest institutions in the African American community (Billingsley, 1974; Billingsley & Morrison-Rodriguez, 2007; Franklin, 1997). From emancipation through the late 1960s, the majority of African Americans upheld the institution of marriage, and families were primarily nuclear in structure (Billingsley, 1968; Billingsley & Morrison-Rodriguez, 2007; Franklin, 1997; Gutman, 1976). However, over the past 30 years, massive changes have occurred within the structure of African American families, resulting in many fathers living apart from their children (Cheadle, Amato, & King, 2010). While fathers across race and ethnicity, as well as socioeconomic status, have increased their level of involvement in caregiving roles, the number of fathers who live apart from their children continues to increase rapidly (Amato, Meyers, & Emery, 2009; Livingston & Parker, 2011).

Research suggests that in 1960, only 11% of children in the United States lived without their fathers (Livingston & Parker, 2011). However, by 2010, this number had more than doubled—to 27% (Livingston & Parker, 2011). Among African Americans, two parent coresident families represent the minority (Johnson, 2014; Perry, 2009). As of 2016, 66% of African American children lived in single-parent families (Kids Count Data Center, 2018). Consequently, many African American fathers now embody *nonresident* father roles. However, it is also important to note that the rapid increase in nonresident father homes is not just unique to African American families, as it has become prevalent among all families across the nation over time. As shown in Table 1, 35% of all children in the United States now reside in single-parent households, compared to 11% in 1960 (Livingston & Parker, 2011). Fueling the high rates of nonresident father families has been consistent increases in rates of nonmarital

Table 1. Percentage of Children Living in Single-Parent Homes by Race, 2016.

Race	Percentage of Children Living in Single-Parent Homes
American Indian	52%
Asian or Pacific Islander	16%
Black or African American	66%
Hispanic or Latino	42%
Non-Hispanic White	24%
Total in the U.S.	35%

Source: Kids Count Data Center (2018).

child bearing over time, particularly among younger and more economically disadvantaged African American couples.

According to recent trends highlighted by Child Trends (2016), in 2013, Black women accounted for 72% of all nonmarital births, in comparison to 53% of Hispanic women, 29% of White women, and 17% of Asian or Pacific Islander women. As evidenced in the data from Childs Trends Data Bank, illustrated in Figure 1, this is a historical trend that has created unique and diverse patterns of family formation and structure among African Americans, thereby shifting the role and place of fathers in family life in fundamental ways (Livingston & Parker, 2011). It should be noted that the intent of this article is not to privilege the nuclear family structure or to suggest that this form of family is more beneficial than another. Rather, the major goal is to examine the social, political, and economic factors that have worked to undermine Black fatherhood involvement and family formation patterns over time.

The basic tenets of Critical Race Theory (CRT) are utilized as a framework for explaining the intersections of race, economics, and social policy and the influence that such forces have had on Black fatherhood and family formation over time. First, CRT and its basic tenets are outlined along with an explanation of Alexander's (2012) notion of "racialized game changing." Second, two of the major arguments—the slavery argument and the cultural argument—offered in the empirical research literature in an attempt to explain the shifts that have occurred within Black families historically are examined. This discussion is followed by an analysis of factors that underlie changes in Black family structure and how the most disadvantaged families are affected. The article concludes with a set of policy recommendations for strengthening Black fatherhood and family formation in the 21st century.

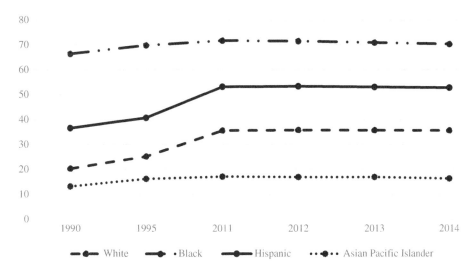

Figure 1. Percentage of all births to unmarried women, by race.
Source: Child Trends Data Bank (2016).

Theoretical framework: critical race theory and alexander's theory of "racialized game changing"

The major tenets of Critical Race Theory (CRT) are utilized as a means for understanding and explaining the intersection between race, social policy, and the structure and functioning of Black families and fatherhood, both past and present. This theory is examined in advance of the argument that a confluence of factors—economic, social, and political, in nature—have contributed to increases in nonresident father families in the Black community over time. Particularly relevant to this thesis is CRT's contextualized perspective and consideration for broader historical, economic, political, and social factors that fuel and perpetuate the relationship between race, racism, and power (Delgado & Stefancic, 2001). As noted by Toldson and Morton (2012), when discussing the structure and functioning of Black families, several issues related to urbanization, employment, poverty, mass incarceration, and institutional racism *must* be taken into consideration.

Additional tenets of CRT that are of particular importance herein are interest convergence, differential racialization, and intersectionality or anti-essentialism. *Interest convergence* suggests that because racism advances the interests of certain groups of elites (i.e., Whites, the working class), the more privileged groups within society have little to no motivation to eliminate it (Delgado & Stefancic, 2001). Furthermore, *differential racism* points to the various ways in which society has racialized minority groups throughout history in response to key shifts in the structure of the economy (Delgado & Stefancic, 2001).

For example, during the U.S. Industrial Revolution, Black men occupied a large portion of the country's high-paying, blue collar manufacturing jobs (Alexander, 2012). However, the onset of deindustrialization and globalization and the shift toward a more service-oriented economy made it difficult for Black men to adapt, given their relatively low level of educational attainment and lack of exposure to formal education (Alexander, 2012). As a new workforce of highly educated members was cultivated, society had little use for less-educated Black men (Alexander, 2012). Finally, the notion of *intersectionality or anti-essentialism* holds that no person has a single, unitary identity (Delgado & Stefancic, 2001).

Precisely, being a Black father often comes with a great deal of ridicule, criticism, and stereotypical verbosity that consistently challenges the paternal role. It is at the intersections of these challenges that the experiences of these men and the state of Black fatherhood and families can be best understood. The concepts of CRT will serve as a lens and framework for delineating and explaining the various factors that have impacted the structure and functioning of Black men in families, both past and present.

Furthermore, in her work entitled *"The New Jim Crow: Mass Incarceration in the Age of Color Blindness*, Alexander (2012) points to the adaptability of racism and suggests that the caste system of slavery in America has not been eradicated but has merely evolved into newer forms of bondage and social control that continue to beset the Black race. As the system is challenged, the "game changes" and newer forms of racism are born that are consistent with the time and historical context. She argues: "racism is highly adaptable. The rules and reasons the political system employs to enforce status relations of any kind, including racial hierarchy, evolve and change as they are challenged" (Alexander, 2012, p. 40). Alexander's (2012) notion of "racialized game changing" is consistent with the tenets or CRT, particularly the concepts of *interest convergence and differential racism*, both of which underscore how shifts within the structure of the economy work to "change the game" for minorities, thereby maintaining the prevailing racial hierarchy and advancing the interests of certain groups of elites.

As shown in Figure 2, three major "game changers" impacting Black fatherhood and families will be highlighted: *deindustrialization of the economy and the onset of joblessness, the war on drugs and subsequent mass incarceration, and welfare reform*. Before providing a detailed analysis of the social, political, and economic factors that have shaped Black families and fatherhood over time, two of the major arguments that have been advanced to explain the structuring and functioning of Black

Figure 2. Game changers for Black fatherhood and family formation.

families historically are presented—the slavery argument and the cultural argument. The former argument emphasizes the impact of slavery on the Black family, while the latter argument advances a culture of poverty thesis to explain Black family functioning. Taken together, both arguments have historically shaped much of the discourse on Black family life.

The slavery argument

The shifts that have occurred within the Black family over time have led to their characterization as unstable (Moynihan, 1965). This so-called instability has been linked to several arguments related to the impact of the slave system on Black family life and supposed cultural norms within the Black community that are claimed to perpetuate the cycle of fatherlessness (Staples, 1999a, 1999b, Staples & Johnson, 1993). For decades, the prevailing thought was that the slave system was responsible for immobilizing Black families and the place of Black fathers within the family unit over time (Toldson & Morton, 2012). The work of scholars such as E. Franklin Frazier (1939) provided the foundation for the advancement of the notion that instability in Black families is a consequence of slavery and assimilation into American culture. In his seminal work entitled *The Negro Family in the United States* (1939), Frazier emphasized the disorganizing effects of the chattel slave system, marginalized freedom, and the crisis that was brought on by emancipation. Rooted in the tenets of the race relations cycle purported by sociologist Robert Park (1950), Frazier's work advanced the viewpoint that Blacks were an assimilationist minority (Mathis, 1978). Central to his thesis was the notion that the African heritage of Negro slaves was essentially obliterated as they transitioned from chattel slavery into the free world wherein the dominant culture was the normative rule (Mathis, 1978). As noted by Ricketts (n.d.):

> According to Frazier, chattel slavery established a pattern of unstable Black families because of lack of consistent marital observance and recognition among slaves and perhaps more importantly, slave owners which often resulted in constant separation of slave families as males and older children were sold. Slavery, therefore, destroyed all family bonds with the exception of mother and child, leading to a pattern of Black families centered on mothers. (p. 32)

The prevailing thought was that, in the aftermath of emancipation, ex-slaves were unable to cope with their newly found freedom, which in turn led to disorganization and instability in Black family life (Ricketts, n.d.). Such arguments gave way to the development of a dysfunctional view of Black families. This view can be traced back to the Moynihan Report of 1965. The report utilized many of the arguments formulated by Frazier and various indices of family stability such as rates of marriage and out-of-wedlock childbearing to characterize the Black family as pathological. The Moynihan Report argued that the patterns of family formation among Blacks were fundamentally different from those of Whites, making the Black family inherently unsteady and dysfunctional (Ricketts, n.d.).

However, historians (Gutman, 1976) and Black family scholars (Billingsley, 1968, 1974; Hill, 1972; Nobles, 1978) have worked tirelessly to revise this thesis by offering the viewpoint that Black families were (and are) in fact highly functional and possess an extraordinary amount of strength and resilience that is built on its African cultural heritage (Mathis, 1978). In contrast to Frazier (1939) and other supporters of the assimilationist viewpoint, scholars such as Billingsley (1968, 1974, 1992), Nobles (1978), and Hill (1972) emphasize the retention and maintenance of African culture and uphold the notion that the slave system, in spite of its efforts, "did not stamp out all vestiges of [Black] family life" (Billingsley, 1974, p. 50). From a strengths-based perspective, they proclaim that Black families have historically possessed a remarkable degree of stability and commitment to marriage and family in slavery and upon emancipation (Gutman, 1976).

The cultural argument

Furthermore, the cultural argument has also been advanced within the literature and public discourse as a means of explaining the patterns of structure and functioning that have become widespread among contemporary Black families. As noted by Staples (1999a, 1999b), it is often argued that economically disadvantaged Blacks possess a system of values that are inherently different and deviate substantially from those of the dominant culture. Values allegedly characterized by female dominance, sexual promiscuity, poor work ethic, and a devaluing of the nuclear family structure are subordinate to the dominant family culture (Staples, 1999a, 1999b, Staples & Johnson, 1993) and also allegedly perpetuate economic deprivation and destabilization of the Black family structure. At its core, this argument advances a "culture of poverty" thesis that is rooted in a pathological orientation toward Black families (Staples, 1999a, 1999b, Staples & Johnson, 1993).

Those who subscribe to these views decidedly ignore other factors that also work to threaten the vitality of Black families (Staples, 1999a, 1999b). Underlying the various shifts that have occurred within the structure and functioning of the Black family over time are several key factors that have unquestionably shaken the foundation of Black family life and relegated Black men to a tangential role in the family unit (Toldson & Morton, 2012). This article provides a comprehensive viewpoint that includes an emphasis on historical and cultural as well as larger social, political, and economic factors that underscore the plight of Black men and Black families (Wilson, 2010).

Undeniably, it is necessary to view our contemporary understanding of family and fatherhood in light of historical developments (Cabrera, Tamis-LeMonda, Bradley, Hofferth, & Lamb, 2000), which means taking into consideration the complex web of forces that have historically placed Black families in a state of disorganization and Black men in positions that have made it difficult for them to meet the demands of fatherhood (Gary, 1981; Hill, 2007; Miller, 2003; Morehouse Research Institute and the Institute for American Values, 1999; Perry, Harmon, & Bright, 2013; Wilson, 1987, 1996). A wide range of factors has been linked to the trend toward "radically fatherless" (Morehouse Research Institute and the Institute for American Values, 1999, p. 6) homes. As noted by Billingsley and Morrison-Rodriguez (2007) and Wilson (2003), such forces are thought to have contributed to a state of disequilibrium within African American Black families. In the following sections, several structural and political factors are outlined, placing a particular emphasis on the role that social welfare policies have played in shaping Black families and fatherhood over time.

Economic, political, and social factors impacting black fatherhood and family formation

Economics and Joblessness

American sociologist William Julius Wilson has written extensively about the impact of systemic structural forces on Black families (Wilson, 1987, 1992, 1996, 2010). In his seminal work *The Truly Disadvantaged* (1987), Wilson argues that increases in Black male joblessness since the 1960s account in large part for the decline in marriage rates and the significant increase in single-parent Black families (Johnson, 2014; Offner, 2001). In 1948, the unemployment rate among Black men was only 5.8%, in comparison to 3.4% for White men (Center for the Study of Social Policy, 1999). However, the 1960s brought with it a collapse in the economic security of Black families. This is due in large part to the deindustrialization of the economy and the erosion of job opportunities that took root in the latter part of the 20th century (American Sociological Association, 2005; Center for the

Study of Social Policy, 1999; Wilson, 1992, 1996). Low-skilled Black male workers were disproportionately impacted and consequently displaced from the workforce (Center for the Study of Social Policy, 1999; Wilson, 1996).

As a result, many young Black males either turned to low-wage or unskilled jobs as a means of employment or left the labor force entirely (American Sociological Association, 2005; Wilson, 1992, 1996). As noted by Wilson (1996), "The proportion of [Black] men who 'permanently' dropped out of the labor force was more than twice as high in the late 1980s than it had been in the late 1960s" (p. 25). Alongside increases in joblessness were a sharp decline in real wages and an overall deterioration of socioeconomic status among low-income Black male workers (American Sociological Association, 2005; Grubb & Wilson, 1989; Hewlett & West, 1998; Wilson, 1992, 1996). Overall, the loss in blue collar manufacturing jobs resulted not only in joblessness but also the concentration of inner-city Black males in low-skilled, high-turnover service jobs (Wilson, 1992).

Many Black men of earlier generations benefited from the unique window of opportunity brought on by industrialization, the Great Migration, and the subsequent rise in well-paying blue collar jobs (Butler, 2000; Roy, 2006). As a result, these men were able to consistently provide for their families and maintain a stable presence in the home. However, while today's Black fathers may desire to imitate their own fathers' parenting behaviors in the area of financial provision, they often face significant challenges in doing so, as the game has changed within the current economic landscape, destabilizing and displacing many of them from the kinds of occupations and jobs that are necessary for forming and sustaining a family (Roy, 2005, 2006).

Racial Disparities in Labor Market Participation and Unemployment Rates

As shown in Figure 3, historically, labor force participation rates among Black men have been the lowest, in comparison to their racial/ethnic counterparts. Today, labor market outcomes for African Americans, especially Black men, continue to be disparate (Lang & Lehmann, 2011). In fact, as documented by the U.S. Bureau of Labor Statistics (2011), "In 2010, Black men were less likely than men in any other racial or ethnic group to be in the labor force" (p. 1). Specifically, in 2010, the unemployment rate for adult Black men was 17.3%, in comparison to 11.7% among adult Hispanic

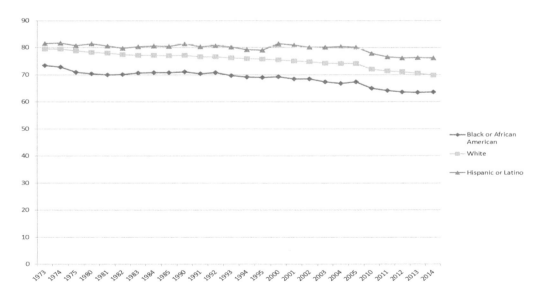

Figure 3. Labor force participation rates among U.S. men by race, 1973–2014 (percent).
Source: U.S. Bureau of Labor Statistics (2015).

men, 8.9% among White adult men, and 7.5% among adult Asian men (U.S. Bureau of Labor Statistics, 2011). Furthermore, the unemployment rate is particularly high among less-educated Black men (U.S. Bureau of Labor Statistics, 2015; American Sociological Association, 2005). As illustrated in Table 2, in 2016, the unemployment rate of Black men with less than a high school diploma was more than twice the rate of White and Hispanic men and more than 4 times the rate of Asian men (U.S. Bureau of Labor Statistics, 2017). Data in Table 2 suggests that, even with a bachelor's degree or higher, Black men still have the highest unemployment rates in the nation, in comparison to their racial/ethnic counterparts (American Sociological Association, 2005; U.S. Bureau of Labor Statistics, 2017).

The Consequences of Joblessness for Black Fatherhood and Black Family Formation

The correlation between poor labor market outcomes, wage deterioration, joblessness, and declines in marriage rates among Blacks has been theorized and speculated about extensively (Center for the Study of Social Policy, 1999; Lewis, 2010; Morehouse Research Institute and the Institute for American Values, 1999; Nock, 2003; Wilson, 1987, 2003). One qualitative study found economic insecurity to be the primary source of contention in many relationships (Charles, Orthner, Jones, & Mancini, 2006). Under many circumstances, chronic work instability contributes to low marriage rates among Black males, particularly young men who tend to have higher rates of unemployment (Edin & Nelson, 2013, Hill, 2007; Johnson, 2014, Mincy, 2014).

Low marriage rates, in turn, contribute to declines in two-parent families and increases in nonmarital childbearing. Both joblessness and low socioeconomic status make Black men less desirable as marriage partners (Center for the Study of Social Policy, 1999; Morehouse Research Institute and the Institute for American Values, 1999; Wilson, 2003). Within the Black community, stable employment is often seen as a prerequisite for marriage as "African American women are more likely than their White and Hispanic peers to expect their male partner to have an adequate income before marriage" (Tucker, 1995; as cited in Mincy & Pouncy, 2004, p. 66). Data from the Fragile Families and Child Well-Being Study also revealed that among unwed low-income parents, "Roughly 90 percent of mothers rated 'husbands having a steady job' as a very important quality for having a successful marriage" (McLanahan, Garfinkel, & Mincy, 2001, p. 2).

As well, qualitative studies have also revealed the importance of human and economic capital assets for the maintenance of couple relationships and the expressed intolerance and frustration of many economically disadvantaged women toward men who fail to provide financially for the household (Charles et al., 2006; Johnson, 2002, 2000). Such expectations have a significant influence on the attitudes of single, economically unstable Black men toward marriage (Billingsley & Morrison-Rodriguez, 1998; Charles et al., 2006; Morehouse Research Institute and the Institute for American Values, 1999). On the other hand, economic viability increases the likelihood that Black men will marry (Center for the Study of Social Policy, 1999; James, 1998; Nock, 2003). Issues of unemployment or income differentials between husband and wife can also cause strain in marital relationships, posing the threat of family disruption and divorce (Bent-Goodley, 2014; Mincy & Pouncy, 2004).

In sum, lack of viable employment options and unfavorable economic conditions make it next to impossible for Black men to fulfill the provider role, thereby obstructing the path to family formation

Table 2. Unemployment Rates Among U.S. Men (25 Years and Older) by Race and Level of Education, 2016 Annual Averages.

Race	Less Than a High School Diploma	High School Graduates, No College	Some College, No Degree	Associate's Degree	Bachelor's Degree and Higher
Black Men	14.1%	8.6%	6.5%	5.3%	3.7%
Hispanic Men	5.9%	5.1%	4.4%	4.0%	3.1%
Asian Men	3.9%	4.0%	4.0%	3.8%	2.8%
White Men	6.5%	4.5%	3.9%	3.3%	2.3%

Source: U.S. Bureau of Labor Statistics (2017).

(Coles & Green, 2009; Johnson, 2014; McAdoo, 1997). As noted by Billingsley and Morrison-Rodriguez (1998), "The employment status of parents, especially fathers, is a direct determinant of the formation maintenance and stability of the Black family" (p. 61). Indeed, financial strain and the inability of Black men to successfully execute the provider role are undeniably at the root of the breakdown in Black marriage and fatherhood (Bent-Goodley, 2014; Morehouse Research Institute and the Institute for American Values, 1999). Additionally, U.S. criminal justice policies have also had a devastating impact on the Black family, namely the War on Drugs and the resultant increase in the incarceration of Blacks, mainly men (Alexander, 2012; Lewis, 2010; Miller, 2003). The next section provides an overview of these policies and their devastating impact on Black fatherhood and families over time.

Criminal Justice Policies and Mass Incarceration

Parallel to the decline in two-parent households and the rise in female-headed homes in the 1980s, urban America was also experiencing an unsettling amount of social disorganization due to drug trafficking and the introduction of crack cocaine into the Black community.

Along with the infiltration of crack cocaine came high rates of crime, violence, and homicide (Aronson, Whitehead, & Baber, 2003; Hill, 2007). As noted by Aronson, Whitehead, and Baber (2003), "From all reports, drug trafficking had a catastrophic effect on inner-city families and communities" (p. 732). The sharp increases in drug addiction during this time period weakened the capacity for parenting and lowered the prospects for marriage (Hill, 2007). Between the years of 1985 and 1995, the trafficking of crack cocaine became a major problem in the United States (Aronson, Whitehead, & Baber, 2003). Such turmoil within the Black community has been linked to the anger and frustration that came as a result of the deindustrialization of the economy and sharp declines in job opportunities, especially for Black men (Alexander, 2012). Despite the gains made during the Civil Rights Movement of the 1960s, yet again the game changed, with the United States federal government launching the "War on Drugs," which sought to punitively enforce drug laws in inner-city communities where the presence of crack cocaine was most prevalent (Aronson, Whitehead, & Baber, 2003; Alexander, 2012).

The Nixon and Reagan Administrations waged the drug war and resultant shift toward punitive punishment. However, the Clinton Administration escalated the war by advancing several "get tough on crime" zero tolerance policies—such as the three strikes laws and mandatory minimum sentencing—that disproportionately impacted the Black community (Alexander, 2012). The "war" essentially resulted in the disparate incarceration of Black males in epidemic proportions (Aronson, Whitehead, & Baber, 2003; Alexander, 2012; Center for the Study of Social Policy, 1999; Miller, 2003). Today, racial disparities in incarceration persist, as evidenced in the statistics presented in the following section.

Racial Disparities in Incarceration

Miller (2003) notes that "In 1985, the incarceration rate of African Americans was 368 per 100,000 in the population, and by 1995, that rate was almost double at 725" (Bureau of Justice Statistics; as cited in Miller, 2003, p. 5). A report by the Center for the Study of Social Policy (1999) also documents the rise in the number of incarcerated Blacks in the 1980s and 1990s. In 1981, Whites (57%) outnumbered Blacks (42%) in the state and federal prison population. However, by 1986, the trend reversed, where 45% of Blacks and 40% of Whites made up the prison populace. Furthermore, in 1991, 49% of the prison populace was made up of Blacks, in comparison to 35% of Whites. In addition, Clayton and Moore (2003) note that in 1997, six times more African Americans were incarcerated than Whites, and of this group, one-third were African American males between the ages of 20 and 29.

Racial discrimination in the application of drug laws has largely been responsible for the dramatic rise in incarceration rates among young, inner-city Black males (Clayton & Moore, 2003; Human

Rights Watch, 2008). Racial inequities in our nation's criminal justice system continue to be apparent today, as incarceration has become a part of the normal life course for many low-income men of color (Lyons & Pettit, 2011), especially Black men. According to the Bureau of Justice Statistics, one in three Black men can expect to go to prison in their lifetime (Lyons & Pettit, 2011). Much of this inequity can be attributed to punitive drug law enforcement policies (Alexander, 2012; Human Rights Watch, 2008).

When examining the intersections of race and U.S. drug enforcement policies, it is evident that, since its inception, the war on drugs has been unfairly targeted toward Blacks (Drug Policy Alliance, 2016; Human Rights Watch, 2008). As noted by the Drug Policy Alliance (2016), Black people comprise 13% of the U.S. population and engage in drug use at similar rates in comparison to other racial/ethnic groups. However, they represent 31% of those arrested for drug offenses and 40% of those incarcerated for such crimes (Drug Policy Alliance, 2016). Spikes in incarceration, both past and present, have many adverse consequences for Black fatherhood and family formation (Drug Policy Alliance, 2016; Lewis, 2010; Swisher & Waller, 2008), which is discussed in detail in the following section.

The Consequences of Mass Incarceration for Black Fatherhood and Family Formation

Research indicates that incarceration negatively impacts family formation and maintenance (Joseph, 2010; Lewis, 2010; Swisher & Waller, 2008; Western, Lopoo, & McLanahan, 2002). Specifically, frequent contacts with the criminal justice system and the stigma attached to incarceration make it difficult for unmarried Black men to establish stable relationships with women, which in turn reduces their prospects for marriage (Hill, 2007; Lewis, 2010; Pate, 2010; Western et al., 2002; Western & McLanahan, 2000). In addition, involvement with the penal system adversely affects the employability and financial stability of Black males, which in turn impacts their ability to function in the provider role in families (Joseph, 2010). Given that one's economic prospects are a significant determinant in the decision to marry (Tucker, 1995; as cited in Joseph, 2010; Lewis, 2010; Mincy & Pouncy, 2004, p. 66), the financial barriers experienced by many men with criminal histories make their opportunities for marriage bleak (Western et al., 2002).

In addition, among married men, imprisonment has a significant impact on their ability to form and maintain an intact family (Lewis, 2010; Western et al., 2002; Western & McLanahan, 2000). Clayton and Moore (2003) suggest that "One of the biggest casualties of the incarceration of African American men has been the nuclear family" (p. 84). Specifically, incarceration contributes to disruptions in relationships, both marital and nonmarital (Lewis, 2010). In addition, even when men are released from prison, the burden of incarceration may continue to damage relationships with significant others (Western et al., 2002; Western & McLanahan, 2000) and children (Currence & Johnson, 2003). The rampant racial disparities in drug law enforcement and rapid increases in the imprisonment of Black males have been offered as an explanation for father absence and the rise in female-headed households in the Black community. In addition to incarceration, social welfare policies and welfare reform have also had a deleterious impact on Black fatherhood and families. These policies are discussed in detail in the following section.

Social Welfare Policies and Welfare Reform

The Aid to Families with Dependent Children (AFDC) Basic program was established under the Social Security Act of 1935 to provide cash assistance to the families of needy children. From 1935 to the early 1960s, this was the principle program under which economically disadvantaged families were able to receive cash assistance (Page & Larner, 1997). To be eligible for AFDC, families were required to have dependent children who were: (a) U.S. citizens; (b) residents of the state in which they were to receive aid; (c) under the age of 18; and (d) deprived of parental support or care usually because the father was absent from the home continuously or because the principle family earner was incapacitated, deceased, or unemployed (Page & Larner, 1997).

AFDC benefit levels were calculated based on the resources of the Basic Family Unit (BFU), which by definition, consisted only of a mother and her dependent children (Harvard Law Review, 1970).

Thus, from its inception, AFDC Basic was designed to provide benefits to one-parent families. Eligibility rules for the program were such that the presence of a male who had a biological relationship with the child either significantly reduced welfare payments or completely disqualified potentially eligible families from receiving aid (Charles et al., 2006; Moffitt, Reville, & Winkler, 1994; Pate, 2010). The "man in the house" (Harvard Law Hill, 2007; Review, 1970) ineligibility rule led many to argue that the policy discouraged marriage and engendered father absence in economically disadvantaged Black families as many fathers left their homes for mothers to qualify for assistance (Hill, 2007; McLanahan et al., 2001).

In August of 1996, Congress passed legislation that significantly altered U.S. welfare policies (Page & Larner, 1997). Under the Clinton Administration, AFDC was replaced with the Temporary Assistance to Needy Families (TANF) Block Grant Program, which is housed within the Personal Responsibility and Work Opportunity Reconciliation Act of 1996 (PRWORA). Like the early AFDC policies, TANF also contains provisions that negatively impact Black family relationships and the presence of Black fathers in the home (Pate, 2010; Roy, 1999; Roy, Dyson, & Jackson, 2010). A major policy goal under TANF is the establishment of paternity and the strict enforcement of child support payments (Doherty, Kouneski, & Erickson, 1998; Hill, 2007; Pate, 2010). According to eligibility rules, for mothers to receive TANF benefits, they must be willing to assist federal government officials with "outing" or locating the nonresident father(s), establishing legal paternity, and collecting child support payments (Doherty et al., 1998; Pate, 2010).

The Consequences of Social Welfare Policies and Welfare Reform for Black Fatherhood and Family Formation

Given the legacy of institutional racism in America and the historically strained and distrusting relationship between Black men and systems of government (i.e., criminal justice system, child welfare system, educational system), these requirements often lead to conflict, tension, and adversarial couple and parental relationships (McLanahan & Carlson, 2002; Pate, 2010; Roy, 1999; Roy et al., 2010). In addition, although some states no longer discourage marriage by favoring single-parent over two-parent families, TANF continues in the tradition of AFDC as a means (i.e., income) tested program (McLanahan et al., 2001). Such programs often encourage economically disadvantaged mothers and fathers to live apart, or deny the existence of their partner, to receive the maximum amount of benefits (Charles et al., 2006; McLanahan et al., 2001). Qualitative studies have revealed the impact that TANF and other contemporary social welfare policies have on family structure and relationships between Black men and women. Charles et al. (2006) highlight the effect of social welfare policies on relationships, revealing that many young mothers feel forced to choose between the economic security provided through federal and state public assistance programs and maintaining relationships with men who demonstrate an inability to consistently provide financial support for them and their children.

In the Charles et al. study (2006), young mothers also expressed a sense of economic vulnerability brought on by means-tested social welfare programs that penalize dual-earner, two-parent families. Although welfare benefits are now made available to two-parent families, eligibility rules continue to be structured in a manner that dejects the presence of men in the home, causing many to go underground to mask their existence (Charles et al., 2006; McLanahan et al., 2001). Engagement in these illusory practices can contribute to disruption and strains in couple relationships, reductions in the prospects for marriage, and increases in the dissolution of marital unions, ultimately undermining the formation and maintenance of two-parent Black families. This article provides an overview of the fundamental structural and political shifts that have occurred over time, adversely impacting the structure and functioning of Black families. The challenges presented herein help to articulate the historical context of Black fatherhood and appropriately contextualize the contemporary circumstances that significantly influence Black family life. Several policy recommendations for strengthening Black fatherhood in the 21st century are offered in the following section.

Policy Recommendations for Strengthening Black Fatherhood and Family Formation in the 21st Century

As evidenced in the previous discussion, Black fathers—as presumed heads of households but also as coparenting contributors to child and family stability—often contend with numerous political and structural barriers that undermine their role as fathers (Johnson, 2014; Johnson, Levine, & Doolittle, 1999). It is important for policy makers to understand the complex nature of Black fatherhood in the 21st century, avoiding overreliance on conventional and stereotypical information and seeking to understand the individual experiences of these men as they are and not as they should or ought to be.

Black Americans of African descent living in the United States continue to be uniquely plagued by the vestiges and institutional effects of chattel slavery (Wright, 1995). Recognized as one of the most severe forms of slavery in the world, chattel slavery was uniquely experienced by Africans and their descendants in America from their arrival in 1619 until the passage of the 13th Amendment to the U.S. Constitution. This was a legal form of enslavement in which Africans were actual property that could be bought, sold, traded, or inherited. Legally recognized as 3/5 of a person, the chattel slave in America was subjected to inhumane treatment that diminished his/her total existence. Following the passage of the 13th Amendment, Jim Crow practices and laws aimed at intimidating and disenfranchising legal and social rights to former chattel slaves and their descendants formed institutional barriers to fully enacting citizenship. More than a century later, contemporary machinations of Jim Crow including voter suppression (Bump, 2016), mass incarceration (Alexander, 2012), and other legal maneuvers and mechanisms designed to discourage Black civic engagement continue to wreak havoc on individual social roles like Black fatherhood as well as collective social roles within Black family and community life in the United States (Johnson, 2014).

In fact, some contemporary machinations of Jim Crow, like mass incarceration, have exacted devastating tolls on personal agency and civic engagement, family formation, and community disempowerment (Miller, 2003). As Black males have been severely impacted by the continuing rise of incarceration in America, it is crucial that a reversal of this growing trend manifest with all deliberate speed. By promoting de-escalation of mass incarceration, especially among African American males, individual and family interventionists and policy practitioners alike can advocate for structural, institutional, and environmental strategies that can foster the development of more traditional and family-sensitive policies and practices. Smart decarceration focuses on reducing the incarceration population within the United States. The Smart Decarceration Initiative (SDI) at the Center for Social Development at the Brown School of Washington University in St. Louis (WUSTL) is one example of this effort (Pettus-Davis & Epperson, 2015).

All in all, ameliorating the smoldering sting of incarceration among ex-offenders and returning citizens is important to the rebuilding of lives, families, and communities. Inequities in the criminal justice system make a history of incarceration the rule rather than the exception among many Black fathers, particularly those of a lower socioeconomic status. Thus, it is imperative that policy makers meet the unique needs of this population, with special attention given to the development of policies and programs that will address the difficulties associated with prison life, such as father-child physical and emotional separation and the reunification process (Harris & Miller, 2003; Lewis, 2010). Furthermore, fathers who spend an extensive period of time in prison consequently experience a loss in wages and subsequent to their release from prison, unstable patterns of employment and joblessness (Joseph, 2010). To make matters worse, they also accumulate massive child support arrearages while incarcerated, making it next to impossible to repay upon their release from prison (Pate, 2010).

As highlighted earlier in this article, the economic prospects of Black men as fathers and providers for their children and families have been have been tenuous and marginalized. Throughout their presence in America, the labor force engagement prospects for Black men have been more sensitive to disruptions and change in structural, environmental, and technological contexts as compared to their racial and ethnic peers (Johnson, 2014). While the more recent Great Recession (December 2007–June 2009) wreaked havoc on many Americans, Black Americans, and Black men in particular, entered this economic downturn severely disadvantaged with higher rates of underemployment and unemployment with respect to labor force participation and were further disproportionately victimized by job loss and economic opportunity (Pitts, 2014). Joblessness among Black males continues to soar.

The U.S. Department of Labor's Bureau of Labor Statistics reports that unemployment among Black males 18–19 has increased from the 2015 3rd Quarter high of 33% to the 2016 3rd Quarter high of 33.9% and correspondingly, from 16.7% to 17.2% for Black males ages 20–24 during the same period (Bureau of Labor Statistics, 2016). Davis (2015) uses recent Current Population Survey data analyses in her Economic Policy Institute report, finding "real unemployment" among African American youth to be as high as 51%. These data are of increasing importance given the preponderance of young Black fatherhood and the subsequent family formation patterns that are complicated by rates of joblessness and unemployment, racial bias, and discrimination in hiring practices and detention and mass incarceration (Currence & Johnson, 2003; Johnson, 2014). The rebounding economy resulting from the Great Recession of 2007–2009 has had a negligible impact on the economic well-being of young Black males collectively. Compared to their racial and ethnic peers, they remain behind with respect to employment gains (Pitts, 2014). To enhance their suitability as parenting and coupling partners, collective individual and societal investments in their overall appeal as fathers and partners in relationships are necessary.

Taken together, the following recommendations are among the highest priorities for creating sustainable efforts to enhance paternal engagement and strengthen Black fatherhood and family formation: (a) enhanced opportunities for family and community reunification, following incarceration, via housing support, in both the public and private markets; (b) pathways to sustainable and living wages through job creation and employment; (c) provision of physical, mental, and behavioral health services; (d) rebuilding of couple, partner, and parenting relationships, as well as legal and cultural pathways to civic engagement; and (e) provision of parenting supports that include preparation for a labor market that yields livable wages and work supports for poor fathers and mothers alike. Such efforts are critical to those who been victimized at the hand of economic and social policies, whether intended or unintended. In fact, given the historical negative impact of these policies, race-targeted efforts to assuage their effect are both appropriate and necessary. Building hope within young Black males can assist them in transcending their current position in the United States, building momentum for brighter futures. In tandem, societal investments that facilitate and bolster their development is also critical to building and sustaining hope for a promising future. Strengthening, recognizing, and positioning young Black males as vital members of their families of origin, choice, and procreation is an important challenge that American society must embrace.

Disclosure statement

No potential conflict of interest was reported by the authors.

Funding

This work was supported by the University of Chicago's Chapin Hall and the Doris Duke Charitable Foundation.

References

Alexander, M. (2012). *The new Jim Crow: Mass incarceration in the age of colorblindness*. New York, NY: The New Press.

Amato, P. R., Meyers, C. E., & Emery, R. E. (2009). Changes in non-resident father-child contact from 1976-2002. *Family Relations*, 58, 41–53. doi:10.1111/j.1741-3729.2008.00533.x

American Sociological Association. (2005). *Race, ethnicity, and the American labor market: What's at work.* Retrieved from http://www.asanet.org/sites/default/files/savvy/images/research/docs/pdf/RaceEthnicity_LaborMarket.pdf

Aronson, R. E., Whitehead, T. L., & Baber, W. L. (2003). Challenges to masculine transformation among urban low-income African American males. *American Journal of Public Health, 93,* 723–741.

Bent-Goodley, T. B. (2014). African American marriages at the intersections: Challenges, strengths and resilience. In T. B. Bent-Goodley (Ed.), *By grace: The challenges, strengths, and promise of African American marriages* (pp. 1–12). Washington, DC: NASW Press.

Billingsley, A. (1968). *Black families in white America.* Englewood Cliffs, NJ: Prentice-Hall, Inc.

Billingsley, A. (1974). *Black families and the struggle for survival: Teaching our children to walk tall.* New York, NY: Friendship Press.

Billingsley, A. (1992). *Climbing Jacob's ladder: The enduring legacy of African-American families.* New York, NY: Simon & Schuster, Inc.

Billingsley, A., & Morrison-Rodriguez, B. (1998). The black family in the twenty-first century and the church as an action system. In L. A. See (Ed.), *Human behavior in the social environment from an African American perspective* (pp. 31–47). Binghamton, New York, NY: The Haworth Press.

Billingsley, A., & Morrison-Rodriguez, B. (2007). The black family in the twenty-first century and the church as an action system: A macro perspective. In L. A. See (Ed.), *Human behavior in the social environment from an African American perspective* (2nd ed., pp. 57–74). New York, NY: The Haworth Press, Inc.

Bump, P. (2016). *The long history of black voter suppression in American politics.* Retrieved from https://www.washingtonpost.com/news/the-fix/wp/2016/11/02/the-long-history-of-black-voter-suppression-in-american-politics/

Bureau of Labor Statistics, US Department of Labor. (2016). *Labor force statistics from the Current Population Survey.* Retrieved from http://www.bls.gov/web/empsit/cpsee_e16.htm

Butler, J. (2000). *Being there: Exploring fatherhood experiences and beliefs of low-income urban African American males.* Paper presented at the meeting of National Association of African American Studies & National Association of Hispanic and Latino Studies, Houston, TX.

Cabrera, N. J., Tamis-LeMonda, C. S., Bradley, R. H., Hofferth, S., & Lamb, M. E. (2000). Fatherhood in the 21st century. *Child Development, 71,* 127–136.

Center for the Study of Social Policy. (1999). World without work: Causes and consequences of black male joblessness. In R. Staples, *The black family: Essays and studies* (6th ed., pp. 291–311). Belmont, CA: Wadsworth Publishing Company.

Charles, P., Orthner, D. K., Jones, A., & Mancini, D. (2006). Poverty and couple relationships: Implications for welfare policy. *Marriage and Family Review, 39,* 27–52. doi:10.1300/J002v39n01_03

Cheadle, J. E., Amato, P. R., & King, V. (2010). Patterns of non-resident father contact. *Demography, 47,* 205–225.

Child Trends Data Bank. (2016). *Births to unmarried women: Indicators of youth well-being.* Retrieved from https://www.childtrends.org/wp-content/uploads/2015/12/75_Births_to_Unmarried_Women.pdf

Clayton, O., & Moore, J. (2003). The effects of crime and imprisonment on family formation. In O. Clayton, R. B. Mincy, & D. Blankenhorn (Eds.), *Black fathers in contemporary American society: Strengths, weaknesses, and strategies for change* (pp. 84–102). New York, NY: Russell Sage Foundation.

Coles, R. L., & Green, C. (2009). Introduction. In R. L. Coles & C. Green (Eds.), *The myth of the missing black father* (pp. 1–18). New York, NY: Columbia University Press.

Currence, P., & Johnson, W. (2003). The negative implications of incarceration on Black fathers. *African American Research Perspectives, 9*(1), 24–32.

Davis, A. (2015). *Young Black high school grads face astonishing underemployment.* Retrieved from http://www.epi.org/blog/young-black-high-school-grads-face-astonishing-underemployment/

Delgado, R., & Stefancic, J. (2001). *Critical race theory: An introduction.* New York, NY: New York University Press.

Doherty, W. J., Kouneski, E. F., & Erickson, M. F. (1998). Responsible fathering: An overview and conceptual framework. *Journal of Marriage and Family, 60,* 277–292. doi:10.2307/353848

Drug Policy Alliance. (2016). *The drug war, mass incarceration, and race.* Retrieved from https://www.drugpolicy.org/sites/default/files/DPA%20Fact%20Sheet_Drug%20War%20Mass%20Incarceration%20and%20Race_%28Feb.%202016%29_0.pdf

Edin, K., & Nelson, T. (2013). *Doing the best I can: Fatherhood in the Inner City.* Berkeley, CA: University of California Press.

Franklin, J. H. (1997). African American families: A historical note. In H. Pipes McAdoo (Ed.), *Black families* (3rd ed., pp. 5–8). Thousand Oaks, CA: Sage Publications.

Frazier, E. F. (1939). *The negro family in the United States.* Chicago, IL: The University of Chicago Press.

Gary, L. E. (1981). *Black men.* Beverly Hills, CA: Sage Publications, Inc.

Grubb, W. N., & Wilson, R. H. (1989). *Sources of increasing inequality in wages and salary.* Retrieved from http://bls.gov/mlr/1989/04/art1full.pdf

Gutman, H. G. (1976). *The black family in slavery and freedom, 1750-1925.* New York, NY: Pantheon Books.

Harris, O., & Miller, R. (2003). *Impacts of incarceration on the African American family.* New Brunswick, NJ: Transaction Press.

Hewlett, S. A., & West, C. (1998). *The war against parents: What we can do for America's beleaguered moms and dads.* New York, NY: Houghton Mifflin Company.

Hill, R. B. (1972). *The strengths of Black families.* New York, NY: Emerson Hall Publishers.

Hill, R. B. (2007). Family roles of non-custodial African American fathers. In L. A. See (Ed.), *Human behavior in the social environment from an African American Perspective* (2nd ed., pp. 117–131). New York, NY: The Haworth Press, Inc.

Human Rights Watch. (2008). *Targeting Blacks: Drug law enforcement and race in the United States.* Retrieved from https://www.hrw.org/sites/default/files/reports/us0508_1.pdf

James, A. D. (1998). What's love got to do with it?: Economic viability and the likelihood of marriage among African American men. *Journal of Comparative Family Studies, 29*, 373–383.

Johnson, E., Levine, A., & Doolittle, F. (1999). *Fathers fair share: Helping poor men manage child support and fatherhood.* New York, NY: Russell Sage Press.

Johnson, W. (2000). Work preparation and labor market experiences among urban, poor, nonresident fathers. In S. Danziger & A. Lin (Eds.), *Coping with poverty: The social contexts of neighborhood, work and family in the African American community* (pp. 224–261). Ann Arbor, MI: University of Michigan Press.

Johnson, W. (2002). Time out of bound: High school completion and work preparation among urban, poor, unwed African American nonresident fathers. In W. Allen, M. Beale Spencer, & C. O'Connor (Eds.), *African American education: Race, community, inequality and achievement-a tribute to Edgar G. Epps* (pp. 229–257). Oxford, UK: Elsevier/JAI Press.

Johnson, W. (2010). *Social work with African American males: Health, mental health and social policy.* New York, NY: Oxford University Press.

Johnson, W. (2014). Black masculinity, manhood and marriage. In T. Bent-Goodley (Ed.), *By grace: The challenges, strengths and promise of African American marriage* (pp. 113–133). Washington, DC: NASW Press.

Joseph, M. L. (2010). Understanding economic costs of incarceration for African American males. In W. Johnson (Ed.), *Social work with African American Males: Health, mental health and social policy* (pp. 311–324). New York, NY: Oxford University Press.

Kids Count Data Center. (2018) *Children in single parent families by race.* Retrieved from https://datacenter.kidscount.org/data/tables/107-children-in-single-parent-families-by#detailed/1/any/false/870,573,869,36,868,867,133,38,35,18/10,11,9,12,1,185,13/432,431

Lang, K., & Lehmann, J. K. (2011). *Racial discrimination in the labor market: Theory and empirics.* Retrieved from http://people.bu.edu/lang/w17450.pdf

Lewis, C. E. (2010). Incarceration and family formation. In W. Johnson (Ed.), *Social work with African American Males: Health, mental health and social policy* (pp. 293–310). New York, NY: Oxford University Press.

Livingston, G., & Parker, K. (2011). *A tale of two fathers: More active, but more absent.* Retrieved from http://www.pewsocialtrends.org/files/2011/06/fathers-FINAL-report.pdf

Lyons, C. J., & Pettit, B. (2011). Compounded disadvantage: Race, incarceration, and wage growth. *Social Problems, 58*, 257–280. doi:10.1525/sp.2011.58.2.257

Mathis, A. (1978). Contrasting approaches to the study of black families. *Journal of Marriage and the Family, 40*, 667–676. doi:10.2307/351187

McAdoo, J. L. (1997). The role of African American fathers in the socialization of their children. In H. Pipes McAdoo (Ed.), *Black families* (3rd ed., pp. 183–197). Thousand Oaks, CA: Sage Publications.

McLanahan, S. S., & Carlson, M. J. (2002). Welfare reform, fertility, and father involvement. *The Future of Children, 42*, 146–165.

McLanahan, S. S., Garfinkel, I., & Mincy, R. B. (2001). *Fragile families, welfare reform, and marriage.* Retrieved from http://www.brookings.edu/~/media/Files/rc/papers/2001/12childrenfamilies_mclanahan/pb10.pdf

Miller, R. R. (2003). Various implications of the "race to incarcerate" on incarcerated African American men in families. In O. Harris & R. Robin Miller (Eds.), *Impacts of incarceration on the African American family* (pp. 3–15). New Brunswick, NJ: Transaction Publishers.

Mincy, R. B. (2014). *Failing our fathers: Confronting the crisis of economically vulnerable nonresident fathers.* New York, NY: Oxford University Press.

Mincy, R. B., & Pouncy, H. W. (2004). The responsible fatherhood field: Evolution and goals. In C. S. Tamis-LeMonda & N. Cabrera (Eds.), *Handbook of father involvement: Multidisciplinary perspectives* (pp. 555–597). Malwah, NJ: Lawrence Earlbaum, Publishers.

Moffitt, R. A., Reville, R. T., & Winkler, A. E. (1994). State AFDC rules regarding the treatment of cohabiters: 1993. *Social Security Bulletin, 57*, 26–33.

Morehouse Research Institute and the Institute for American Values. (1999). *A statement from the Morehouse Conference on African American Fathers: Turning the corner on father absence in Black America.* Retrieved from http://www.americanvalues.org/turning_the_corner.pdf

Moynihan, D. P. (1965). *The negro family: The case for national action.* Retrieved from http://www.dol.gov/oasam/programs/history/webid-meynihan.htm

Nobles, W. (1978). Toward an empirical and theoretical framework for defining Black families. *Journal of Marriage and Family, 40*, 679–690. doi:10.2307/351188

Nock. (2003). Marriage and fatherhood in the lives of African American men. In O. Clayton, R. B. Mincy, & D. Blankenhorn (Eds.), *Black fathers in contemporary American society: Strengths, weaknesses, and strategies for change* (pp. 30–42). New York, NY: Russell Sage Foundation.

Offner, P. (2001). *Reducing non-marital births*. Retrieved from http://www.brookings.edu/es/wrb/publications/pb/pb05.pdf

Page, S. B., & Larner, M. B. (1997). Introduction to the AFDC program. *Welfare to Work, 7*, 20–27.

Park, R. (1950). *The race relations cycle in Hawaii*. Retrieved from http://faculty.washington.edu/charles/562_f2011/Week%203/Park_ch14PDF.PDF

Pate, D. J. (2010). Life after PRWORA: The involvement of African American fathers with welfare-reliant children and the child support enforcement system. In W. Johnson (Ed.), *Social work with African American Males: Health, mental health and social policy* (pp. 61–80). New York, NY: Oxford University Press.

Perry, A., Harmon, D., & Bright, M. (2013). A package deal?: African American men's perspectives on the intersection of marriage and fatherhood. *Women, Gender, and Families of Color, 1*, 124–142. doi:10.5406/womgenfamcol.1.2.0124

Perry, A. R. (2009). The influence of the extended family on the involvement of nonresident African American fathers. *Journal of Family Social Work, 12*, 211–226. doi:10.1080/10522150903046390

Pettus-Davis, C., & Epperson, M. (2015). From mass incarceration to smart decarceration. *Grand Challenges for Social Work Initiative Working Paper No. 4*. Cleveland, OH: American Academy of Social Work and Social Welfare.

Pitts, S. C. (2014). *Black employment and unemployment in 2013*. Center for Labor Research and Education, UC Berkeley Labor Center.

Review, H. L. (1970). AFDC income attribution: The man-in-the-house and welfare grant reductions. *Harvard Law Review, 83*, 1370–1386. doi:10.2307/1339820

Ricketts, E. (n.d.). *The origin of black female-headed households*. Retrieved from http://www.irp.wisc.edu/publications/focus/pdfs/foc121e.pdf

Roy, K. M. (1999). Low-income single fathers in an African American community and the requirements of welfare reform. *Journal of Family Issues, 20*, 432–457. doi:10.1177/019251399020004002

Roy, K. M. (2005). Transitions on the margins of work and family life for low-income African American fathers. *Journal of Family and Economic Issues, 26*, 77–100. doi:10.1007/s10834-004-1413-3

Roy, K. M. (2006). Father stories: A life course examination of paternal identity among low-income African American men. *Journal of Family Issues, 27*, 31–54. doi:10.1177/0192513X05275432

Roy, K. M., Dyson, O. L., & Jackson, J. (2010). Intergenerational support and reciprocity between low-income African American fathers and their aging mothers. In W. Johnson (Ed.), *Social work with African American Males: Health, mental health and social policy* (pp. 42–60). New York, NY: Oxford University Press.

Staples, R. (1999a). The changing black family. In R. Staples (Ed.), *The black family: Essays and studies* (6th ed., pp. 2–6). Belmont, CA: Wadsworth Publishing Company.

Staples, R. (1999b). Patterns of change in the postindustrial black family. In R. Staples (Ed.), *The black family: Essays and studies* (6th ed., pp. 281–290). Belmont, CA: Wadsworth Publishing Company.

Staples, R., & Johnson, L. B. (1993). *Black families at the crossroads: Challenges and prospects*. San Francisco, CA: Jossey-Bass Publishers.

Swisher, R. R., & Waller, M. R. (2008). Confining fatherhood: Incarceration and paternal involvement among nonresident White, African American and Latino fathers. *Journal of Family Issues, 29*, 1067–1088. doi:10.1177/0192513X08316273

Toldson, I. A., & Morton, J. (2012). *Black people don't read: The definitive guide to dismantling stereotypes and negative statistical claims about Black Americans*. Washington, DC: iYAGO Entertainment Group.

U.S. Bureau of Labor Statistics. (2011). *Labor force characteristics by race and ethnicity, 2010*. Retrieved from http://www.bls.gov/opub/reports/race-and-ethnicity/archive/race_ethnicity_2010.pdf

U.S. Bureau of Labor Statistics. (2015). *Labor force characteristics by race and ethnicity, 2014*. Retrieved from https://data.bls.gov/search/query/results?cx=013738036195919377644%3A6ih0hfrgl50&q=BLS+Reports+%E2%94%82+November+2015+%E2%80%A2+www.bls.gov+1+Labor+Force+Characteristics+by+Race+and+Ethnicity%2C+2014

U.S. Bureau of Labor Statistics. (2017). *Labor force characteristics by race and ethnicity, 2016*. Retrieved from https://www.bls.gov/opub/reports/race-and-ethnicity/2016/pdf/home.pdf

Western, B., Lopoo, L. M., & McLanahan, S. (2002). *Incarceration and the bonds among parents in fragile families*. Retrieved from http://www.rwjf.org/files/research/Incarceration%20-%20Fragile%20Families.pdf

Western, B., & McLanahan, S. (2000). *Fathers behind bars: The impact of incarceration on family formation*. Retrieved from http://www.rwjf.org/files/research/Incarceration%20-%20Fragile%20Families.pdf

Wilson, W. J. (1987). *The truly disadvantaged: The inner-city, the underclass, and public policy*. Chicago, IL: The University of Chicago Press.

Wilson, W. J. (1992). The plight of the inner-city Black male. *Proceedings of the American Philosophical Society, 136*, 320–325.

Wilson, W. J. (1996). *When work disappears: The world of the new urban poor.* New York, NY: Alfred A. Knopf, Inc.
Wilson, W. J. (2003). The woes of the inner-city African American father. In O. Clayton, R. B. Mincy, & D. Blankenhorn (Eds.), *Black fathers in contemporary American society: Strengths, weaknesses, and strategies for change* (pp. 9–29). New York, NY: Russell Sage Foundation.
Wilson, W. J. (2010). Why both social structure and culture matter in a holistic analysis of inner-city poverty. *The Annals of the American Academy of Political and Social Science, 629,* 200–219. doi:10.1177/0002716209357403
Wright, J. A. (1995). *Good news!: Sermons of hope for today's families.* Valley Forge, PA: Judson Press.

Inequities in Family Quality of Life for African-American Families Raising Children with Disabilities

Carl Algood and Amber M. Davis

ABSTRACT
Over time, groundbreaking changes in societies' views and treatment of persons with disabilities, along with significant legislative and policy changes, have impacted the quality of life of African-American families raising children with disabilities. This article presents some of the challenges and inequities faced by African-American families that impact their quality of life using critical race theory (CRT). Also, it reviews results obtained by a study of 123 African-American families raising children with disabilities. The article offers implications for policy and practice and discusses the role for social workers in addressing disparities in healthcare and other areas.

Introduction

Family quality of life has been defined as "conditions where the family's needs are met, family members enjoy their life together and have the chance to do things that are important" (Poston et al., 2003, p. 96). Since the 1970s, the concept, family quality of life (FQOL), has gained recognition as an important concept linked to family supports for families of children with disabilities, as a new extension of individual quality of life (QOL), a framework that has been widely embraced in the field of disability to affect policymaking, guide service delivery, and enhance outcomes of individuals with disabilities (Wang & Brown, 2009)

Historically, African-American families raising children with disabilities experienced a different plight than the majority population, with implications for impact on their quality of life. King (1998) noted that in the past, African-American parents raising children with disabilities were not involved in the disability rights movement, tended to keep their children at home as a protection from institutional placements (Daly, Jennings, Beckett, & Leashore, 1995), and lacked an abundance of services and supports (Popple & Leighninger, 2005). African-American parents also faced challenges in relating to the public education system policies and fear of unwelcoming environments. There existed a disproportionate representation of minority students in special education.

The Mills v. Board of Education case of 1972 attempted to address disparities experienced by minorities with disabilities in the educational system. Following this was the passage of the special education legislation of PL 94-142, the 1975 Education of All Handicapped Children Act, subsequently amended to the Individual with Disabilities Education Act (IDEA) of 1990. Racial inequality and denial of rights to education regardless of ability were key factors in the passage of the legislation (Skiba, Poloni-Staudinger, Gallini, Simmons, & Feggins-Azziz, 2008).

Mills v. Board of Education was initiated by the caregivers of seven children diagnosed with diverse disabilities consisting of physical disabilities, mental retardation (intellectual disability), seizure disorders, hyperactivity, and problem behaviors (Yell, Rogers, & Rogers, 1998). The legal action concluded with a judgement against the Board of Education that restated the requirement that all children with disabilities, regardless of race or ethnicity, be provided education that is publicly supported.

Background

In the United States, over several decades a more sensitive view of persons with disabilities evolved. These more sensitive views positively impacted the family quality of life of families raising children with disabilities. The changes occurred because of demands from family advocates and the passage of laws to ensure that those with disabilities were guaranteed civil rights. Antiquated views of persons with disabilities included the view that they were cursed by God, incompetent, or sick (Mackelprang & Salsgiver, 2016). These longstanding negative perceptions and stereotypes birthed during the 18th and 19th centuries impacted quality of life for individuals and their families. A majority of persons facing developmental and mental disabilities were placed in asylums, reform schools, and other institutions away from the general population (Ferguson, 2002). Throughout the 20th century and 21st centuries, negative stereotypes embedded in the antiquated views of the medical and moral models have persisted (Mackelprang & Salsgiver, 2016, Marini, Glover-Graf, & Millington, 2012, Wolfensenberger, 1972).

Up until the period of community integration in the 1960s and 1970s, individuals with disabilities had limited or no voice in society and were not able to enjoy a high quality of life, largely due to systemic disfranchisement including not being able to attend mainstream schools (Seligman & Darling, 2017; Wituk, Bomhoff, Hinde, & Meissen, 2007). The normalization movement in the 1960s fought for the rights of persons with developmental disabilities to have the opportunity to live, learn, and excel in conditions similar to the general population (Dodd, Zabriskie, Widner, & Eggett, 2009). This movement gained impetus from the civil rights movement of the 1960s, when the crusade for equal rights of African Americans culminated in the Civil Rights Act of 1964.

The predominant view prior to the 1960s was that persons with disabilities required a great deal of care in settings apart from the regular population. This medical model has changed for the most part, with a new focus on protecting and promoting the civil rights of people with disabilities and making more efforts to treat them in a humane manner (Parish & Lutwick, 2005). The principle of normalization promoted the inclusion of persons with developmental disabilities in nonsegregated settings (Parish & Lutwick, 2005), where nondisabled persons reside, are employed, and have educational and recreational opportunities available to them (Renzaglia, Karvonen, Drasgow & Stoxcen, 2003).

Conceptualization of family quality of life

Campbell, Converse, and Rodgers (1975) conducted some of the early studies on FQOL and assessed predictions of satisfaction with family life by set measures of early circumstances, set of personal characteristics, and perceptions of relationships with family members. The authors concluded that a major contributor to satisfaction with family is the relationship between children and spouse.

In their seminal study, Campbell et al. (1975) found a lower life satisfaction and quality of well-being in African-American families than Caucasian families in such domains as standard of living, level of savings, housing, amount of schooling, and neighborhood.

Campbell et al. (1975) concluded that the consistent, less-than-positive tone in which African Americans described their satisfaction with quality of life was based on being poorly employed, poorly paid, and poorly housed. In addition, the authors asserted that the dissatisfaction in African-American families originates from experiences and viewpoints associated with being Black in a society which is only beginning to accord African Americans equal recognition as citizens. In their study, citing results from logistic regression on the research question of whether being of African American race, with a disability, and perceived racism decrease life satisfaction, (Smith & Alston, 2009) concluded that unequal treatment in the workplace or medical setting based on race, and experiencing physical or emotional symptoms based on race, lowers levels of satisfaction with life.

The movement toward understanding FQOL is rooted in the premises that the individual and the family must be viewed from a holistic perspective. Programs of intervention, historically, in intellectual and developmental disabilities have focused on special needs of individuals, separate from the environment and the family (Samuel, Rillotta, & Brown, 2012) "The emerging focus on conceptualizing and researching FQOL addresses, in part, whether or not assumptions that most families are both able and willing to act as the main caregivers and decision makers, over time, are valid" (Samuel et al., 2012, p. 2).

The issue of accountability for family outcomes has brought forward an expanding focus on family-centered approaches to services and supports for families of children with disabilities, which has led researchers to focus their efforts on FQOL (Summers et al., 2005). One of the key reasons for the increased interest in FQOL is the global trend toward deinstitutionalization and the corresponding growing reliance on the family home as an ongoing residence (Werner et al., 2009).

Conceptualization of disability

In this study, the disabilities that will be discussed are those covered under the Individual with Disabilities Education Act of 2004 (IDEA). As defined by the act, the term *child with a disability* means:

> a child with mental retardation (intellectual disability), hearing impairments (including deafness), speech or language impairments, visual impairments (including blindness), serious emotional disturbance, orthopedic impairments, autism, traumatic brain injury, other health impairments, or specific learning disabilities; and who, by reason thereof, needs special education and related services. (PL-108-446-2004, p. 6)

Critical race theory/racial inequities

Critical race theory (CRT) has been cultivated in various fields in contemporary times (i.e., education, legal studies, and public health) to help situate racial inequities. As a theory, CRT situates paradigms of racial power, racial dominance, and racial disadvantage as a result of the enduring legacy of discrimination, segregation, and inequality leading to a continuous plight of minorities (Pinn-Wiggins, 1990). Aspects of race and race relations are unapologetically and continuous framed with an eye on the current manifestation of inequality, with consideration for past patterns of injustice that are perpetuated by systemic factors. The impact of inequality and the actual life experiences of minorities impacted by the staunch effects of racism and an unequal distribution of power and privilege through the course of the nation's inception into the present are inner workings of CRT that continue to raise scholastic focus (Bell, 2009; Delgado & Stefancic; Taylor, 1998).

Quality of life has been critically considered by Duncan (2002), who asserted that "it is fashionable nowadays to downplay and even dismiss race as a factor shaping the quality of life in the United States and instead to favor class-based and gender-based approaches to understanding social oppression" (p. 93). Further, CRT is useful to understand the societal impact on FQOL in African-American families raising children with disabilities.

The perspective that racism is not isolated but instead is the normal order of American life is CRT's key theme (Asch, 2001). CRT can guide the study and theorizing of race and disability because both are considered compatible markers of oppression that interact in subgroups such as minority children disproportionately receiving special education services (Annamma, Connor, & Ferri, 2013; Connor, 2008, 2008; Erevelles & Minear, 2010).

Health disparities/inequities

There are major inequalities in healthcare, housing, employment, finances, and education that impact the quality of life of African-American families raising child(ren) with disabilities. Gupta (2007) found that as a group, minorities with disabilities in the United States have fewer resources and less knowledge and understanding of available resources than others. Several researchers have documented the connection between poverty and disability and have explored how the lack of employment, finances, education, transportation, and other resources results in the family's isolation, exclusion, and overall difficulty in the adjustment process (Emerson, 2007; Ghosh & Parish, 2013; Kelly-Moore & Ferraro, 2004; Parish & Cloud, 2006; Parish, Rose, Grinstein-Weiss, Richman, & Andrews, 2008; Terhune, 2005).

In a national context, children with disabilities are more likely to reside in households that are deemed impoverished (Ghosh & Parish, 2013; Parish et al., 2008). Families of children with disabilities face added burdens financially when compared to families of children without disabilities, such as increased therapy costs, specialized day care, and adapting the home environment (Newacheck, Stein, & Bauman, 2003; Parish & Cloud, 2006). From a quality-of-life standpoint, families of children who have increased personal care, medical, and therapeutic service needs were found to have increased financial concerns, as well as problems with work and sleep (Neely-Barnes & Marcenko, 2004). Further, African-American families raising children with disabilities raises the concern of intersectionality, or double disadvantages, when disability-related inequities are added to racial inequality.

A significant area that impacts quality of life for minority families is healthcare. There are major disparities in the healthcare system between Whites and racial/ethnic minorities and many researchers have documented that, as opposed to non-Hispanic White children, African-American children had a greater likelihood of being identified as having disabilities (Algood, Harris, & Hong, 2013). For minority families, two groups have disproportionately encountered disparities in healthcare: children with developmental disabilities including autism, and children who are Black and Latino as compared with White children within the population of children with special healthcare needs (Gourdine & Algood, 2014; Magaña, Parish, Rose, Timberlake, & Swaine, 2012). Despite their challenges, it is important to discuss some of the strengths African-American families possess that lead to enhancement of quality of life as they raise their child with disability. It is also important to note that the challenges families face far outweigh the strengths and should not mask the fact of the struggles they endure and the services and supports required.

Coping in the face of inequities

Despite enduring stressors, all families have their diverse ways of coping and being resilient to challenges and adversity, including those raising a child with a disability, resulting in an improved quality of life. Several authors (Crewe & Gadling- Cole, 2015; Crewe & Wilson, 2007; Gourdine, 2007; Taylor, Seaton, & Dominguez, 2008) state that strong kinship bonds, religious connections, and extended family networks remain a current, relevant source of social support for the African-American family on their quality of life. The authors contend that, in instances when mainstream services are not available or accessible, or are difficult to obtain, the importance of the family and community networks becomes even more salient. They further note that it is important to consider that socioeconomic status, class, financial resources, and parenting skills impact minority families and the services they seek and/or receive from the community, particular as they raise children with disabilities.

Method

To better understand the needs of African-American families, the authors conducted research to address the question, "What are the effects of the levels of family coping on the level of quality of life in African-American families caring for a child with a disability?"

Demographic characteristics

This research was conducted in 2011 at two medical centers located in the mid-eastern section of the United States. These parents were engaged in services for their children at these facilities.

The study included 123 families, with 94.3% of the families identifying themselves as African American, whereas the remaining 4.9% identified themselves as "other," which included categories of multiracial participants and included some of African-American heritage. The majority of the respondents were female (81.3%). The age of the parents ranged from 20–79 years, with the average age of 42.17 years ($SD = 12.07$).

The marital status of the respondents was varied, with three of the most frequent marital status categories being single/never married ($n = 54$), married ($n = 40$), and divorced ($n = 16$). Other categories included: widowed ($n = 4$), separated ($n = 5$), and other ($n = 2$). When examining employment status, 116 respondents provided their current employment status as having full-time or part-time employment (46%), whereas, the remaining 54% were unemployed. The annual income reported by the participants ranged from $900 per month to $180,000 per year, with 50% of the respondents reporting a median income of at least $30,000 or more per year.

The majority of the families reported having, on average, three children in their households. The vast majority of the sample reported having one child with a disability (81.3%), 22.2% reported having two children with a disability, and less than 1% reported having three children with disabilities.

The respondents' familial relationship to the child with a disability was distributed as follows: 77.9% biological parent, 11.5% legal guardian, 9.0% adoptive parent, and 1.6% foster parent. The age range of the disabled children was between eight months and 21 years,, with the average age being around 10 years old ($M = 9.69$ years, $SD = 5.44$ years). Consistent with most research findings, most of the children with disabilities reported in this study were male (57%).

Figure 1 provides details on type of disability and Figure 2 provides severity of disability of children in the sample. Further, Figure 2 provides additional demographic information on the study. As shown in Figure 1, the three most frequently reported disabilities were speech or language impairment (51%), orthopedic impairments (45%), and intellectual disability (41%).

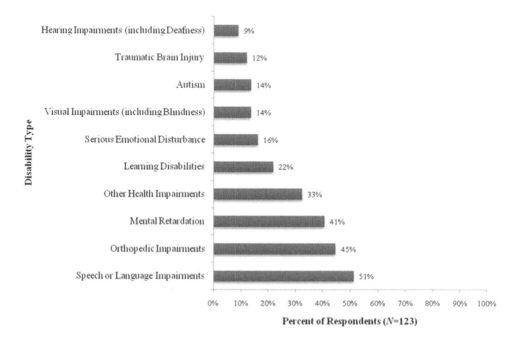

Figure 1. Type of disability.

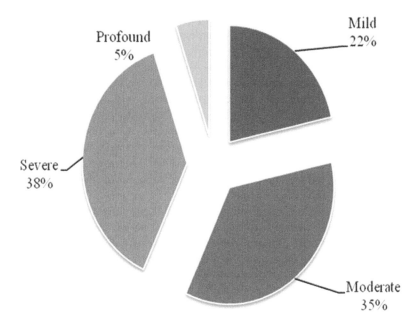

Figure 2. Severity of disability.

The families participating in this study provided information about their child's disability in terms of severity and type of disability. As shown in Figure 2, most of the families reported that their children had moderate or severe disabilities (36%) (Algood & Gourdine, 2015).

Measures

The research used the following instruments to measure coping and quality of life: Beach Family Quality of Life (FQOL) (Summer et al. 2005), Family Functioning Style Scale (Dunst, Trivette, & Deal, 1988), and the Coping Health Inventory for Parents (McCubbin & Thompson,1991; McCubbin and Huang, 1989).
This hypothesis specified that, as levels of coping increase, the quality of life in African-American families raising a child with a developmental disability will increase. Bivariate analysis indicated a statistically significant, positive relationship between coping and family quality [r (96) = 0.43, $p < .001$, one-tailed].

Analysis

An analysis of information from the families concluded that families raising a child with a developmental disability experience a range of negative challenges along with some positive outcomes. The levels of caregiver burden were associated with the severity and type of disability. Of the four levels of intellectual disability, the severe level was rated at 35%. While caregivers raising children with intellectual disability were experiencing a higher quality of life, those caring for children with traumatic brain injury were experiencing more caregiver burden. Other indicators of caregiver impact include the characteristics of the household structure and the nature of the parent/child attachment.

For example, demographic data results showed that 50% of the respondents in the study were making an income of $30,000 dollars or more. Despite this income level, they were found to be experiencing a higher quality of life. However, the demographic data point to a host of challenges also, in that it revealed that 54% of the respondents were from single female–headed households and the unemployment rate for participants was 54%. When examining employment status, 116 respondents provided their current employment status as reported having full-time or part-time employment (46%). This indicates an almost even split among the participants and suggests that while many families are in the ranks of the employed and a slightly greater number of families raising children with disabilities are unemployed, it is unclear if they desired this status or if caregiver responsibilities limited their opportunities for employment. Several authors have documented the low ranks that families with children with disabilities fall in with regard to income, unemployment, housing, and education (Park, Turnbull, & Turnbull III, 2002; Parish, Rose, Grinstein-Weiss, Richman, & Andrews, 2008).

Coping resources also impacted FQOL in parents raising children with disabilities, which points to the fact that they need an abundance of resources and supports to help them cope while raising a child with a disability (Algood & Gourdine, 2015).

Finally, information sharing had a major impact on FQOL for caregivers. This is indicative of the importance and high priority parents place on sharing information through parent groups to help cope and assist each other in obtaining support and services, particularly after initially learning the child has a disability. After being made aware that their infant has a disability, there is a necessity for parents to receive information that is accurate and timely and for immediate resources to be available (Resch et al., 2010).

Discussion

Practice and policy implications

From the perspective of this study, there are important practice and policy implications as well as key roles for social workers and public health workers to perform. CRT informs the discussions because practitioners and policymakers must be cognizant of the inequities when working with minorities and their families with disabilities who experience discrimination and other forms of marginalization in areas such as healthcare, housing, insurance, and social services.

Practice implications

Social workers and public health workers alike must think critically about race as they engage on a daily basis in many areas and in doing so must consider how racial inequality impacts the quality of life of the parent and child. Social workers intervening with this population to insure effective service delivery should be knowledgeable about disability types and conduct a family-centered assessment to determine level of family functioning and coping capacities of the families.

Social workers also need to be aware of the importance placed by parents on information sharing as a means of support for family functioning and coping to improve their quality of life. Information sharing is a key element that empowers families to advocate for their own needs (King, Tepplicky, King and Rosenbaum, 2004). Through this process, parents are able to network with other caregivers to share information and resources, and to secure training opportunities and services and supports for the child and the caregiver. The social worker also helps the family, to the greatest extent possible, to navigate in an environment where a "gap in provision" exists. The social worker meets the family where they are at, reducing their burden by linking to available services. This role of the social worker can stabilize family functioning and improve FQOL by reducing stress, frustration, and strife while increasing the coping capacity within the family.

Policy implications

Social welfare policies directly impact quality of life of African-American families raising children with disabilities. Given this fact, policymakers must be aware of systemic inequality that exists and develop policies that adequately address disenfranchised populations like minorities with disabilities.

With various pieces of federal and state legislation in place for persons with disabilities, social workers have necessary information for the families to use in raising a child with disabilities. Also, parents can be encouraged, in the absence of a policy, to form support groups for the purpose of offering information sharing around the needs of their children. Social workers have a significant role as advocates to ensure that agency-based policies continue to be updated and reach persons with disabilities and their families who can benefit. For example, it might be helpful to parents for agencies to have a policy on information sharing to ensure that families obtain necessary information for the families' use in raising a child with disabilities.

Engaging parents to enhance their level of awareness of federal and state policies that directly impact the child and the overall family system is also a vital role of the social worker. The quality of life of the family becomes compromised if policies intended to improve the outcomes of children and youth with disabilities are not effectual in moving the children along in the areas of education, health, and transition to adulthood, most commonly (Ghosh & Parish, 2013; Ihara, Wolf-Branigin, White, 2012; Okumura, Saunders, & Rehm, 2015).

Entitlement programs such as Supplemental Security Income (SSI), medical assistance, and food stamps provide needed resources and financial support for parents and their children with developmental disabilities and families with limited incomes (Trachtenberg, Batshaw, & Batshaw, 2007). However, disparities exist in the process because many of these programs fall short in meeting the needs of families. For example, managed-care plans may not cover all long-term medications, rehabilitation therapies, and technologies that are presently funded by mandated programs (Trachtenberg et al., 2007). Other disparities arise as well in access to healthcare facilities for persons with disabilities. Health facilities and services often are not fully accessible, despite passage of the ADA more than 20 years ago. Because equipment such as weight scales, examining tables, and mammography equipment do not accommodate their disability, many people with disabilities do not receive complete medical examinations (Krahn, Walker, and Correa-De-Araujo (2015).

In the scope of policy, social workers play a significant, delicate role in promoting policies that address the needs of families who have children with disabilities. In the vein of policy informing practice, social workers work in a professional and interdisciplinary role to improve the delivery of and access to family supports through effective outreach, education, service coordination, and advocacy. These roles extend from state and federal policy, such as social workers performing a significant role under the "related services" area that is mandated under the Individual with Disabilities Education Act (IDEA) of 2004. These social-work tasks include providing psychosocial histories, therapeutic interventions, organizing community resources, and intervening in the home, community, and school to insure a seamless transition for the child-to-school setting, thus helping to fulfill federal IDEA policy (Heward, 2006).

Limitations

There were several limitations to consider in this study. The parents in the sample were provided a questionnaire to self-report their experiences in raising their child with a disability. Another limitation is the cross-sectional design of the study because it limits the ability to make a causal statement about the relationships of the variables. Finally, the absence of a qualitative sample can be a limitation of the study. If qualitative methods were to be implemented in the study, a more in-depth narrative would be gained from the research subjects. Thus, the mixed-methods, qualitative and quantitative approach would provide a better picture of the lived experiences of this population.

Conclusion

Research cited in this discussion shows that inequities that negatively impact family quality of life in African-American families are pervasive. Inequities in basic requirements—housing, healthcare, income, and education—are discussed in this article. Social workers and public health professionals must be diligent in their advocacy on the local, state, and federal laws and other supports and services that lead to enhanced quality of life for this population. Social workers need to be culturally aware of the importance of the extended family network, strong bonds and work ethic, and the role that spirituality and religion perform as coping mechanisms that aid in positive FQOL outcomes. Successful intervention to enhance FQOL must not only target macro-level systems such as service delivery systems and policies, but all aspects of the social ecology.

Critical race theory (CRT) is especially important to consider in seeking an understanding of the impact of society on FQOL in African-American families raising children with disabilities. Further, the use of the CRT in an intersectionality context allowed the opportunity to explore race and disability in the lives of these families. Race and disability often compound the struggle in the lives of Black families, despite their ability to show strong resilience as they cope with the challenges they face in these situations. The sample from our study revealed that 54% of the respondents were from single female–headed households and the unemployment rate for participants was at 54%. Supportive policies and practices that are available and accessible will significantly increase the possibility that African-American families raising children with disabilities will experience an enhanced quality of life.

References

Algood, C. L., & Gourdine, R. M. (2015). African American caregivers raising children with disabilities: Doing more with less. In S. E. Crewe & C. Gadding- Cole (Eds.), *Seasons of care: Practice and policy perspectives for social workers and human service professionals* (pp. 127–141). Hauppauge, NY: Nova Science Publishers.

Algood, C. L., Harris, C., & Hong, J. S. (2013). Parenting success and challenges for families of children with disabilities: An ecological systems analysis. *Journal of Human Behavior in the Social Environment, 23*(2), 126–136. doi:10.1080/10911359.2012.747408

Annamma, S. A., Connor, D., & Ferri, B. (2013). Dis/ability critical race studies (DisCrit): Theorizing at the intersections of race and dis/ability. *Race Ethnicity and Education, 16*(1), 1–31. doi:10.1080/13613324.2012.730511

Asch, A. (2001). Critical race theory, feminism, and disability: Reflections on social justice and personal identity. *Ohio St. LJ, 62*, 391.

Bell, D. (2009). Who's afraid of Critical Race Theory? In E. Taylor, D. Gillborn, & G. Ladson-Billings (Eds.), Foundations of Critical Race Theory in Education (pp. 37–50). New York, NY: Routledge.

Campbell, A., Converse, P. E., & Rodgers, W. (1975). The quality of American life-perceptions, evaluations, satisfactions. New York, NY: Russell Sage Foundation.

Connor, D. J. (2008). Not so strange bedfellows: The promise of disability studies and critical race theory. In *Disability and the politics of education: The international reader* (pp. 451–476). New York, NY: Peter Lang.

Crewe, S., & Wilson, R. (2007). Kinship care: From family tradition to social policy in the African American community. *Journal of Health & Social Policy, 22*(3/4), 1–7. doi:10.1300/J045v22n03_01

Crewe, S. E., & Gadling- Cole, C. (Eds). (2015). *Seasons of care: Practice and policy perspectives for social workers and human service professionals*. Hauppauge, NY: Nova Science Publisher.

Daly, A., Jennings, J., Beckett, J. O., & Leashore, B. R. (1995). Effective coping strategies of African Americans. *Social Work, 40*(2), 240–248.

Dodd, C. H., Zabriskie, R. B., Midner, M. A., & Eggett, D. (2009). Contributions of family leisure to family among families that include children with developmental disabilities. *Journal of Leisure Research, 41*(2), 261–286. doi:10.1080/00222216.2009.11950169

Duncan, G. A. (2002). Critical race theory and method: Rendering race in urban ethnographic research. *Qualitative Inquiry, 8*(1), 85–104. doi:10.1177/107780040200800106

Dunst, C. J., Trivette, C. M., & Deal, A. G. (1988). *Enabling and empowering families: Principles and guidelines for practice*. Cambridge, MA: Brookline Books.

Emerson, E. (2007). Poverty and people with intellectual disabilities. *Mental Retardation & Developmental Disabilities Research Reviews, 13*(2), 107–113. doi:10.1002/mrdd.20144

Erevelles, N., & Minear, A. (2010). Unspeakable offenses: Untangling race and disability in discourses of intersectionality. *Journal of Literary & Cultural Disability Studies, 4*(2), 127–145. doi:10.3828/jlcds.2010.11

Ferguson, P. M. (2002). A place in the family: An historical interpretation of research on parental reactions to having a child with a disability. *The Journal of Special Education, 36*(3), 124–130. doi:10.1177/00224669020360030201

Ghosh, S., & Parish, S. (2013). Prevalence and economic well-being of families raising multiple children with disabilities. *Children and Youth Services Review, 35*(9), 1431–1439. doi:10.1016/j.childyouth.2013.05.018

Gourdine, R. M. (2007). Child only kinship care cases: The unintended consequences of TANF policies for families who have health problems and disabilities. *Journal of Health & Social Policy, 22*(3/4), 44–64.

Gourdine, R. M., & Algood, C. L. (2014). Autism in the African American population. A comprehensive guide to autism. New York, NY: Springer Publishing.

Gupta, V. B. (2007). Comparison of parenting stress in different developmental disabilities. *Journal of Developmental and Physical Disabilities, 19*(4), 417–425. doi:10.1007/s10882-007-9060-x

Heward, W. L. (2006). *Exceptional Children: An Introduction to Special Education* (8th ed.). Upper Saddle River, NJ: Pearson.

Ihara, E. S., Wolf-Branigin, M., & White, P. (2012). Quality of life and life skill baseline measures of urban adolescents with disabilities. *Social work in public health, 27*(7), 658–670. doi:10.1080/19371910903269596

Kelley-Moore, J. A., & Ferraro, K. F. (2004). The black/white disability gap: Persistent inequality in later life? *Journal of Gerontology: Social Sciences, 59*(1), 34–43. doi:10.1093/geronb/59.1.S34

King, S., Teplicky, R., King, G., & Rosenbaum, P. (2004). Family-centered services for children with cerebral palsy and their families: A review of the literature. *Seminars in Pediatric Neurology, 11*(1), 78–86.

King, S. V. (1998). The beam in thine eye: Disability and the Black church. *Western Journal of Black Studies, 22*(1), 37–48.

Krahn, G. L., Walker, D. K., & Correa-De-Araujo, R. (2015). Persons with disabilities as an unrecognized health disparity population. *American journal of public health, 105*(S2), S198–S206. doi:10.2105/AJPH.2014.302182

Mackelprang, R. W., & Salsgiver, R. O. (2016). *Disability: A diversity model approach in human service practice* (2nd ed.). Pacific Grove, CA: Brooks/Cole.

Magaña, S., Parish, S. L., Rose, R. A., Timberlake, M., & Swaine, J. G. (2012). Racial and ethnic disparities in quality of health care among children with autism and other developmental disabilities. *Journal of Intellectual & Developmental Disabilities, 50*(4), 287–299. doi:10.1352/1934-9556-50.4.287

Marini, I., Glover-Graf, N. M., & Millington, M. (2012). Psychosocial aspects of disability. New York, NY: Springer.

McCubbin, H. I., & Thompson, A. I. (1991). Coping h and Practice. Madison: University of Wisconsin Madison.

McCubbin, M. A., & Huang, S. T. T. (1989). Family strengths in the care of handicapped children: Targets for intervention. *Family Relations, 38*, 436–443. doi:10.2307/585750

Neeley-Barnes, S., & Marcenko, M. (2004). Predicting impact of childhood disability on families: Results from the 1995 national health interview survey disability supplement. *Mental Retardation, 42*(4), 284–293. doi:10.1352/0047-6765(2004)42<284:PIOCDO>2.0.CO;2

Newacheck, P. W., Stein, R. E. K., & Bauman, L. (2003). Disparities in the prevalence of disability between Black and White children. *Archives of Pediatric Adolescent Medicine, 157*, 244–248. doi:10.1001/archpedi.157.3.244

Okumura, M. J., Saunders, M., & Rehm, R. S. (2015). The role of health advocacy in transitions from pediatric to adult care for children with special health care needs: bridging families, provider and community services. *Journal of pediatric nursing, 30*(5), 714–723. doi:10.1016/j.pedn.2015.05.015

Parish, S., & Cloud, J. (2006). Financial well-being of young children with disabilities and their families. *Social Work, 51*(3), 223 232.

Parish, S., & Lutwick, Z. (2005). A Critical analysis of the emerging crisis in long-term care for people with developmental disabilities. *Social Work, 50*(4), 345–354. Retrieved from Academic Search Premier database

Parish, S., Rose, R., Grinatein-Weiss, M., Richman, E., & Andrews, M. (2008). Material hardship in US families raising children with disabilities. *Exceptional Children, 75*(1), 71–92. Retrieved from Academic Search Premier database. doi:10.1177/001440290807500104

Park, J., Turnbull, A. P., & Turnbull, III. (2002). Impacts of poverty on quality of life in families of children with disabilities. *Exceptional Children, 68*(2), 151–172.

Pinn-Wiggins, V. W. (1990). Recognition of the plight of minorities in the educational process and health care system. *Journal of the National Medical Association, 82*(5), 333.

Popple, P. R., & Leighninger, L. (2005). *Social work, social welfare, and American society* (6th ed.). New York, NY: Allan Bacon.

Poston, D. J., Turnbull, A. P., Park, J., Mannan, H., Marquis, J., & Wang, M. (2003). Family quality of life outcomes: A qualitative inquiry launching a long-term research program. *Mental Retardation, 41*, 313–328. doi:10.1352/0047-6765(2003)41<313:FQOLAQ>2.0.CO;2

Renzaglia, A., Karvonen, M., Drasgow., E., & Stoxen, C. C. (2003). Promoting a lifetime of inclusion. Focus on Autism and other developmental disabilities, 18(3), 140–149. doi:10.1177/10883576030180030201

Resch, J. A., Mireles, G., Benz, M. R., Grenwelge, C., Peterson, R., & Zhang, D. (2010). Giving parents a voice: A qualitative study of the challenges experienced by parents of children with disabilities. *Rehabilitation Psychology, 55*(2), 139–150. doi:10.1037/a0019473

Samuel, P. S., Rillotta, F., & Brown, I. (2012). Review: The development of family quality of life concepts and measures. *Journal of Intellectual Disability Research*, 56(1), 1-16. doi:10.1111/j.1365-2788.2011.01486.x

Seligman, M., & Darling, R. B. (2017). *Ordinary families, special children: A systems approach to childhood disability*. New York: Guilford Publications.

Skiba, R., Poloni-Staudinger, L., Gallini, S., Simmons, A., & Feggins-Azziz, R. (2008). Disparate access: The disproportionally of African American students with disabilities across educational environments. *Exceptional Children*, 72(4), 411-424. doi:10.1177/001440290607200402

Smith, D. L., & Alston, R. J. (2009). The relationship of race and disability to life satisfaction in the United States. *Journal of Rehabilitation*, 75(12), 3-9.

Summers, J. A., Poston, D. J., Turnbull, A. P., Marquis, J., Hoffman, L., Mannan, M., & Wang, M. (2005). Conceptualizing and measuring family quality of life. *Journal of Intellectual Disability Research*, 49(1), 777-780. doi:10.1111/j.1365-2788.2005.00751.x

Taylor, E. (1998). A primer on critical race theory: Who are the critical race theorists and what are they saying? *The journal of blacks in higher education*, 122. doi:10.2307/2998940

Taylor, R., Seaton, E., & Dominguez, A. (2008). Kinship support, family relations, and psychological adjustment among low-income African American mothers and adolescents. *Journal of Research on Adolescence*, 18(1), 1-22. doi:10.1111/jora.2008.18.issue-1

Terhune, P. S. (2005). African-American developmental disability discourses: Implications for social policy. *Journal of Policy and Practice in Intellectual Disabilities*, 2(1), 18-28. doi:10.1111/j.1741-1130.2005.00004.x

Trachtenberg, S. W., Batshaw, K., & Batshaw, M. (2007). Caring and coping: Helping the family of a child with a disability. In M. L. Batshaw, L. Pellegrino, & N. J. Roizen (Eds.), *Children with Disabilities* (6th ed.), (pp. 601-612). Baltimore, MD: Paul H. Brookes.

Wang, M., & Brown, R. (2009). Family quality of life: A framework for policy and social service provisions to support families of children with disabilities. *Journal of Family Social Work*, 12(2), 144-167. doi:10.1080/10522150902874842

Werner, S., Edwards, M., Baum, N., Brown, I., Brown, R. I., & Isaacs, B. J. (2009). Family quality of life among families with a member who has an intellectual disability: an exploratory examination of key domains and dimensions of the revised FQOL Survey. *Journal of Intellectual Disability Research*, 53(6), 501-511. doi:10.1111/j.1365-2788.2009.01164.x

Wituk, S., Pearson, R., Bomhoff, K., Hinde, M., & Meissen, G. (2007). A Participatory process involving people with development disabilities in community development. *Journal of Developmental & Physical Disabilities*, 19(4), 323-335. doi:10.1007/s10882-007-9052

Wolfensenberger. (1972). Normalization: The Principles of Normalization in human services. Toronto, Canada: National Institute on Mental Retardation.

Yell, M. L., Rogers, D., & Rogers, E. L. (1998). The Legal History of Special Education What a Long, Strange Trip It's Been! *Remedial and Special Education*, 19(4), 219-228. doi:10.1177/074193259801900405

Justice Is Not Blind: Disproportionate Incarceration Rate of People of Color

Janie L. Jeffers

ABSTRACT
Understanding both the impact and intersection of race in the criminal justice system is critical to understanding cyclical factors driving the disproportionate minority incarceration rate. Through the Critical Race Theory (CRT) lens, this article examines race and the criminal justice system by reviewing specific aspects of the legal system and its arbitrary application of the system's significant discretionary power, which is a major influencer in the disparate incarceration rates for people of color.

The Sentencing Project reports that racial disparity the criminal justice system exists when the proportion of a racial or ethnic group, within the control of the system, is greater than the proportion of such groups in the general population.

Introduction

The racial dimension of mass incarceration is its most striking feature. No other country in the world imprisons so many of its racial or ethnic minorities. The United States imprisons a larger percentage of its black population than South Africa did at the height of apartheid. In Washington, D.C., our nation's capitol, it is estimated that three out of four young black men (and nearly all those in the poorest neighborhoods) can expect to serve time in prison. Similar rates of incarceration can be found in black communities across America (Alexander, 2010, p. 6).

The literature is replete with graphic and unassailable data revealing that the United States of America has significant challenges in its criminal justice system. For the past 35 years, this author has worked on operational and policy issues within the criminal justice system in over 42 states and counties, resulting in an intimate and detailed knowledge of its inner workings. As a criminal justice professional and advocate this article reflects both conceptual, practical experiences and knowledge. The goal is to provide additional insight from a policy and political perspective.

America is the most racially diverse democratic and wealthiest nation in the world. However, the gains in economic prosperity and stated values of American society are not uniformly shared across society. Specifically, significant portions of communities of color are not treated in the same manner as the dominant culture. One fundamental aspect of this marginalization is the disparate treatment of persons of color, which occurs across the entire spectrum of America's criminal justice system. Racial and ethnic disparity fosters public mistrust of the criminal justice system and impedes the ability to promote public safety (Nellis, Greene, & Mauer, 2008).

In 1954, the year of the historic *Brown v. Board of Education* decision, about 100,000 African Americans were incarcerated in America's prisons and jails. Following that decision, there was a half a century of enhanced opportunity for many people who were previously denied access to equity in education and employment. Yet, despite this sustained progress, the rate of incarceration in the criminal justice system increased, from 100,000 African Americans to nearly 900,000.

Attendant to the continued inequity resulted in unequal access to critical services such as housing, education, health and mental health, and employment opportunities. Sustained denial of these critical life-sustaining services plays a major role in determining who are vulnerable to interface with law enforcement and subsequently the criminal justice system.

The Dellums Commission (2006) seminal findings substantiated the negative impact of flawed public policy by stating "The social cost of such policies for families of color have been enormous. Incarceration also limits the life options of young men of color upon release, as they struggle to re-enter society and the workforce with limited skills and resources. The social costs to communities of color have been and continue to be enormous in both scale and scope" (p. 2).

It is within this understanding that we can document the "mass incarceration of African Americans and other people of color.

For example, Mauer (2011) reports that racial disparities in the use of imprisonment result in communities of color being disproportionately affected by the collateral effects of incarceration. Other factors include family stress and dissolution, neighborhoods experiencing high mobility of residents cycling in and out of prison, and growing numbers of people with limited employment prospects.

The critical race theory and disparate incarceration rates

The over representation of people of color in the criminal justice system will be examined through the Critical Race Theory (CRT) lens because it provides an appropriate context and applicable framework to examine how the uneven and inconsistent manipulation of the criminal justice system has resulted in the current crisis.

Critical Race Theory emanates from the legal profession composed of activists and scholars who are interested in transforming the relationship between race, racism and power (Delgado & Stefancic, 2006, p. 1). It addresses the role racism has in in discriminatory practices in our American Society. Further it addresses the foundations of the liberal order, equality theory and legal reasoning and its ultimate goal is to transform to improve the way society functions (Delgado & Stefancic, 2006, p. 1). As theoretical formulations go it is relatively new as it came about in the 1970s. This theory is applicable to the thesis of this article in that it questions the role of race and racism has on those characteristics determined by society and how people of certain racial groups are treated. It is this disparate treatment that regulates certain groups to certain practices in society. The criminal justice system is such a system. One has only to look at how laws are applied. A quick example is the disparate sentencing for the use of cocaine and crack. African Americans were sentenced to longer sentences than white Americans. Most recently Caucasians experiencing substance abuse issues are considered as a medical problem whereas African Americans substance abusers are considered to be criminal. These disparate views are the ones that result in the mass incarceration of African Americans and this practice has in some cases decimated communities. This results in low employment and other societal issues which are sometimes linked to risks for incarceration. It creates the notion that there is an inherent pipeline to prison that can be traced back to education achievement of children as early as the third grade.

The impact of racial disparities in the legal system

The American Bar Association Commission on Effective Criminal Sanctions (2007) lays the foundation for understanding the impact race has on the criminalization of people of color; they state, "available data supports some theories about racial disparities in prosecution and punishment. However, the existing research does not support a conclusion that African Americans and Latinos disproportionately offend in all crime categories. It seems clear that there is a proportionate offending in certain crime categories and there are discretionary decisions made by criminal justice officials that contribute to the racial disparity that exists in the criminal justice system" (p. 71). Although data does not support that there are disproportionate offending among people of color there is a general perception that there is. One only has to listen to the nightly news and read newspapers which highlight offenses of people of color. The American Bar Association concludes that "When the Commission viewed the criminal justice system as a whole – all crime categories and all communities – we could only conclude that both disproportionate offending (and the various causes thereof) and discretionary law enforcement decisions contribute to racial disparities in our criminal justice system" (2007, p. 71).

It is this behavior on the part of the legal systems that resulted the fight against police brutality and the organization of groups like "Black Lives Matter." The idea that a group could be so presumptuous to make this claim has anger many in American society despite the evidence that Black lives don't matter as much. If one protests again police inappropriate behavior then they became the target of criticism and this is exactly the point made by critical race theory.

Intersection of race and criminal justice

Mass incarceration has not touched all communities equally. The Sentencing Project Fact Sheet indicates that sentencing policies, implicit racial bias, and socioeconomic inequity contribute to racial disparities at every level of the criminal justice system. Today, people of color make up 37% of the U.S. population but 67% of the prison population. Overall, African Americans are more likely than white Americans to be arrested; once arrested, they are more likely to be convicted; and once convicted, they are more likely to face stiff sentences. Black men are six times as likely to be incarcerated as white men and Hispanic men are more than twice as likely to be incarcerated as non-Hispanic white men.

Beginning with law enforcement, we find the first intersection of race and the criminal justice system. Having contact with law enforcement typically is detrimental for African Americans. The police exercise wide discretionary judgment in who is to be arrested. The phenomenon of "driving while black" is an excellent example of police discretion – in many instances the white driver and the black driver have both committed the same traffic violation but the black driver is stopped while the white driver is allowed to continue (Nellis et al., 2008). The infractions by Blacks are usually punished but with Whites there appears more latitude. There are numerous of antidotal stories of how Black males describe their experiences. These situations have arisen to the point that Black parents have had to implement a practice with their Black children called "the talk." The Talk is an explanation to Black youth of how they are perceived by police and what they should do if stopped and basically they are told to be subservient to them and keep their hands in sight for fear that they will be accused of reaching for a weapon (Whitaker & Snell, 2016). Society has endorsed implicit support for being guilty before found innocent especially among African Americans.

Next, the arraignment, release, and pre-adjudicatory decisions too, are discriminatory. The criminal system is disparate in parts of the system. In some jurisdictions, large proportions of misdemeanor cases are disposed and given non-incarceration sentences at arraignment. The absence of pre-trial services often leads to an assumption that money bail should be set in all but capital cases and that the bail amount should simply reflect the seriousness of the charge. Such assumptions discriminate against low-income minorities and result in unnecessarily high rates of detention. Detention, in turn, increases the likelihood of conviction and incarceration (Nellis et al., 2008). In these cases presumptions of guilt may be made prior to trial and the poor does not have adequate legal representation to avert these decisions.

A rather recent and troubling phenomenon in criminal justice practice is the high rate of incarceration for failure to pay court imposed fines. In 2014, a young African American male, Mike Brown, was shot and killed by the Ferguson, Missouri police and as a consequence the Justice Department investigated. One of its findings highlighted the use of excessive court imposed fines as one of the causes of racial discord in Black communities (Maciag, 2014).

While there is not comprehensive national data on what percentage of municipal revenue is typically generated by court fines, Governing Magazine (2014) compiled financial data for other nearby municipalities in northern St. Louis County with at least 5,000 residents. Of 19 local governments with available data, Ferguson relies more on fines to fund government than all but two smaller jurisdictions. So one might conclude that incarceration for not paying fines for arbitrarily imposed funds the municipal operations and are relied upon to support and maintain other services. Who are the vulnerable to these citations? It is typically the poor and people of color. This is exactly the point of CRT.

In general, traffic fines tend to account for a larger share of revenue in smaller communities. State law, however, prohibits Missouri municipalities from collecting more than 35% of operating revenues from traffic fines and court costs, requiring excess money be turned over to the state Department of Revenue for schools (Maciag, 2014).

Christine Cole, executive director of the Harvard University Kennedy School of criminal justice policy and management program states, "If cities decide to ramp up traffic enforcement, they shouldn't do so primarily to raise revenue. It can put police in a difficult place because then the several municipalities in Missouri become reliant on this stream of revenue. Any increase in law enforcement must be clearly tied to public safety gains. It's also equally crucial that city officials and law enforcement communicate such safety benefits to residents" (Maciag, 2014, p. 11).

It's difficult to gauge the extent to which the increased enforcement and hefty fines added to Ferguson residents' discontent in the years leading up to shooting death of Michael Brown. Legal advocates, though, argue that it helped foster negative perceptions of law enforcement and government in general. Also, Arch City Defenders, a local legal and social advocacy firm, recently issued a scathing white paper that identified the Ferguson Municipal Court as one of the region's most "chronic offenders of " using traffic fines as a source of revenue (Maciag, 2014).

Throughout the next phases of the criminal justice system – adjudication through sentencing – offers new opportunities for discretion and bias to control by race. The quality of representation at the adjudication stage can affect the outcome of the case. There is some evidence that sentencing outcomes are dependent on type of counsel (i.e. no counsel, public counsel or private counsel) even when relevant factors are controlled. Since minorities are less likely to have a private attorney who generally has more time to devote to the case than a public defender – it is especially important to monitor this decision point for racial disparity (Nellis et al., 2008).

Equal Justice USA reports bias in the application of the death penalty in sentencing and indicates that race had an impact on death penalties and the race of the victim (i.e., white) resulted in death penalty; over half murders are of African Americans but their murderers were less than 15% of the people executed; as a result there is the risk that those executed for murder could be innocent. (Equal Justice USA, n.d.).

After sentencing and the defendant has served his or her sentence – the next stage is parole. As US Parole Commissioner, this author was tasked with making decisions when a federal, military, or District of Columbia prisoner could be released or returned to custody for violating a condition of release. Although release decisions were governed by a set of rules, discretion determined who and when a prisoner would be released from prison. A parolee could be returned to prison if he or she violated any of the conditions surrounding their release such as, getting rearrested, failing to find work and failing a drug test.

While serving as a Parole Commissioner, this author was frequently asked to sign a warrant for the arrest of a parolee who had not been accused of committing a new crime but had failed to report to his or her parole officer. It was my practice not to issue a warrant until the parole officer proved to my satisfaction that all other remedies were exhausted – such as directly confirming if the parolee was gainfully employed, had a good reporting record and no positive drug tests. Invariably the warrant was requested for a parolee was a person of color.

It was within author's discretion to return the parolee with no questions asked. It is that discretion that contributes significantly to the revocation of parolees in generally and specifically to those of color.

There is documented evidence that racial disparity exists in the number of parolees returned for technical violations of their conditions of release. Technical violations are essentially rule breaking. These violations do not involve new convictions, although it can involve a new arrest. The general conditions of parole can include positive test results for drug use; failure to report for drug testing/ treatment, alcohol treatment or other counseling. Any violation of these rules can subject the parolee to being returned to prison through an administrative hearing process. Indeed, parole offices have the power to immediately incarcerate parolees who are accused of a technical violation. The administrative process to determine whether the violation actually occurred, and the penalty to ensue takes place while the parolee is locked up in the local jail or state prison. The reason parole officers have this extraordinary power is because people on parole are still considered prisoners while they have the right to representation by an attorney, during their technical violation hearings, they can be immediately re-incarcerated (Jacobson, 2005).

Promising practices

After reviewing and analyzing the data through the Critical Race Theory, it is clear that this theory of biased race-based discretionary decision points in the criminal justice system are major factors contributing to and resulting in the disproportionate incarceration of people of color. What, then is the call to action? There is a current climate in the political arena suggesting that both major political parties agree that the current incarceration rate of people of color is unsustainable and the need for reform to the criminal justice system is critical. The 2010 Fair Sentencing Act passed by Congress reduced the disparity in sentencing between crack and powder cocaine and is an example of bipartisan cooperation (Department of Justice, 2010) The passage of this landmark legislation is movement in the right direction but the challenge and opportunity is to demonstrate that reforms to the system do not represent a threat to public safety. To that end, this author has compiled a listing of potential promising models and significant reforms, which are operating in just a few local jurisdictions; but the hope is that more localities will see the value of these constructs. The challenge is to continue to monitor, evaluate, and study the outcomes of these initiatives to ensure their implementation, efficacy and result in the elimination of a biased and race-based legal system.

Models to curb prosecutorial bias

The Vera Institute of Justice, 2014 prosecutors have broad discretion and immense power, in making critical decisions in such as charging, bail, pleas bargaining and sentencing that impact defendants and victims at every stage of the criminal justice continuum.

This author has witnessed a major power shift in the criminal justice system from the judiciary to the prosecutors with the onset of sentencing guidelines requiring, with little variance, a set of rigidly prescribed and mandatory sentences. It is within the exclusive province of the prosecutor to determine if the arrested individual is released or charged and the prosecutor and also determines the level or severity of charges. These decisions, in turn, can effect if the individual is eligible for bail or is held in custody.

The Vera Institute of Justice (2014) further reports the creation of the Vera's Prosecution and Racial Justice Program (PRJ) in New York City to enhance prosecutorial accountability and performance through partnerships with prosecutors' offices nationwide. PRJ works collaboratively with its partners to analyze data about the exercise and impact of prosecutorial discretion; assists in developing routine policies and practices that promote fairness, efficiency, and professionalism in prosecution; and provides technical assistance to help prosecutors implement those measures. By collaborating with prosecutors, analyzing data and devising solutions, PRJ works to improve their performance by:

- Partnering with prosecutors to analyze the impact of their decisions and develop policies to address unwarranted racial and ethnic disparities;
- Serving as a resource for research, technical assistance, innovation, and policy development in the areas of prosecution and racial justice; and
- Engaging communities in improving prosecutorial accountability and enhancing public safety.

Restorative justice model

Restorative justice is a theory of justice that emphasizes repairing the harm caused by criminal behavior (Centre for Justice & Reconciliation, 2016). It is best accomplished through cooperative processes that include all stakeholders. This can lead to transformation of people, relationships, and communities.

Practices and programs reflecting restorative purposes will respond to crime by:

(1) identifying and taking steps to repair harm,
(2) involving all stakeholders, and
(3) transforming the traditional relationship between communities and their governments in responding to crime.

The foundational principles of restorative justice have been summarized as follows:

(1) Crime causes harm and justice should focus on repairing that harm.
(2) The people most affected by the crime should be able to participate in its resolution.
(3) The responsibility of the government is to maintain order and of the community to build peace.

The four major components are:

(1) Inclusion of all parties
(2) Encountering the other side
(3) Making amends for the harm
(4) Reintegration of the parties into their communities.

This author was first introduced to the restorative justice model over 30 years ago at the National Institute of Corrections, a technical assistance arm to local correctional agencies, as a promising alternative to the criminal justice system. Nearly three decades later, only a handful of jurisdictions have adopted this model most notably because it was labeled as a soft on crime option.

Public health model

Dr. Deborah Prothrow-Stith in her 1991 ground breaking book, *Deadly Consequences*, was one of the first major proponents of considering the benefits of a public health model to stem and prevent violence. She updated her work in a 2004 article in the *Journal of Law, Medicine, and Ethics* and suggested that the two disciplines complement rather than compete in preventing violence. "The utilization of public health approaches has generated contributions to the understanding and prevention of violence including new and expanded knowledge in surveillance, delineation of risk factors and program design, including implementation and evaluation strategies" (Prothrow-Stith, 2004, p. 84).

The Public Health Approach consists of four basic elements as described by the Centers for Disease Control, Injury Center (CDC):

- **Define and monitor the problem**: The first step in preventing violence is to understand the "who," "what," "when," "where" and "how" associated with it.
- **Identify risk and protective factors**: Understanding what factors protect people or put them at risk for experiencing or perpetrating violence is also important.
- **Develop and test prevention strategies**: Research data and findings from needs assessments, community surveys, stakeholder interviews, and focus groups are useful for designing prevention programs. Once programs are implemented, they are evaluated. **Ensure widespread adoption**: Once prevention programs have been proven effective, they must be implemented and adopted more broadly. Dissemination techniques to promote widespread adoption include training, networking, technical assistance, and evaluation (CDC, 2015).

A promising collaboration is New York City's $130 million allocation to implement a public health approach to criminal justice. One of its goals is to "break the revolving door of arrest, incarceration, release that has trapped many troubled individuals. This is in recognition that almost 40% of those in New York City's jails are mentally ill and that people were cycling in and out of jail repeatedly as a result of substance abuse and mental health problems, the City will implement public health programs throughout the criminal justice system…including pretrial diversion programs to increasing the amount of resources devoted to easing the transition from jail back into society" (Heller, 2014, p. 1).

Department of justice – fairness in public safety

The following quote from former Attorney General Holder ushered in a long overdue and delayed reset to the Justice Department public policy approach to combating crime. With the utterance of these words from the Attorney General, the Justice Department initiated a series of recommendations to reform the criminal justice system, after a comprehensive review, to ensure that federal laws are implemented without bias. This was a seismic shift from the "get tough" policies advanced and funded by the federal government and General Holder was roundly criticized for moving toward a more fair and just system consistent with the principles of the Critical Race Theory. The author served as a United States Parole Commissioner when Eric Holder was Deputy Attorney General and benefitted from his innovative thinking. Attorney

General Holder states:

"By targeting the most serious offenses, prosecuting the most dangerous criminals, directing assistance to crime 'hot spots,' and pursuing new ways to promote public safety, deterrence, efficiency, and fairness – we can become both smarter *and* tougher on crime"

(Holder, 2013, para, p. 17)

As a part of its 2013 Smart on Crime Initiative, the Department of Justice proposed three goals that are particularly relevant to disproportionate minority confinement:

- To promote fairer law enforcement laws and to alleviate disparate impact;
- To ensure just punishments for low-level, nonviolent convictions;
- To bolster prevention and reentry efforts to deter crime and reduce recidivism; In the Smart on Crime Initiative (2013), the Department studied all phases of the criminal justice system – including charging, sentencing, incarceration, and reentry – to examine which practices are most successful at deterring crime and protecting the public, and which are not. The above cited DOJ review also considered demographic disparities that have provoked questions about the fundamental fairness of the criminal justice system.

Limiting the use of pretrial detention to individuals who pose a threat to public safety; Increasing diversion programs for low-level offenses at the arrest, pre-charge and pretrial phases to reduce the number of people entering jails;

Setting specific goals to reduce racial disparities, including incentives to steer decisions and success measures to track progress;

Creating cross-departmental task forces to identify drivers of racial disparities and devise strategies to address them;

- Requiring training to reduce implicit racial bias for all justice system actors – including police, judges, prosecutors, probation officers, parole board members, correctional officers and court administrators;
- Encouraging prosecutors to prioritize serious and violent offenses;
- Increasing public defense representation for misdemeanor offenses;
- Developing checklists (referred to as "bench cards") for judges to use in hearings to combat implicit biases in decision-making and encourage alternatives to incarceration.These represent what the roundtable considers as being contributing a fairer system for those facing and experiencing incarceration. Former Attorney General Eric Holder exhibit a boldness in his request to both protect citizens and reform a criminal justice system that unfairly targets certain population based upon perceptions and categories of race.

Conclusion

The Great Hall lobby at the Justice Department, in the nation's Capitol, has a life-size picture of a blind-folded statue of Lady Justice denoting that the justice system is blind and therefore fair and impartial. Like most symbols, it represents the ideal and like most goals, it is more aspirational than actual.

There is opportunity for bias at every phase of the criminal justice system from the initial encounter with the police where discretion determines who is held and charged and who is released. These types of discretionary and frequently race based decisions can follow a defendant beyond the courtroom to parole and release. This author served as a probation officer in New York City Criminal Courts, a United States Parole Commissioner, and a policy advisor at the highest levels of government. These positions gave witness to the enormously detrimental impact and negative outcomes of both deliberate and unconscious bias on people of color.

However, there appears to be encouraging signs on the horizon that may bring about positive change and improvement to the criminal justice system. As referenced earlier, conservative and progressive congressional leaders on both sides of the political aisle are working together to stem the tide of mass and disproportionate incarceration of people of color.

The current rate of mass incarceration and by definition, disparate race-based incarceration, is unsustainable both in terms of human and financial cost to our society. Financial because county, state and the federal budget cannot continue to fund prisons at the expense of hospitals, schools, and infrastructure required to promote effective commerce and the well being of its citizens, and human costs of incarceration to people of color are even more egregiously damaging because it decimates entire neighborhoods, promotes unemployment, and tears at the fabric and underpinning that defines and binds this country together – the family.

The proposed models and promising practices offer an array of alternatives to augment, complement, and replace the utterly failed existing criminal justice system. The restorative justice model and the public health model, with sufficient study and extensive evaluation can be expanded into smaller jurisdictions with the ultimate goal of bringing them to scale.

Policymakers would be wise to consider the proposed doctrine of fairness proposed by the Justice Department as it proposed new legislation to improve the disparate incarceration rates of people of color. The field of social work is uniquely positioned through its rich history of advocacy and research, to play a key role in reframing and rethinking creative, effective, and culturally competent public policy options to restructure the criminal justice system with the Critical Race Theory as the guiding precept.

Disclosure statement

No potential conflict of interest was reported by the author.

References

Alexander, M. (2010). *The New Jim Crow: Mass incarceration in the age of colorblindness*. New York, NY: The New Press
American Bar Association. (2007). *Second chances in the criminal justice system: Alternatives to incarceration and reentry strategies*. Retrieved from http://www.aba.org
Centers for Disease Control and Prevention. (2015, March 25). *The public health approach to violence prevention*. Retrieved from http://www.cdc.gov/violenceprevention/overview/publichealthapproach.html
Centre for Justice and Reconciliation. (2016). *Lesson 1: What is restorative justice?* Retrieved from http://restorativejustice.org/restorative-justice/about-restorative-justice/tutorialintro-to-restorative-justice/lesson-1-what-is-restorative-justice/
Delgado, R., & Stefancic, J. (2006) *Critical race theory: An introduction*. New York, NY: NYU Press.
Dellums Commission. (2006). *A way out: Better health through stronger communities: Public policy reform to expand life paths of young men of color*. Washington, DC: The Joint Center for Health, Policy Institute.
Department of Justice. (2010). *Statement of the attorney general on passage of the fair sentencing act*. Washington, DC: United States Government Printing Office.
Department of Justice. (2013). *The Attorney's smart on crime initiative*. Washington, DC: United States Government Printing Office.
Equal Justice USA. (n.d.). *Fair and equal under the law?* Retrieved from http://ejusa.org/learn/fairness/
Heller, J. (2014). *A new public health approach to criminal justice reform in New York city*. Human Impact Partners. Retrieved from http://www.humanimpact.org
Holder, E. (2013). Attorney General Eric Holder Delivers Remarks at the Annual Meeting of the American Bar Association's House of Delegates, San Francisco, August, 12.
Jacobson, M. (2005). *Downsizing prisons: How to reduce crime and end mass incarceration*. New York, NY: University Press.
Kutateladze, B., Tymas, W., & Crowley, M. (2014). *Vera institute of justice*, Retrieved from http://www.vera.org/race-and-prosecutiin-research-summary
Maciag, M. (2014). *Public safety and justice: Skyrocketing court fines are major revenue generator for Ferguson*. Governing: The States and Localities. Retrieved from http://www.governing.com
Nellis, A., Greene, J. A., & Mauer, M. (2008). *Reducing racial disparity in the criminal justice system: A manual for practitioners and policymakers*. Washington, DC: Sentencing Project.
Prothrow-Stith, D. (2004). Strengthening the collaboration between public health and criminal justice to prevent violence. *The Journal of Law, Medicine & Ethics, 32*(1), 82–88. The Sentencing Project, Criminal Justice Facts, 2016. Retrieved from http://www.sentencingproject.org
Prothrow-Stith, D., & Weissman, M. (1991). *Deadly consequences: How violence is destroying our teenage population and a plan to begin solving the problem*. New York, NY: Harper Collins.
Whitaker, T. R., & Snell, C. L. (2016). Parenting while powerless: Consequences of "the talk". *Journal Of Human Behavior In The Social Environment, 26*(3–4), 303–309. doi: 10.1080/10911359.2015.1127736

The Task is Far from Completed: Double Jeopardy and Older African Americans

Sandra Edmonds Crewe

ABSTRACT
The National Urban League released a seminal report on the state of older African Americans in 1964. This report titled *Double Jeopardy: The Older Negro in America Today* presented data that documented the hardships faced by African Americans as they aged in a society that marginalized them. Using critical race theory (CRT), this article reviews the report and addresses the contemporary state of African Americans. It specifically focuses on income, education, poverty, and health status. The article also includes the scholarship of seminal scholars on the Black aged as context. It ends with policy implications that address changes that will continue to improve quality of life for older African Americans.

Older African Americans are more likely to be in poverty and to have poorer health than their White counterparts. This holds true despite the unprecedented reduction of poverty among older African Americans that has occurred since the National Urban League's (1964) seminal and impactful report titled "Double Jeopardy: The Older Negro in America Today" [hereafter referred to as NUL Double Jeopardy report]. Current U.S. Census data reports that the poverty rate for older African Americans is almost 2.5 times higher than that of Whites. This gap prevails despite the passage of social welfare policies such as the Older Americans Act in 1964 and Medicare in 1965. In his last book, *Where Do We Go From Now: Chaos or Crisis*, Martin Luther King (1968) stated that the Civil Rights movement "unconsciously patterned a crisis policy and program, and summoned support *not* for daily commitment but for explosive events alone" (p. 167). Nowhere is this more evident than in the aforementioned data that document the persistence of poverty despite the sweeping changes brought about through the Older Americans Act. Unlike the older persons who lived in 1964. during the time of the seminal double-jeopardy report, most of today's older persons enter old age with the protection or coverage of these programs as well as the Civil Rights and Voting Rights Acts. Thus, the persistence of the higher rates of poverty and health disparities among a segment of African Americans calls into question the effectiveness of social welfare policy in removing cumulative disadvantage. Through a 50-year examination, the article also draws attention to the length of time it takes to "undo" harm caused by racism and other "isms."

This article builds upon the 1964 National Urban League Report, *Double Jeopardy*, which describes the plight of the Negro during old age as double jeopardy (National Urban Leagu, 1964). It provides a summary of this seminal report and other valuable research related to the Black aged. Using critical race theory, the article reviews the contemporary socioeconomic status of the African American aged and addresses whether double jeopardy prevails today. Finally, the author makes policy recommendations to address poverty and income insecurity among the Black aged.

Social welfare policy is "the formal expression of a community's values, principles, and beliefs" that "become reality through a program and its resulting services" (Colby, 2016). For the Black aged, social welfare policy in the United States is a reflection of its sanctioned oppression throughout their life course. Despite the social and economic advances experienced by the majority of African Americans, generations of unbridled racism find many older African Americans in poverty and dependent on the social welfare safety net programs for survival. According to the 2015 Administration on Aging (AoA) report, the number of people aged 65 years and older is expected to more than double by 2060 and 12% (12 million) of older persons will be African Americans. This unprecedented growth of older persons presents an important opportunity to examine the well-being of older African Americans using the NUL *Double Jeopardy Report* as a benchmark and to demonstrate the impotence of piecemeal approaches to poverty eradication.

The NUL report was sandwiched between two important pieces of legislation: The Civil Rights Act of 1964 and the Older Americans Act (OAA) in 1965. Both of these acts provided access to programs and resources that were heretofore absent for many older African Americans. Additionally, the controversial 1965 Moynihan report titled "Negro Families in America" that introduced the widely disdained characterization of the black family as a "tangle of pathology" was issued in the same time period (Moynihan, 1965). Among the organizations advocating for the needs of African American families and particularly the aged, using a strengths-based perspective, was the National Urban League.

National Urban League

An understanding of the significance of the NUL *Double Jeopardy* report is linked to the values of the corporate author, the National Urban League. Founded in 1910, almost a half-century after the end of slavery, the National Urban League had two major goals—to remove barriers to racial equality and to achieve economic empowerment for the country's Negro citizens (National Urban League, 2016, 2). Over 100 years old, this organization exists today and continues to be in the vanguard of raising issues of economic and other disparities (Smith, 2010). Today, the mission of the National Urban League movement is to enable African Americans to secure economic self-reliance, parity, power, and civil rights (National Urban League, 1964). During its 107-year history, NUL has been led by several prominent professional social work leaders including Lester Granger (1940–61); Whitney Young, Jr. (1961–1971); and John Jacob (1981–1994). The NUL *Double Jeopardy* report was produced under the leadership of Whitney M. Young, Jr. Consistent with the intersecting values of the social work profession, the eradication of poverty for African Americans was a major policy initiative during his tenure as executive secretary. Thus, the *Double Jeopardy* report was inextricably linked to the overall NUL agenda to address persistent poverty. Embedded in the philosophy of the NUL was "cultural pride and self-help" (Smith, 2010). In 1963, the NUL established a Subcommittee on Aging of its Health and Welfare Committee. The committee worked for two years and developed the seminal report on the profile of the older Black person in America (Special Senate Report) that has been influential in social welfare policy and research.

Double jeopardy—the older Negro in America today

We know that Negroes bring to their older years a whole lifetime of economic and social indignities, a lifetime of struggle to get and keep a job, more often than not at unskilled hard labor; a lifetime of overcrowded, substandard housing in slum neighborhoods; of inadequate medical care; of unequal opportunities for education and the cultural and social activities that nourish the spirit; a lifetime of second-class citizenship; a lifetime of watching their children learn the high cost of being a Negro in America (National Urban League, 1964, p. 1).

According to the 1964 NUL Double Jeopardy report, the older black in America was placed in double jeopardy because of the inequities and indignities described above. The "cumulative effects of the wear and tear of a lifetime" (p. 1) form the theses that older Blacks suffer from the intersectionality of ageism and racism. Using data from federal agencies and publications, the report cited a number of inequalities in areas such as housing, education, health, old age assistance benefits, employment/unemployment, earnings, life expectancy, mortality rates, disability, and long-term care. In addition to citing these problems, the report focused on the urgency of the need for improved social welfare standards. Among the needs articulated were programs addressing income maintenance, better housing, health and mental health services, higher social security benefits, increased old age assistance grants, vocational training and retraining, special housing to address unique needs of both infirm and well-aged, homemaker services, friendly visitors, portable meals, protective services, multiservice centers, education, and recreation programs. This list of critical unmet needs is presented as an opportunity for the social welfare system to improve the outcomes of older African Americans. The report noted, however, that even if the changes were put in place immediately, it would be too late "for hundreds of thousands of these Americans—whatever we do now will be too late" (p. 27). Thus, the reality of the *Double Jeopardy* report is that it was written for today's generation—children and great-grandchildren of the aged in 1964. Today's generation of older persons was born at the time of the writing of this report. Thus, we have an opportunity to see what the subsequent 50-plus years of social welfare policy have contributed to removing the inequalities pointed out by this seminal report.

According to Manuel (1994), the concepts of double jeopardy (theory of interaction between age and race) and differential mortality have been underdeveloped. The prominent black gerontologist, Jacqueline Jackson, and Hobart Jackson, founder of the National Center and Caucus for the Back Aged, agreed that there had been inadequate attention given to the needs of older Blacks and that there was "systematic exclusion of the Negro aged" in the sociocultural and psychological studies of the aged (Golden, 1980, p. 329). There was scholarly consensus, particularly among Black scholars, on the importance of this report in addressing a void in the literature. They emphasized its value in calling attention to the neglected and unmet needs of older Blacks. Critics of the report argued that it was an oversimplification because it did not address differentials within the group (Golden, 1980).

An alternative to double jeopardy was the multiple jeopardy concept that addressed socioeconomic variables as well, including gender, levels of education, employment, and a sense of well-being. Accordingly, restricting analysis to race had the undesired effect of overlooking class and other differences, and this in turn could be a serious setback to more useful research that would improve social service delivery. The concern was that double jeopardy centered around the stigmatizing of all Blacks rather than a focus on a subset of the Black poor as compared to multiple jeopardy that considered more variables. A more concerning, perhaps subtle, argument against double jeopardy was that it would offer special services to Blacks at the expense of poor Whites who also shared some of the problems noted in the report. The RAND report stated:

> Providing services to blacks as a group in a fashion that is appropriate for only a subset of the black population would be a serious error. Similarly, it would be unfortunate to provide services only to the black poor when they should in fact be provided to a larger set of poor persons. (Golden, 1980, p. 335)

This reasoning prevailed despite the evidence of the time that the poverty level among blacks was three times higher than that of whites. According to Golden, The RAND Report went on to criticize the NUL *Double Jeopardy* report because "it fails to define any problems that would indicate a need for methods of services delivered that are unique to blacks (p. 335)." Similar claims are made about the Black Lives Matter movement, whose critics quickly respond by stating that *all* lives matter and reject the singling out of a group despite evidence of persistent and growing disparities. In a 2016 *New York Times* article, Victor (2016) describes "*all* lives matter" as a perilous phrase because it "suggests to them that all people are in equal danger, invalidating the specific concerns of black people." The same flawed logic fueled the critics of the NUL *Double Jeopardy* report.

Despite NUL *Double Jeopardy* report critics, prominent African-American social scientists of the time, such as Jacqueline Jackson, Barbara Solomon, and Inabel Lindsay, called attention to and forcefully pointed out the effects of racism on the quality of life of African Americans. Jackson stated:

> Racism is a reality and we should not deny it....Insofar as black old people are concerned, I think we should not begin to treat them as if they were the same as white old people. They are not. Racism has adversely affected their preparation for old age. (Golden, 1980, p. 336).

It is important to call attention to Jackson's resistance to the notion that equality of treatment starts at the point of older age with disregard to the lawful discrimination that paved the treacherous pathway to older age for African Americans. Similarly, noted Black sociologist Barbara Solomon emphasized that the focus should be on differential versus preferential treatment. She stated that

> Those of us who are practicing in the helping profession need to gain some understanding of when black elderly people are like all older people, when they are only like some older people, and when they are like no other older people. (Golden, 1980, p. 336).

Inabel Burns Lindsay authored a 1971 working paper, "The Multiple Hazards of Age and Race: The Situation of Aged Blacks in the United States" for the Special Committee on Aging for the United States Senate that also affirmed the importance of a sociocultural examination of the intersection age and race. She stated:

> The facts have been well established that poverty (by whatever definition) bears more heavily upon the old than upon the young and there are proportionately more poor [people] among nonwhites than among whites. Thus, in 1964, the National Urban League was able to forcefully document the "double jeopardy" of the aged black. That study took for granted that poverty was a fact of life for aged blacks and focused upon race and age as the conditions leading to "jeopardy." (Lindsay, 1971, p. 9)

Further authenticating her support for the particular focus on the Black aged is the following excerpt from the report that raises the following profound question. "If progress for the total aged population has lagged noticeably in comparison with enlightened measures for all citizens, how much more acute must be the adverse condition of black Americans?" Lindsay, Dean Emerita of Howard University's School of Social Work, elaborates further with the following facts:

> Negroes as a group constitute more than 10 percent of the total population. Negroes, for more than 300 years, have suffered all of the deprivations and handicaps of second-class citizenship, or even of "noncitizenship." One social work educator has aptly described the Negro's position in the American society as that of "nonperson." This definition was basic in the "Black Codes" of certain Southern States in the post-reconstruction era and implied in the historic Dred Scott decision of an early Supreme Court. The scars from those early struggles against involuntary servitude and the efforts to achieve true manhood have remained throughout the history of the Negro in the United States. (p. 1)

Other authors also affirmed the importance of race and ethnicity in examining disparities that followed older Blacks. Manuel (1994) noted that ethnicity was a powerful variable in predicting familial network patterns and that it was consistently more important than socioeconomic status and gender.

These scholars of the 1960s and 1970s rejected the premise that previous hardships could be replaced with a leveled playing field on the basis of others having hardships as well. Instead they stood firm on the cumulative disparities that were the result of White privilege sanctioned by legislation that denied or severely limited opportunities for older Blacks in a way that it did not for poor Whites. Rather than age being a leveler, they argued that racism in early life was inextricably linked to the disparities suffered in early life. A life-course perspective supports this argument. Scholars and social workers who focus on a life-course perspective rely on concepts including cohorts, transitions, trajectories, life events, and turning points. In addressing African Americans, life course is very relevant because of the uniqueness of their experiences. Scholars have found the concept of cohort to be very useful in examining their experiences. A cohort, according to the life-course perspective, is a group of persons who were born at the same historical time and who experience particular social changes within a given culture in the same sequence and at the same age. According to Gee, Walsemann, and Brondolo (2012), a life-course perspective emphasizes the importance of change. Exposure to racism can change in nature, importance, and intensity.

Similarly, health and the factors that produce health can change. A growing body of research shows that health is not merely the result of risks that occur sporadically at one point in time. Failure to attend to these temporal changes not only shortchanges our knowledge base, but also can lead to missed opportunities for intervention (p. 967).

Clearly, the *Double Jeopardy* report is a cohort analysis that fits into the life-course perspective. Those who were 65 at the time of the report were born in 1899–1900, at the turn of the century, and their life expectancy was 33 years compared to 46 years for Whites. According to Lindsay, along with the aged poor of any race, aged Negroes suffer loss of dignity, loneliness, and isolation. Probably more so than youth, they identify themselves as Negroes first and Americans second, for this is the concept of self which their lives in the United States had taught them. Efforts to achieve the goals of democracy through integration into the mainstream were marked by attempts at self-improvement and acceptance of the values of the White majority. For most Negroes, such efforts have been repeatedly thwarted by barriers of race.

Another challenge to the NUL *Double Jeopardy* report was the fact that some African-American older persons defied the pernicious effect of decreased longevity and exceeded the longevity of their White counterparts. Known as the crossover effect or the racial mortality crossover, according to Ferraro and Farmer (1996) it addresses that longer life of Blacks when compared to Whites over age 80, which has posed a challenge for double-jeopardy theory. On the surface, this seems to weaken the existence of double jeopardy or cumulative disadvantage. Although not systematically tested, it has been hypothesized that the crossover effect is associated with the older of the oldest Blacks representing an elite group that is highly resilient. Selective survival, according to Ferraro and Farmer (1996), actually supports health inequities being present early in life and persisting throughout the life course. They state that:

> These health inequities contribute to the higher mortality risk of Black adults, but the survivors—Black older adults—appear to have overcome considerable disadvantage in maintaining their health.... the hypothesis specified by as aging as aleveler should be recast as selective survival as leveler among populations. (Ferraro & Farmer, p. S327)

Another, less supported, hypothesis, the artifact thesis, claimed that inflated age reports of older Blacks result in the crossover effect or the narrowed Black disadvantage among persons 80 years and older (The Black-White mortality crossover). Today, the crossover effect, while not as pronounced, still exists. Rather than it diminishing the double-jeopardy theory, it most likely speaks to other protective factors among this group of Black elders.

The 1964 NUL *Double Jeopardy* report clearly cast attention to the lifelong inequities faced by African Americans and presented data to support the claim. Despite the counterarguments about the relevance of the term *double jeopardy*, the evidence of the time pointed to some differences that were likely the result of racism. This lends itself to further examination using critical race theory.

Critical race theory

After passage of the 1964 Civil Rights Act, there were likely great expectations that social and economic inequities would quickly dissipate. This was not the case. Critical race theory (CRT) emerged in part to address the slow progress following Civil Rights in the 1960s." CRT asserts that racism for African Americans influences all aspects of life and that racial hierarchy is perpetuated in social policies as well as the educational system that prepares professionals to practice. According to Delgado and Stefanic (2013), the CRT movement consists of a collection of activists and scholars focused on transforming the relationships among race, racism, and power and rejects assumptions of neutrality of laws and policies. They note that its basic tenets are that racism is ordinary and because large sectors of society benefit from it there is little incentive to eradicate it (interest convergence and material determinism). Although CRT started as a movement within the field of law (Bell, 1994), other disciplines, including social work, subscribe to the tenets that racism is ubiquitous and social policies often mirror this. Gee et al. (2012) use a public health lens to recommend that efforts to eliminate health inequalities consider how racism not only creates adverse exposure but structures time as well. Thus, CRT is a very important framework to use in examining the progress made since the *Double Jeopardy* report was written over 50 years ago. Given the intensity of the disagreement about the importance of the NUL *Double Jeopardy* report during the 1960s, it is important to examine it using a contemporary context. Critical race theory has been selected to analyze the progress or lack of progress in addressing the contemporary relevance of the double jeopardy claimed in the 1964 NUL report.

Social welfare policy and the Black aged

According to Colby (2016), social policy is a "formal expression of a community's values, principles and beliefs" (p. 3). Social policy refers to goals of collective responsibility as well as services related to carrying out those agreed-upon responsibilities. The goals of social welfare policy are congruent with societal views representing a subset of the larger social policy arena (Colby, 2016, p. 3; Stern & Axinn, 2012, p. 2). Further, Colby (2016) states that "macro social welfare policy provides a framework and means to strengthen larger communities. As an instrument of change, social welfare policy can reduce or eliminate a particular issue that impacts at-risk and marginalized population groups such as children, families, seniors, and people of color. Conversely, social policy may exacerbate or penalize a particular population group" (p. 3.)

Very often, social welfare policy is presented in reference to distinct vulnerable groups in society including families with children, persons with disabilities, and the aged. While the groups are not segregated in society, social welfare policy sometimes imposes a silo approach. In reality, the groups are nested and intersectionality is a better lens for social policy, especially among historically oppressed groups. For example, policies that address quality of life for older persons (the aged) should be mindful of the caregiving responsibilities that older persons have for disabled adult children and grandchildren. This self-help philosophy is linked to the failure of early social welfare efforts to be made available to them as well as a developed sense of family responsibility linked to African ancestry (Martin & Martin, 1985). Thus, social welfare policy for African Americans is further defined by critical race theory, which emphasizes that racism is "engrained in the fabric and system of American society" (UCLA, n.d., p. 1). Social welfare policy for African Americans focuses simultaneously on restorative justice and opportunity. For African Americans, there is wide consensus that race matters and policies that are color blind are also blind to the systemic barriers they encounter. There is evidence of this in the 2016 Pew research report on views of race and inequality. This report titled "on Views of Race and Inequality, Blacks and Whites are Worlds Apart" (Pew Research Center, 2016, p. 4) states "an overwhelming majority of blacks (88%) say the country needs to continue making changes for blacks to have equal rights with whites, but 43% are skeptical that such changes will ever occur." According to Mouzon, Taylor, Woodward, and Chatters (2016), "Exhaustive reviews of the literature find that perceived major and everyday discrimination have deleterious effects on physical and mental health" (p. 1). Additionally, the authors identify everyday discrimination as a psychosocial stressor that negatively impacts well-being and quality of life. Their findings underscore the importance of race in discussion of social welfare policy and the use of critical race theory as a theoretical framework.

Modern social welfare policy in the United States is often traced to the 1935 Social Security Act (Day & Schiele, 2012; Trattner, 1999). This act focused specifically on the needs of older persons as well as other vulnerable groups in the U.S. population. The Social Security Act (Act of August 14, 1935) [H. R. 7260] describes it as:

> An act to provide for the general welfare by establishing a system of Federal old-age benefits, and by enabling the several States to make more adequate provision for aged persons, blind persons, dependent and crippled

children, maternal and child welfare, public health, and the administration of their unemployment compensation laws; to establish a Social Security Board; to raise revenue; and for other purposes (Social Security).

Social Security created a greatly needed source of income for the Black aged. In the 1960s, many Blacks for the first time had a source of income to support them during old age. Although the program is often cited for institutional racism from its inception, those that were assisted cannot be marginalized. Yet, there were categories of excluded groups that scholars have claimed disparately impacted African Americans receiving benefits. Specifically, the exclusion of farm workers and domestic workers is often cited as intentional racism. Others, however, argue no racial disparity in that categories of *all* racial groups were denied based upon their occupation.

The following excerpt from a 2010 Social Security Brief authored by Larry DeWitt states:

> The Social Security Act of 1935 excluded from coverage about half the workers in the American economy. Among the excluded groups were agricultural and domestic workers—a large percentage of whom were African Americans. This has led some scholars to conclude that policymakers in 1935 deliberately excluded African Americans from the Social Security system because of prevailing racial biases during that period (p. 1).

DeWitt (2010) disputes the claim and draws the conclusion that "the racial-bias thesis is both conceptually flawed and unsupported by the existing empirical evidence. The exclusion of agricultural and domestic workers from the early program was due to considerations of administrative feasibility involving tax-collection procedures. The author finds no evidence of any other policy motive involving racial bias" (p. 1).

The author argues the familiar position that more Whites were excluded than Blacks. He wrote that, "Indeed, of the 20.1 million gainfully employed workers that the president's Committee on Economic Security estimated were excluded from participation in the Social Security system, at least 15 million were white" (p. 1). What he does not say is that categories of Blacks who were excluded were more likely to be in greater need because of historical disparities. A more salient discussion likely centers around the impact of the exclusion rather than the number of the excluded. Of interest is the following statement by the author that seems to point out a contradiction in his argument:

> Although 65 percent of the African American workforce was excluded by this provision, it was also the case that 27 percent of the white workforce was likewise excluded from coverage. Moreover, African Americans were not the most heavily impacted group: 66 percent of "other" races were excluded as well. Of those individuals excluded under the provision, 74 percent were white, and only 23 percent were African American. This hardly constitutes a compelling initial case for the assumption that the provision targeted African Americans (p. 6).

Spriggs & Furman (2006) note that the lower life expectancy of African Americans results in them collecting social security benefits for fewer years. They also document that African American workers earnings are 73% of white workers and this contributes to the retirments benefits equalling 85% of the average benefits for whites.

The compelling case for those advocating institutional disparities is the assumption that need was the same across racial groups and totally misses the enslaved period of African Americans. The ahistorical nature of the argument reflects the marginalization of the impact of the cruel institution of slavery and its byproduct, Jim Crow. It also speaks to the ease at which the nonimpacted group embraces the need to include "all" when blacks are identified as a targeted group for affirmative or corrective treatment. Ironically it appears that the focus on "all" is less present when punishment, penalty, or neglect is the point of discussion. When we lift all at the same rate, those who were at the bottom remain there.

Additional evidence that Social Security was needed more by Blacks to address historical inequalities is found in the (2006) report from the Center on Budget and Policy Priorities regarding African Americans and Social Security authored by Spriggs and Furman (2006). They stated that:

> Social Security also makes up a larger share of the income of elderly African Americans than of elderly white people. This reflects, in part, the fact that African Americans are less likely to have retirement accounts or life insurance than whites. Elderly African Americans also have a harder time finding work and have less in earnings than do elderly whites. These factors make Social Security an even more important component of African Americans' retirement security. (p. 2)

This analysis makes a compelling argument of persistent inequalities that continue to plague African-American older persons. Despite the gains of 50 years, these gaps indicate the deep hold that historical disparities have and the inability of social welfare policy in isolation to eradicate differences.

The 1965 Older Americans Act (OAA) is another key piece of legislation that was aimed at serving the unmet of the needs of older persons. The Administration on Aging (AoA) states that the OAA was passed in response to concern by policymakers about a lack of community social services for older persons. The original legislation established authority for grants to states for community planning and social services, research and development projects, and personnel training in the field of aging. The law also established the Administration on Aging (AoA) to administer the newly created grant programs and to serve as the federal focal point on matters concerning older persons.

The previously mentioned 1971 report to the Special Senate Committee also addressed the Older Americans Act. It stated:

> Until passage of the Older Americans Act in 1965, the various provisions of the Social Security Act constituted the major attempt of the Federal Government to aid the elderly. The provisions in the latter act for payment of benefits for work in covered employment had little impact on black wage earners until various amendments—over 35 years—belatedly brought more blacks within its scope. Consequently, the present groups of blacks in the age group of 65-and-over enjoy these benefits to a much more limited degree than whites in the same age group. It was not surprising therefore that the major provision of the Social Security Act which afforded significant help to aged blacks was in the public assistance sections—which offered some relief through the Old Age Assistance Program

Even here, however, elderly Negroes—often unaware of, and culturally unprepared to cope with, legislative routines—did not share to the extent to which they were entitled. The administration of the program was in the hands of the states and thus were philosophically and legally influenced by old poor-law ideology (p. 34).

A key policy recommendation that emerged from this 1971 Senate Special Committee on Aging report was to bring greater equity to disadvantaged non-White minorities through amendments that would provide benefits to non-White minorities at an earlier age because of their higher mortality and lower longevity. This was never enacted.

Today, older persons receive services under many federal programs. The Administration for Community Living (ACL) (2017) states that the Older Americans Act however, served as the major vehicle for the organization and delivery of social and nutrition services to this group and their caregivers:

> It authorizes a wide array of service programs through a national network of 56 State agencies on aging, 629 area agencies on aging, nearly 20,000 service providers, 244 Tribal organizations, and 2 Native Hawaiian organizations representing 400 Tribes. The OAA also includes community service employment for low-income older Americans; training, research, and demonstration activities in the field of aging; and vulnerable elder rights protection activities (ACL, p. 1).

The OAA responded to many of the gaps/needs noted in the *Double Jeopardy* report.

The timing of passage of the Older Americans Act, in 1965, lends credence to its influence in the inclusion of programs that focused on quality-of-life issues that were pointed out in the NUL Double Jeopardy report. According to the Administration of Community Living (2017), the OAA places emphasis on serving persons with the greatest need, including racial and ethnic and minority groups. In 2013 they reported serving 11.1 million older persons using the following targeted approach: Consistent with the targeting requirements of the OAA, state and area agencies on aging placed considerable emphasis on services to persons with the greatest social and economic need, including members of racial and ethnic minority groups, especially those who are poor. Among the older persons who received Title III OAA home and community-based registered services, 12% were African American (Administration on Aging, 2015).

An advocacy group for the Black aged emerged in the 1970s as well. This group was composed of persons from the fields of sociology, social work, housing, psychology, gerontology, education, housing, research, and others representing no particular organization or discipline. The National Caucus on the Black Aged was organized in response to the absence of other organizations targeting the needs of the Black aged. Black organizations of the time "were perhaps justifiably preoccupied with other priorities—one of the unfortunate kinds of developments when there are so many inequities to overcome. Their efforts toward social revolution seemed not to include the elderly, for whatever reasons" (Special Senate Report Multiple Hazards, p. 66). To address this unmet need, the National Caucus for the Black Aged was launched and still exists today as a resource for the needs of the Black aged. According the its current website,

> The National Caucus & Center on Black Aging, Inc. was founded in 1970 to ensure that the particular concerns of elderly minorities would be addressed in the then-upcoming 1971 White House Conference on Aging. Since then, NCBA has helped protect and improve the quality of life for elderly populations, making certain that legislators, policy makers, philanthropists, advocacy groups, service organizations, thought leaders and the public at-large include minority seniors in their programs, policy- and law-making, and giving. (NCBA, 2014)

The unique needs of older African Americans continue and as one of the country's oldest organizations dedicated to aging issues and the only national organization devoted to minority and low-income aging, NCBA continues to be a strong advocate.

African-American aged

According to the 2015 Profile of Older Americans (AoA), the population age 65 years and older numbered 46.2 million in 2014, an increase of 10 million, or 28%, since 2004. Consistent with projects of a substantial increase of older persons, between 2004 and 2014 the population age 60 and older increased 32.5%, from 48.9 million to 64. 8 million. About one in every seven, or 14.5%, of the population is an older American. The number of people aged 65 and older is projected to increase to 98.2 million by 2060—nearly doubling the current numbers.

A targeted look at non-Hispanic African Americans over 65 years of age indicated that in 2014 there were four million and by 2060, the number will be 12 million—a three-fold increase. In 2014, African Americans represented 9% of older populations and this will increase to 12% by 2060. The key variables examined to address the persistence of double jeopardy are life expectancy, education, income and poverty, and health.

Education

Seventy-four percent of African Americans age 65 and older had finished high school and 17% had a college degree (bachelors degree). This compared with 84% of all older persons with high school degrees and 26% with a bachelors degree or higher. While there has been a substantial increase in the past decades, the gap in educational attainment still exists.

Poverty

In 2013, African Americans age 65 and older reported a median income of $42,805. The comparable number for all older households was $54,184. The median personal income for older African-American men was $23,026 and $14,633 for women. For all older persons, the comparable figures were $29,854 for men and $17,366 for women. Consistent with the worse economic security for African Americans, the poverty rate for African Americans age 65 and older was 18.7% as compared to 10.2% for all older Americans. When the comparisons are between Blacks and Whites alone, the gap is even wider.

Health

The Centers for Disease Control and Prevention (CDC) reports closing the longevity gap between Blacks and Whites. Based upon a 2015 CDC report, between 1999 and 2013 Blacks made notable progress in rates of heart disease, cancer, HIV, unintentional injuries, and perinatal conditions, which together accounted for 59% of the decline in the Black-White life expectancy gap. Whites could expect to live 79.1 years at birth in 2013, a steady 2.3% improvement since 1999. Men could expect to live 76.7 years and women 81.4 years. Black life expectancy rose to 75.5 years, a solid 5.7 percent gain over the 14-year period. Men could expect to live 72.3 years and women 78.4 years, according to the report. According to the *Washington Post* coverage of the report (Bernstein, 2015), greater progress against death from heart disease and HIV in particular helped African Americans catch up to Whites.

Although there is welcomed improvement, data also document that African Americans are still more prone to chronic conditions. Data from 2012–13 provided in Table 1 show the following prevalence of chronicity for African-American older persons when compared with all older persons.

Among the five most frequently occurring conditions among older Americans, African Americans have a higher prevalence in three of them. Consistent with these data, older African Americans (non-Hispanic) are less likely to rate their health as excellent or very good (27%) as compared to 47% of older Whites (Non-Hispanic). Additionally, among older African Americans, 34% had Medicare and supplementary health insurance. Eleven percent were covered by both Medicare and Medicaid. Among all older adults, 50% had Medicare and supplemental insurance and 6% received both Medicare and Medicaid. These numbers also reflect a gap in coverage.

Conclusion

Marking a half-century after the passage of the 1964 Civil Rights Act (and coincidentally, the NUL *Double Jeopardy* report), in 2014 the Congressional Black Caucus Foundation stated:

> Fifty years after this landmark legislation, African Americans are active and present participants in major domains of the US labor market unlike ever before, as the percentage of African Americans 25 years or older with at least a high school education has increased from 27 percent in 1964 to 86 percent in 2012. (Pew Research). There have been increases in African-American life expectancies and, accordingly, voter turnout. However, persistent challenges remain with regard to the quality of life of African Americans (Grant, 2014, p. 1).

And for many older African Americans who grew up under the indignation of Jim Crow, in their older age, the inequalities are more persistent. While some have been able to escape economic hardships, too many continue to reap the deficits of discrimination through the end of their lives. For many, the cycle of neglect followed through to the future generations, resulting in what is referred to as generational or chronic poverty. Miller-Cribbs and Farber (2008) caution that an overreliance on African-American kin networks to provide material and socioemotional support contributes to the chronicity of poverty or generational transfers of poverty. Thus, the increased emphasis by social welfare policy on personal and family responsibility can result in the continuation of poverty because the networks are fragile.

For older African Americans, this can mean that older people are not only meeting their own needs but are forced to take on the needs of multiple generations. This policy shift to personal responsibility of younger generations can have the unintended or under-investigated impact of keeping older Blacks in poverty as they age. The rise in grandparents raising grandchildren is an example of this (Bertera & Crewe, 2013). These grandparent-headed households stand in the gap for birth parents and assume responsibilities that too often compromise their own well-being.

Table 1. Prevalence of Chronic Conditions (Percentage).

CHRONIC CONDITION	African American Older Persons	All Older Persons
Hypertension	85	71
Arthritis	51	49
Heart Disease	27	31
Diabetes	39	21
Cancer	17	25

Administration on Community Living (2015)

There are important lessons to be learned from this examination of progress. First, the improvements in the quality of life of the Black aged came about because of advocacy from diverse disciplines and constituencies. The pioneers of these seminal programs used a variety of tactics to bring attention to the plight of the Black aged, including the establishment of a new advocacy group and threatening a counter–White House Conference on Aging to bring into focus the needs of a marginalized group of persons. Additionally, the NUL *Double Jeopardy* report used timing effectively to get its message out. The fact that it raised the voices of critics was in itself a victory because it allowed the opportunity to reinforce the intersectionality of race, age, and economic status. Equally important, it allowed for the forceful rejection of ahistorical accounts of the plight of the African-American aged and the pioneers stood their ground that no research, no matter how rigorous, could discount the subjective experience of growing old Black in America. As stated by the Special Senate Commission, "Facts and statistics withstanding, growing old black is a peculiar and perilous experience" (p. 64). For too many, this is still the case today. As we focus on potential changes to the Patient Protection and Affordable Care Act, there are advocacy lessons to be garnered by the early champions of equity for the Black aged.

I conclude that although multiple layers of legislation resulted in progress in removing some of the critical quality-of life-gaps, disparities continue. These disparities cannot be reduced to personal deficits. Systemic injustices are not easily erased and the next generation of social welfare policy must resist the historical cynicism about inequity and disparities that endures for many throughout their life course. The success of many does not negate the struggle of others. There is a clear pattern that many African Americans continue to enter older age with the burden of poverty and unfilled promises of liberty and justice for all. As we face possible changes to the Patient Protection and Affordable Care Act, it is imperative that special attention be given to the impact on older African Americans. A colorblind approach has not been successful in eradicating the gaps. CRT would lead us to think about race and use our knowledge of systemic racism to examine the impact of policies and practices on the most vulnerable older persons. Whether we are examining social security, long-term care, or any other aspect of aging, a racial lens is important. We must reject the false hope that by lifting all we will provide an adequate safety net for the most vulnerable and at risk for poverty and disparities. An appropriate end to this article is the words that Inabel Burns Lindsay made to the Special Senate Committee on Aging in 1971. She stated, "Some progress has been made toward removing injustice and toward equality, but the task is far from completed" (p. 1). Forty-five years later, as the current dean of the Howard University School of Social Work, I affirm the statement of my predecessor and embrace the need for social welfare policies that acknowledge the disparities and put in place programs and protections that make old age a time of integrity versus despair for the African-American aged.

References

Administration for Community Living. (2017). Older Americans Act. Retrieved 2018, January https://acl.gov/about-acl/authorizing-statutes/older-americans-act.

Administration on Aging. (2015). *A profile of older Americans 2015*. Retrieved from http://www.aoa.acl.gov/aging_statistics/Profile/index.aspx

Administration on Community Living (2015). A statistical profile of older african americans. Retrieved https://www.aoa,acl,gov/Aging_https://acl.gov/sites/default/files/Aging%20and%20Disability%20in%20America/Statistical-Profile-Older-African-Ameri.pdf

Bell, D. A. (1994). Who's Afraid of Critical Race Theory? *University of Illinois Law Review, 4*, 893–910. (November 6, 2015). https://www.washingtonpost.com/news/to-your-health/wp/2015/11/06/the-black-whitegap-in-life-expectancy-is-narrowing-as-african-americans-get-healthier/

Bernstein, L. (November 6, 2015). Black-white gap in life expectancy is narrowing as African Americans get healthier. Washington Post. Retrieved https://www.washingtonpost.com

Bertera, E., & Crewe, S. E. (2013). Parenthood in the twenty-first century: African American grandparents as surrogate parents. *Journal Of Human Behavior In The Social Environment, 23*, 178–192. doi:10.1080/10911359.2013.747348

Pew Research Center, June 17. 2016. On Views of Race and Inequality, Blacks and Whites are Worlds Apart.

Colby, I. C. (2016). Social work education: Social welfare policy. In *Encyclopedia of social work*. PRINTED FROM the Encyclopedia ofSocial Work, accessed online. (c) National Association of Social Workers and Oxford University Press USA. doi:10.1093/acrefore/9780199975839.013.619.

Day, P. J., & Schiele, J. (2012). *A new history of social welfare* (7th ed.). Upper Saddle River, NJ, USA: Pearson Education.

Delgado, R., & Stefanic, J. (2013). *Critical race theory: The cutting edge* (3rd.), Philadelphia, PA: Temple University Press.

DeWitt. (2010). The Decision to Exclude Agricultural and Domestic Workers from the 1935 Social Security Act. Retrieved from https://www.ssa.gov/policy/docs/ssb/v70n4/v70n4p49.html

Ferraro, K. F., & Farmer, M. M. (1996). Double jeopardy, aging as leveler,or persistent healthinequality? A longitudinal analysis of White and Black Americans. *Journal of Gerontology, 51B*(6), S319–S3. doi:10.1093/geronb/51B.6.S319

Gee, G. C., Walsemann, K. M., & Brondolo, E. (2012). A life course perspective on how racism may be related to health inequities. *American Journal of Public Health, 102*(5), 967–974. doi:10.2105/AJPH.2012.300666

Golden, H. M. (1980). Black ageism: Relative deprivation revisited. In B. B. Hess (Ed.), *Growing old in America* (pp. 327–346). New Brunswick, NJ: Transaction, Inc.

Grant, B. O. (2014). Fifty Years of the Civil Rights Act of 1964- Progress, Problems and the Way Forward. Retrieved from Congressional Black Caucus Foundation: http://www.cbcfinc.org/thevillage/2014/07/03/fifty-years-of-the-civil-rights-act-of-1964progress-problems-and-the-way-forward/

King, M. L. (1968). *Where do we go from here: Community or chaos*. Boston, Mass, USA: Beacon Press.

National Urban League (1964). Double jeopardy, the older Negro in America today. New York: National Urban League.

Lindsay, I. B. (1971). *Multiple hazards of age and race: the situation of aged blacks in the United States. A preliminary survey for the Special Committee on Aging*. United States Senate. Retrieved from http://www.aging.senate.gov/imo/media/doc/reports/rpt771.pdf?

Manuel, R. C. (1994). The physical, psychological, and social health of black older Americans. In I. L. Livingston (Ed.), *Handbook of Black American health* (pp. 300–314). Westport, Conn: Greenwood Press.

Martin, E., & Martin, J. (1985). *The helping tradition of the Black family*. Washington, DC: NASW press.

Milller-Cribbs, J. E., & Farber, N. B. (2008). Kinship networks and poverty among African Americans: Past and present. *Social Work, 53*(1), 43–45.

Mouzon, D. M., Taylor, R. J., Woodward, A. T., & Chatters, L. M. (2016). Everyday racial discrimination, everyday nonracial discrimination, and physical health among African Americans. *Journal of Ethnic and Cultural Diversity in Social Work*, 1–13.

Moynihan, D. P. (1965, March). *The Negro family: the case for national action*. United States Department of Labor. Office of Policy Planning and Research. Retrieved 2016, November from http://web.stanford.edu/~mrosenfe/Moynihan's%20The%20Negro%20Family.pdf

National Caucus and Center on the Black Aged (NCBA). (1964). *History*. Retrieved 2016, October from http://www.ncba-aged.org/about/National Urban League

National Urban League. (2016). Retrieved from http://socialwelfare.library.vcu.edu/organizations/national-urbanleague

Smith, A. N. (2010). *Empowering communities-changing lives: 100 years of the national urban league and black America (1910–2010)*. New York, NY, USA: National Urban League.

Social Security Administration. *History*. Retrieved from https://www.ssa.gov/history/35act.html

Spriggs, W., & Furman, J. (2006). *African Americans and Social Security: The Implications of Reform Proposals*. Center for Budget and Policy Priorities. Retrieved from http://www.cbpp.org/research/african-americans-and-social-security-the-implications-ofreform-proposals

Stern, M. J., & Axinn, J. (2012). *Social welfare-A history of the American response to need* (8th ed.). Boston, MA: Allyn and Bacon.

Trattner, W. I. (1999). *From poor law to welfare state* (6th ed.). New York, NY: The Free Press.

UCLA School of Public Affairs. (n.d.). *What is critical race theory?* Retrieved from https://spacrs.wordpress.com/what-is-critical-race-theory/

Victor, D. (July 15, 2016). *Why 'All Lives Matter' is such a perilous phrase*. Retrieved from http://www.nytimes.com/2016/07/16/us/all-lives-matter-black-lives-matter.html?_r=0

Racism and the Christian Church in America: Caught between the Knowledge of Good and Evil

Annie Woodley Brown

ABSTRACT
Those persons with church membership or professing a faith or relationship with God represent a microcosm of society. Therefore, the demons of racism, bigotry, and prejudice found in society at large are found in the church. Despite the very nature of Christianity that calls on Christians to be a countervoice in the world against evil, many have capitulated to various strains of racism in the world and in the Church. Some Christian denominations have begun to explore racism in the church and have developed responses to addressing the issues in the church and in the world. This article examines the historical context of race and religion in the Christian church in the United States, and addresses the current efforts of some Christian denominations to become proactive in the struggle against racism.

Introduction

It seems an oxymoron to speak of racism in the church because the tenets of Christianity are the opposite of the tenets of racism.

> "All world religions proclaim universal brotherly and sisterly love. Yet history is littered with moments in which religion has provided a justification, for, or has given cause to, all kinds of atrocities directed towards people of a different race or culture: the Crusades, slavery, the Holocaust, etc." (Duriez & Hutsebaut, 2000, p. 1)

Therefore, the Christian church has not been immune to racism and, in some ways, may have made it easier for its members to profess Christianity while remaining bigoted and supportive of racist policies. The focus of this article is the relation of racism and the church resulting from that peculiar institution of slavery in the United States of America.

Many Americans think that the United States was founded as a Christian nation. But in fact, this nation was founded on the principle of religious freedom; there was no state religion. Many of the founders of this nation were Christian or nonaffiliated. I surmise a question to be asked is, "How could a nation where so many believe that it is a Christian nation and identify themselves as religious, maintain the attitude, and societal structures that sustained racism?" Gomes (1996) suggests that just as many people in the Bible did wrong when they knew the right; that they acted not out of ignorance, but from what is known in theology as a "corrupted will." Caught between the knowledge of good and evil, Christians are often unable to avoid the easy, acceptable wrong in favor of the difficult right behavior. Although it is difficult to grasp the magnitude of the Christian church's complicity in its ongoing support of racism, understanding certain concepts related to racism may shed light on the matter.

Take the concept of race, defined as "a group of people identified as distinct from other groups because of supposed physical or genetic traits shared by the group," most biological and social scientists do not recognize race as a valid classification of humans (Free Dictionary.com, 2013).

Another view of race that emphasizes the social aspect is provided by the Aspen Institute (2004), "Race is historically and socially constructed (and recreated) by how people are perceived and treated in the normal actions of everyday life" (p. 8). Africans, imported into the colonies as indentured servants, bondsmen, laborers, and slaves, in time, through a series of statutes in the 1600s, became free blacks, or slaves with little or no legal standing. Antimiscegenation laws in Maryland (1681) and Virginia (1691) began to provide the language to separate people. Battalora (2013), in her *Birth of a White Nation*, describes "whiteness" from a social developmental perspective. She links Bacon's rebellion (that time in 1676 in Virginia, when White servants, tenant farmers, free Blacks, and slaves banded together to attack the colonial power structure) as a time when identity references changed. White colonists were referenced in law primarily as British and other Christians; later they were referenced as English and freeborn; then in Maryland's 1681 antimiscegenation law, referenced as "Freeborn English" and other Whites. The change in the labeling of Black and White people in at least two of the colonies, resulted in part, from the Bacon Rebellion of 1676, and efforts of the elite class to quash any alliance between laborers of European and African descent, bond and free. Battalora (2013) noted that those who were members of native tribes or of African descent were viewed as sufficiently unlike the British so as to warrant separate labels and exclusion from the full package of rights and privileges that the British and those who looked sufficiently like them enjoyed. Further evidence of the changes in the way African Americans were treated was stated by Nash (p. 22):

> In rapid succession Afro-Americans lost their right to testify before a Court, to engage in any kind of commercial activity, either as buyer or seller; to hold property; to participate in the political process; to congregate in public places with more than two or three of their fellows; to travel without permission and to engage in legal marriage or parenthood. (Nash, 1992, p. 159).

Thus, was set in motion the structure of a racialized system of power and dominance that defined the privileged relationship of Whites to others – Africans, Native Americans, Mexicans, and Asians, to the present times.

The Western church had already acquiesced to the social and political realities of race. It is important to note that the creation of race as a social construct did not occur in a vacuum. Europeans had already labeled the cargo of the ships of the slave trade as heathens.

> From the very beginning of the Atlantic slave trade, conversion of slaves to Christianity was viewed by Western Christendom as justification of enslavement of Africans. Pangs of guilt over the inherent cruelty in enslaving fellow human beings were assuaged by emphasizing the grace of faith made available to the Africans, who otherwise would die as pagans. (Raboteau, 1978, p. 96).

So, what had occurred in Europe and South America occurred in the colonies when Maryland passed laws clarifying that conversion to Christianity held no relevance to one's status as a slave and would not lead to manumission (Battalora, 2013). Thus, the Church could keep about its mission of converting the "heathens" to Christ without challenging the economic system that needed slave labor.

There was no collective outcry from the Christian church against slavery, and in the Constitution of the United States of America, written in 1789, slaves were counted as three fifths of a person. And in the mid-1700s, Dr. Carl von Linnaeus, who developed the taxonomy to classify plants and animals, expanded this thinking to include human beings. He set forth a race classification system using color as a criterion for classifying races and assigning moral and intellectual capacities to each race (DeGruy, 2005, p. 57). When the need for cheap labor in the American colonies outstripped the indentured servant, forced labor system using mostly Whites; and Native Americans proved not a good fit to be enslaved (could not be contained), it was not a huge move to increase the importation Africans. They were already determined to be inferior beings by the European slave traders.

On the other hand, the term *racism* speaks to a system that offers advantages based on race. White Christians might consciously reject racial prejudice ("I don't have a prejudiced bone in my body" is often declared) but fail to grasp how the structure of our society continues to advantage Whites over other groups. This view of racism is not just about the beliefs one holds as much as the fact that racism involves systemic inequity maintained through individual and institutional means (Tochluk, 2010).

Racism is the backdrop to White privilege, another term which has recently gained explanatory stature, as the context within which our major institutions or opportunity areas such as health care, education, the labor market, the criminal justice system or the media operate. Although some people, White Christians among them, want to see the policies and practices of our institutions as race neutral, they fail to account for the cumulative effects of 400 years of discrimination and inequity. There is a kind of willful scotosis in assessing the racially disparate outcomes for African Americans and other people of color in the highly racialized society that is the United States of America.

Critical race theory

A useful theory for examining the Christian church and racism in the United States of America is critical race theory. "Critical race theory recognizes that racism is engrained in the fabric and system of the American society. This is the analytical lens that CRT uses in examining existing power structures" (UCLA School of Public Health, 2016, p. 1). Although CRT got its start in scholarship related to law, it has become an interdisciplinary tool for examining the relationship between the oppressor and the oppressed in many areas – law, education, feminism, gender bias, Native American rights, and so on. With the notion of race and the creation of White privilege, using CRT can assist in our understanding of ongoing racism in the Christian church.

On the surface racism would appear an anathema to the Christian church. Yet in the USA, White supremacy and White privilege have been maintained despite the rue of law and the professed value that all "men" are created equal. The church as an institution failed from the beginning to take a moral stand against oppression. And that persists even though this nation perceives itself as a Christian nation answerable to the higher authority of moral law. There are factors that can account for this dissonance. The "other" as less than, especially the African American other, has a long and tortuous history in this country. The foundation for racism in the United States of America was laid very early in the formation of the nation. The manner, scope, and depth of chattel slavery created a system that challenged the moral underpinnings of the country, from its incipiency. Human beings (African slaves) were objectified and designated as property. Thus, they were no longer considered children of God, or one's neighbor, and not considered subject to the protection afforded citizens. Despite the fact that both the Old Testament and the New Testament contain many verses admonishing believers to love their neighbors, slaves and Native Americans were not considered neighbors in a civic sense and, therefore, not considered neighbors in a Christian sense. They were thought of as heathens needing to be converted, but that state of being did not render them fully human with the rights and privileges of citizens.

Historical perspective of racism and religion in America

European nations expanded overseas and into the New World with an inherent sense of superiority competing for colonial power and the conversion of "heathen natives." The development of race and color prejudice can be roughly traced to four major historical world events: (1) the discovery of America and the establishment of the slave trade, (2) the development of the slave trade, (3) the scientifically based industrial revolution and its contribution to the enormous economic wealth of Europe and the Americas, and (4) Darwin's theory of evolution with its emphasis on the "survival of the fittest." Herbert Spencer expanded Darwin's theory of natural selection to applicability to cultures positing that some cultures were inherently inferior (Koranteng-Pipim, 2001). This perspective allowed domination of people without the constraints of religion. They could explain their behavior by their claim of superior intellectual endowments. In colonies in North America, that sense of superiority was further heightened and strengthened through the development of White as an identity reference. The construction of White identity, and the term *construction* is used here because Whiteness as a race identifier did not burst on the scene fully formed as a concept. Over a period of time, the legal basis for a White identity was developed by systematically making laws that restricted the rights of Blacks and providing privileges to Whites based on their color.

The fact that the American colonies were formed during a period of religious fervor and reformation, with many people coming to this country seeking religious freedom did not stem the tide of enslavement of Africans. The pressure for cheap labor drove the importation of slaves. It must be noted that many of the Christian Protestants did not get along with each other and often banned fellow Christians. Therefore, it is highly unlikely Christian denominations would have taken on the economic system regarding slavery. However, one denomination did raise the issue and became known as a group, to be against slavery, and were active participants in the abolitionist movement and Underground Railroad; that denomination was the Quakers. Even though some Quakers owned slaves and many were not abolitionists, they came closer than any other organized religious group to be seen as standing against the evil of slavery. Individuals in other denominations were inspired by their religion and could always be found among those who opposed the system of slavery. Radical abolitionism was partly fueled by the religious fervor of the Second Great Awakening that prompted many people to advocate for emancipation on religious grounds. In the 1830s, American abolitionists were led by Evangelical Protestants. Abolitionists believed slavery to be a national sin, and it was the moral obligation of every American to help eradicate it (Division of Rare & Manuscript Collections, 2002). Although this agitation helped lead to the Civil War, there was no sustained effort in the years following the War to treat African Americans as anything but second-class citizens whose problems emanated from their individual behaviors and choices they made. The White Church as an institution accommodated to the social, political, and economic realities of the times; and was, therefore, complicit in the conditions that fostered racism in this country. Howard Thurman, an African American theologian explains the dilemma for the church in America in this way:

> Given segregation as a factor determining relations, the resources of the environment are made into instruments to enforce the artificial position. Most of the accepted behavior-patterns assume segregation to be normal – if normal than correct; if correct than moral; if moral, then religious. Religion is thus made the defender and guarantor of the presumptions (Thurman, 1976, p. 43).

Once in this position, it appeared almost impossible for the Christian church to take up the cross, to become the voice for the poor, oppressed, and disenfranchised citizens of the United States of America. Instead it became a de facto "religion of the nation" with a very narrow perspective of the moral teachings of the Christ of Christianity.

There are other factors that must be considered in examining how racism remained so entrenched in the Christian church in America and society as a whole. One is psychological and the other organizational. From a psychological perspective, it is necessary to consider concepts from the realm of psychoanalysis. The defense mechanisms developed by Freud that explains coping mechanisms to maintain one's psychic health include the concept of compartmentalization. Compartmentalization is defined as "an unconscious psychological defense mechanism used to avoid cognitive dissonance, or the mental discomfort and anxiety caused by a person having conflicting values, cognitions and emotions, beliefs, etc. within themselves" (Wikipedia, 2016).

The story of the White church in America is a story of theology and culture, where the church failed to grapple with its theodicy and the norms of society prevailed. Once slavery was accepted as a legitimate form of labor in the colonies, the psychological work of reconciling human beings as property and human beings as children of God began. From a psychological perspective, the church could be viewed as the super ego of a society—that part that calls forth the norms and values of a society. Historically, it was never really able to fully assume this role in America. Rather it propped up the worst aspects of society by the convenient adage in support of religious freedom, that of separation of church and state. Separation of church and state prevented the establishment of a state church in the United States of America and avoided some of the turmoil experienced by European countries during the reformation as different denominations and sects fought for primacy as the state religion. Many of the early colonists settling America were refugees from the religious wars of Europe. However, this strict separation of church and state seemingly absolved the church as an institution from advocating for humane treatment of Africans and Native Americans. For it then supported the strict separation of people based on fear. How can this be? Howard Thurman in his book, Jesus and the Disinherited (1976) captures the slippery slope of the Church in embracing and supporting first slavery and then segregation:

> The fear that segregation inspires among the weak in turn breeds fear among the strong and dominant. This fear insulates the conscience against a sense of wrong doing in carrying out a policy of segregation. For it counsels if there were no segregation, there would be no protection against the invasion of the home, the church, the school. (pp. 33–34)

The other explanatory perspective (organizational) of how racism persisted in the Christian church in America is really rather extraordinary. Africans brought to this country as slaves were not without culture and a sense of themselves as persons of worth. They were religious. Besides their indigenous religions, some were even Christians and Muslims when they were imported to the Americas. A factor that would assert itself when they had the opportunity to exercise some personal agency and self-determination around religion even while enslaved. So, the very racism in the early American church that led to Africans walking out of the St. Georges Methodist Church in Philadelphia in 1787 provided the impetus for the establishment and growth of a vibrant African American Christian church in America, wholly owned and led by persons of African descent. These churches grew up across denominations but more importantly led to the establishment of an independent Black Christian church, the African Methodist Episcopal Church led by Richard Allen. He along with Absalom Jones established the Free African Society (FAS) in Philadelphia in 1787. Officials at St. Georges Methodist Church, fearful of the increased numbers of Blacks attending the Church, one Sunday, pulled Blacks off their knees to send them to the balcony. FAS members discovered the lengths to which the American Methodists would go to enforce racial discrimination against Africans and walked out of the church. The Black members of St. Georges made plans to transform their mutual aid society into the First African Church. Most of the members of FAS wanted to affiliate with the Protestant Episcopal Church, but Richard Allen led a small group who resolved to remain Methodists. In 1794, Bethel AME was established with Allen as its pastor. To prevent continuing interference from American Methodists, Allen had to sue the Methodist Church in 1807 and 1815 for the right of his congregation to exist as an independent institution. Black Methodists in other Atlantic states faced racism and wanted their own autonomy. Allen called them to meet in Philadelphia to form a Wesleyan denomination, the African Methodist Episcopal Church (2016).

In 1794, those members in the First African Church who followed Absalom Jones applied to join the Protestant Episcopal Church. Meeting the requirements of the Diocese of Pennsylvania that the church be an organized body, in control of its own affairs, and with a leader that could become a licensed lay leader and eventually be ordained a priest, the First African Church was accepted by the Diocese of Pennsylvania and renamed the African Episcopal Church of St. Thomas on the condition that it would not send any clergy or deputies to the Diocesan Convention, thus depriving Blacks of any representation of voice in church governance. The following year Jones became a deacon and was ordained 8 years later as America's first Black priest in the Protestant Episcopal Church. Beginning in 1794 with the founding of St Thomas in Philadelphia, people of African descent established themselves in separate communities especially along the Atlantic seaboard – often carrying on services for years without any sponsorship, recognition, or oversight by an episcopal jurisdiction. At some point these churches became loosely connected to the National Episcopal Church, not their local dioceses. The church reflected the norms of society and endorsed a separate cultivation of Black religious life throughout the 19th and early 20th century (The Archives of the Episcopal Church, 2008). It is safe to say that other mainline protestant churches in America followed a similar pattern of marginalized Black participation in the predominately

White denominations of the Christian church. This contributed mightily to the growth and development of the Black church as an independent institution.

Before and after the Civil War, Black churches formed faith communities independent of the White church. The National Baptist Convention, USA, Inc. traces a history of significant growth and achievement attended sometimes by periods of turbulence to November 1880 (National Baptist Convention, 1988). The Church of God in Christ was chartered in 1897, the first Pentecostal church in America to obtain such recognition (Charisma Magazine,). Black churches flourished in communities as independent entities, loosely organized into associations or marginally connected to the mainline Protestant and Catholic Church.

The Black Church is mentioned here to emphasize the fact that the racism of the White church made it easier for Blacks to establish their own church institutions. Mainline Christian churches had sought to relegate their Black members to second-class status within the church, but even in those instances in which Blacks remained in the White church, they had their own churches, served for the most part by their own leaders. The Black church became the most important institution in Black communities across this country. It became the vanguard in the fight for social justice from the beginning of its existence. Even while still a deacon, before he was ordained a priest, Absalom Jones called upon Congress to abolish the slave trade and to provide for gradual emancipation of existing slaves. Historically, the Black church has functioned as an incubator of the spiritual and cultural life of Black Americans. It has filled many roles: spiritual, physical, educational, cultural, and financial. The Black church has nurtured the talent and aspirations of a people. Many artists across the spectrum of entertainment, politicians, teachers, leaders in a variety of fields, found their voices in the Black church. The Black church has been the initiator of practically every vestige of institutional life extant in the Black community (Lincoln & Mamiya, 1990) It has been the voice for the poor and oppressed, the call for social justice. Barbara Solomon (1976) stated that the Black church facilitated and nurtured Black empowerment as providing the opportunity for those oppressed to participate in valued social roles. Specifically, she defines empowerment as, "a process whereby persons who belong to a stigmatized social category throughout their lives can be assisted to develop and increase skills in the exercise of interpersonal influence and the performance of valued social roles" (p. 29).

Within the segregated system of the United States of America, Blacks developed a parallel society of leadership and achievements often initiated by and in the rich religious and cultural heritage of the Black church. Evangelicalism and social responsibility were not inimical in the Black church.

The white Christian church and racism

After the Civil War, and a brief flowering of hope for the newly freed slaves, the South (but really all of the United States of America) quickly settled into the Black codes and Jim Crow laws and attitudes that kept Blacks in a state of second-class citizenship at best and subject to lynching and other indignities at worst. The White Christian church as an institution continued its alliance with the American power structure. Individual churches and denominations developed their own responses to the poor and oppressed by founding and/or supporting educational institutions (some Historically Black Colleges and Universities [HBCUs]) and social service organizations (such as Lutheran Social Services, Methodist and Baptist Children's Homes, Catholic Charities, etc.) to carry out the mission of the church in service to others; to do "good works." It should be noted, however, that it was only in the second half of the 20th century that these agencies served African Americans, and even then, it was sometimes through a "colored branch." This kind of separation allowed Christians in these churches to feel that they were responding to the call of Christ to "love thy neighbor." But this involvement was in the abstract; it did not promote the kind of engagement that would help White Christians understand the history of the other, the cumulative effects of racism, or their own privilege resulting from this racism. Although the tone of this article has focused on Protestant Christian churches, it should be noted that the Catholic church in the United States followed the same behavior in terms of race. Though in 1839, Pope Gregory, in an apostalic letter condemmned the slave trade as the "inhuman traffic in Negroes", Bishop John England of Charleston, S.C. defended the American slave trade; claiming it only applied to slaves imported by Spain and Portugal Many U.S. bshops as well as religious men's and women's orders owned slaves (Catholic News Herald, 2017).

Strict de jure segregation in the South and de facto segregation in the North left Black Americans discriminated against in every sphere of society. These years of entrenched segregation in society and in the Christian church in America left the Black church as the institution leading the fight against discrimination and injustice, in effect, carrying the gospel of freedom. No less a theologian than the esteemed Dietrich Bonhoeffer, when he visited the United States in 1930 as a teaching fellow at Union Theological Seminary, proclaimed that:

> As long as I have been here, I heard only one sermon in which you could hear something like a genuine proclamation and that was delivered by a Negro (indeed I'm increasingly discovering greater religious power and originality in Negroes), (The Editors of Leben, 2013, p. 2).

Left to itself because of the racism in society, the Black church became an asset not only to African Americans, but to the country.

Racism and religion: contemporary responses

The organized Civil Rights movement of the 1950s, 1960s, and 1970s did bring forth, especially from the mainline White Christian churches, support for legislation against discrimination in public accommodations and housing; and for voting rights. But when the secular government passed laws to address some of the inequities of the past through "affirmative action," the Church as an institution was lukewarm (and in some instances antagonistic) in support of the legislation, as well as education of its members about the need for such redress. In the struggle of the Civil Rights movement, some White Christian leaders were on the frontlines of the struggle. Yet Dr. King's Letter from a Birmingham Jail was in response to eight White clergyman who made an "Appeal for Law and Order and Common Sense," thus criticizing Dr. King for his involvement in the civil rights protest. Three clergy identified themselves as Episcopal bishops, one a Methodist bishop, one a moderator in the Presbyterian church, one a Baptist pastor, and one a Rabbi (Washington National Cathedral, 2016). Even then there was no unified response from the church as an institution, though many lay and clergy from the White Christin church marched with Dr. King and provided financial support for the Civil Rights Movement.

The fissures in the church community were clearly on display in the 1960s and widened in the 1970s with the advent of Rev. Jerry Falwell's moral majority and have continued to this day with the rise of the Evangelical Right and the declining membership in the mainline Protestant churches, due in part to their support of civil rights and social justice in the 1960s and 1970s.

Pete Scazzero, in a blog on healthy spirituality focused on transforming people who transform the world, developed Ten Top Reasons Racism continues in the church today:

(1) Failure to capture Scripture's vision of the church as a multiracial community that transcends racial, cultural, economic and gender barriers.
(2) Measuring success primarily by numbers.
(3) Superficial discipleship
(4) Failure to break the power of the past.
(5) An inadequate, biblical theology of grief and loss.
(6) Isolation
(7) Niavete regarding demonic power and principalities.
(8) Lack of skills to love well.
(9) Obliviousness of systemic racism.
(10) Emotional immaturity. (Scazzero, 2015, p. 1)

These reasons resonate with some American Christians' thinking on this matter, but shouldn't obliviousness to systemic racism be placed at the top of th list? At a Washington National Cathedral conversation on race, Jim Wallis, a panelist observed in one of his contributions, "If white Christians acted more like Christians than white, black parents would have less reason to fear for their children. That's a fact." He paraphrased a verse in the book of Corinthians that says when one part of the body of Christ hurts, all of the body feels the pain. "Not happening" Wallis said. "When the black part of the body hurts, the white part doesn't know what's happening most of the time" (quoted in Milloy, 2016, p. B2). There is a kind of willful ignorance on the part of some Christians; a defense against knowing the truth. White Christians who consider themselves intelligent and otherwise well informed, often know little about the history of African Americans in the history of America; or about the breadth and depth of the effects of systemic racism on every aspect of Black life. Some mainline Christian churches are beginning to find their voices to speak to issues of race in this country. "What is it about recent events that have caused white church leaders to feel the need to engage on a deeper level," as Rev. Gradye, former leader of the Presbyterian Church (USA) declared (Washington National Cathedral, 2016).

Some parts of the White Christian church in America are experiencing an awakening: a renewed sensitivity to the role of the church in relation to social justice – a recognition of the racism that exists among its members and even its leadership. And it has resolved to do something about it. Many of the mainline White Christian denominations have developed antiracism training curricula. In the Presbyterian church (USA) there is *Facing Racism: A View of the Beloved Community*. A call for the Presbyterian church to adopt an antiracism identity. The Evangelical Lutheran Church of America (ELCA, not to be confused with the conservative Evangelicals of the right) have a program for training called *Freed in Christ: Race, Ethnicity, and Culture*. The United Methodist Church (UMC) has a study guide that addresses the church's role in racism called *Steps Toward Wholeness: Learning and Repentance*. It requests all local congregations in the United States to engage in study sessions around the issue of racism (UMC.org, 2008). The Seventh Day Adventists (SDA) have addressed the issue of racism in their church and a church administrator concluded that:

> Institutional racism is a costly separation, and when African Americans speak frankly to their white counterparts, they receive apathy, indifference, or the attitude that the issue is not really important. White racism in white institutions must be eradicated by white people And not just black people. In fact, white racism is primarily a white responsibility. This includes the Seventh-day Adventist Church. We must get our house in order. (Lee, 2000, p. 14)

This author is a member of The Episcopal **Church of America**. For the past 3 ½ years, she has been one of the leaders in her local parish facilitating a conversation on race. These conversations preceded the events in Ferguson, Baltimore, and the highlighted acts of police brutality against Black men. The conversations were supported by readings such as *The Warmth of Other Suns*, Isabel Wilkerson; *The New Jim Crow*, Michelle Alexander; *Birth of a White Nation*, Jacqueline Battalora; and numerous articles on the economic status of poor Blacks and Whites and how these conditions contributed to ongoing racism in this country. Often when people, Black and White, are called on to discuss race, there is a lack of knowledge of the history and language needed to have a meaningful discussion. But knowledge of the historical background of an issue such as race, can give people the confidence to think and speak more clearly. From the conversations in my local parish, a desire to do something was articulated. Because I was a delegate to our Diocesan convention, resolution was developed to be presented at the convention calling on the Church to address issues of systemic racism and mass incarceration. The resolution was passed at the Diocesan level and became part of resolutions addressing racism at The General Convention of the Episcopal Church in Utah in 2015. Resolution C019 directed the Episcopal Church to establish a response to systemic racism. You can see how difficult this issue is for churches when you read one of the explanations supporting the resolution and how long the church has grappled with addressing racism.

Resolved, that the House of Bishops concurring, that the 78th General Convention of the Episcopal Church confesses that, despite repeated efforts at anti-racism training as well as racial justice and racial reconciliation initiatives including the passage of more than 30 General Convention resolutions dating back to 1952, the abomination and sin of racism continue to plague our society and our Church at great cost to life and human dignity; we formally acknowledge our historic and contemporary participation in this evil and repent of it. (General Convention, 2015, p. 310)

The General Convention further asked the Standing Committee on Program, Budget and Finance to consider an allocation of $1.5 million for the Triennium **(the three years before the next convention)** for the implementation of this resolution. The Episcopal Church like the other major White denominations has an antiracism training package titled "Seeing the Face of God in Each Other." This author is a member of the Episcopal Diocese of Washington's Social Justice Task Force and a member of leadership teams that provide the antiracism training to congregations in the Diocese. A retired Episcopal priest has taken this training to the interfaith community of Montgomery County, for provision of antiracism training for clergy and lay leaders across the county. This is an instance of the Church moving into the public square to broaden the discussion of racism and its impact on communities.

Conclusion

The story of racism in the White Christian church of America has its roots in slavery and in the Civil War when major White Protestant groups were torn apart by disputes over slavery, forcing interdenominational schisms that persists to this day (Jones, 2016). The voice of the Christian church for tolerance and social justice are needed now more than ever. The White Christian church, especially the Protestant branch, has declined in membership, influence, power, and wealth. Instead, the ascendency of the Southern Baptists (that never reconciled with the northern American Baptist Churches USA headquartered in the Northeast) and a radical right Evangelical movement fueled to some extent by the Southern Baptists, have emerged as a dominant voice in the moral direction of this country. They have manufactured a fictitious war on religion and under the guise of "religious liberty" condone the right to discriminate against African Americans, other people of color, gays and lesbians and atheists if they determine that what these people represent or who they are is against their evangelical religious beliefs. There is a strain of religious intolerance in the theology of a segment of evangelical fundamentalists. Although it is difficult to measure the concept of religion, early sociological research by Allport and Kramer in 1948 as cited by Duriez and Hutsebaut (2000) concluded that Christians and Protestants were more prejudiced than those who did not attend church (Dittes, 1973).

The election of 2016 exposed a strong undercurrent of racism in the United States of America that many thought had dissipated with the election of an African American president in 2008 and again in 2012. Yet, an unconventional outsider candidate, captured the Republican presidential nomination and rode to victory on a message of racism, bigotry, misogyny and hate and was propelled to this victory by a large segment of the Christian right. It is ironic that the most fundamental segment of the Christian church in America, the most outspoken against their perception of immoral behavior, blinded by racism, helped propel a message of divisiveness in the highest office in this nation. The virulent racism that emerged during the 2016 election reflects the deep division in the White Christian church, reminiscent of the state of the church at the time of the Civil War and the civil rights struggles of the 1950s and 1960s. Even someone as conservative as Reverend Billy Graham in an article in Christianity Today in 1993 acknowledged the failure of evangelical Christians to address the issue of racism. Even though he characterized racial and ethnic hostility as the number one social problem in the world and the church, he noted, "evangelical Christians have turned a blind eye to racism or have been willing to stand aside while others take the lead in racial reconciliation, saying it was not our responsibility" (Graham, 1993, p. 27). The evangelical Christians of the right's lack of sensitivity to race as an issue except as it threatens their privilege is even more pronounced in 2016.

The work of eliminating racism in the Church and in society:

> will require trailblazing both by majority – white congregations and by individual white Christians. At the congregational level, majority white congregations will need to initiate more cross pollination efforts, such as conducting joint services or initiating regular pulpit exchanges. (Jones, 2016, p. 193)

White Christians have always been welcome in African American churches, though few attend predominately Black churches. Spatial segregation, geographical segregation, and issues of White privilege, over time, continue to make it difficult to form meaningful relationships between Black and White Christians. W.E.B. DuBois was prescient in his understanding that the issue for America in the 20th century would be the color line. We are well into the 21st century and the issue of race is still very much with us as a nation and with us as a Christian church in America.

Disclosure statement

No potential conflict of interest was reported by the author.

References

African Methodist Episcopal Church. (2016, September). *Our history – AME church*. Retrieved from https://www.ame-church.com/our-church/our-history/
Aspen Institute (2004). *Structural racism and community building*. The Aspen Roundtable on Community Change. p.8. Retrieved from Racialequitytools.org/resourcefiles/aspeninst3.pdf.
Battalora, J. (2013). *The birth of a white nation: The invention of white people and its relevance today*. Houston, Texas: Strategic Book Publishing and Rights Co.
DeGruy, J. (2005). *Post traumatic slave syndrome*. Portland, OR: Joy DeGruy Publications
Dittes, J. E. (1973). *Bias and the pious: The relationship between prejudice and religion*. Minneapolis, MN: Augsburg Publishing House.
Division of Rare & Manuscript Collections. (2002). *I will be heard!* Abolitionism in America. Retrieved from http://rmc.library.cornell.edu/abolitionism/abolitionists.htm.
Duriez, B., & Hutsebaut, D. (2000). The relation between religion and racism: The role of post-critical beliefs. *Mental Health, Religion & Culture*, 3, 85–102. doi:10.1080/13674670050002135
Free Dictionary.com. (2013). *Race*. Retrieved from http://www.thefreedictionary.com/race
General Convention (2015). The 78th general convention of the episcopal church in Salt Lake City Utah. *Resolution C019*. Archives of the Episcopal Church. Utah, USA.
Gomes, P. J. (1996). *The case for slavery: The good book*. New York, NY: Avon Books.
Graham, B. (1993, October). Racism and the Evangelical Church. *Christianity Today*, 4, 27.
Catholic News Herald. (2017). Living stones: Black Catholics in America. Retrieved from http:/catholicnewsherald.com/88/fp/2394-living-stones-black-catholics-in-america.
Jones, R. P. (2016). *The end of white Christian America*. New York, NY: Simon and Schuster.
Koranteng-Pipim, S. (2001). *Racism in the church: The history, scope, and nature of the problem*. Retrieved from http://www.drpipim.org/church-racism-contemporaryissues-51/102-racism-and-the-church.
Lee, H. L. (2000). *Church leadership in a multicultural world: Directions for cultural harmony in the Adventist church* (pp. 14). Lincoln, NE: Center for Creative Ministry.
Lincoln, C. E., & Mamiya, L. H. (1990). *The black church in the African American experience*. North Carolina, USA: Duke University Press.
Milloy, C. (2016). Talking race in good faith. The Washington Post, July 20, p.B2. Washington, D.C
Nash, G. B. (1992). *Red, white and black: The peoples of early America* (3rd ed.). Englewood Cliffs, NJ: Prentice-Hall.
National Baptist Convention, 1988. (2019, February) *History of the national baptist convention*. Retrieved from www.nationalbaptist.com/aboutus/ourhistory/index.hmtl/
Raboteau, A. J. (1978). *Slave religion: The "invisible institution" in the Antebellum South*. New York, USA: Oxford University Press.
Scazzero, P. (2015). *Ten top reasons racism continues in the church today*. Blog. Retrieved from. Emotionallyhealthg.org/10-top-reasons-racism-continues-in-the-church-today.
Solomon, B. (1976). *Black empowermant*. New York, NY: Columbia University Press.
The Editors of Leben (2013). *How Harlem influenced Dietrich Bonhoeffer*. Retrieved from http://www.wnd.com/2013/03/how-a-harlem-church-nearly-killed-hitler/.
Thurman, H. (1976). *Jesus and the disinherited*. Boston, MA.: Beacon Press.

Tochluk, S. (2010). *Witnessing whiteness: The need to talk about race and how to do it* (2nd ed.). Lanham, Maryland, USA: Rowman and Littlefield Education.

UCLA School of Public Health (2016). *What is critical race theory*. Retrieved from https:/spacrs.wordpress.com/what-is-critical-race-theory/

UMC.org (2008). *Step toward wholeness: Learning and repentance.* Retrieved from Umc.org/what-we-believe5/act-of-repentance-for-racism

Washington National Cathedral (2016, July 17). *Race and reconciliation: What the church must do?* Prep notes and talking points for roundtable discussion. Washington, D.C.: Author.

Wikipedia. (2016, December 14). *Compartmentalization (psychology)*. Retrieved from https://en.wikipedia.org/wiki/Compartmentalization_psychology

Index

Adams, E. A. 67
Adams, P. L. 16
affirmative action 64, 65, 71, 140
affordable housing 4, 48–50, 54–58
African-American children 61–63, 67–71, 75–79, 81–84
African-American families 5, 10, 75–77, 81, 84, 86, 102–105, 108–110, 123
African American population 61–72
African Americans 3, 5, 10, 16, 22–25, 30, 62–65, 71, 86, 114, 123, 128, 130, 131; mass incarceration of 114
African-American students 62–65, 67, 70
agencies 75, 78–81, 83, 109, 139
Alexander, M. 35, 87, 88
American Bar Association 82, 115
American Public Health Association 61, 62, 68, 70
American Sociological Association 90–92
American Values 37, 90, 92, 93
antiracism training 142
Aronson, R. E. 93

Baber, W. L. 93
Baker, H. 6, 83
Barker, R. L. 3
Battalora, J. 135
Bell, D. A. 6
Bertrand, M. 23
Billingsley, A. 75, 90, 93
Black adults 2, 126
Black America 61, 66, 72
Black Americans 6, 34, 61–63, 71, 96, 97, 125, 139
Black church 139, 140, 143
Black families 47, 48, 87–90, 95, 110
Black family formation 92
Black fatherhood 87, 88, 90, 92, 94–97
Black females 63
Black males 63, 67, 92–94, 96, 97, 115
Black nationalism 43
Black power 2, 10, 40, 41, 44–47, 57
Black students 63, 65–68
Bowser, Mayor Muriel 44, 53, 54, 58

Brondolo, E. 125
Brown, A. F. 23

campaigning accountant 49
Campbell, A. 103
Campbell, T. 68
Charles, P. 95
chattel slavery 89, 96, 136
Chatters, L. M. 127
Chibnall, S. 76
child welfare 5–8, 75–79, 82, 83; disproportionality in 76; racial bias in 77; services 5, 75, 82, 83; system 5, 75–79, 82–84, 95
Christians 134, 135, 138, 139, 141, 142
citizenship 34
Civil Rights Act 24, 28, 103, 123, 126, 131
civil rights movement 31, 44, 55, 93, 103, 140
class 23, 25, 30–32, 41, 43, 44, 47, 51, 63
Clayton, O. 93–94
Coates, T. 1, 9
Colby, I. C. 127
colleague attendance 63
college readiness 63, 71
color 2, 3, 7, 16, 28–30, 34–37, 76, 79–82, 113, 114, 116, 120; children of 30, 76, 79–83; communities of 3, 7, 8, 113, 114; families of 34, 77, 80, 81, 114
compartmentalization 137
Comprehensive Merit Personnel Act 48
Congress, E. P. 9
contemporary responses 140
Converse, P. E. 103
Cooper, T. A. 78
Council on Accreditation (COA) 78, 79
crack cocaine 8, 35, 93
Crewe, S. E. 5
criminal justice 115; policies 36, 93, 116; system 5, 7, 8, 94–96, 113–121
criminal records 23, 24
critical race theory (CRT) 3, 4, 6, 7, 30–32, 36, 76, 86–88, 104, 110, 114, 115, 126, 127, 136; use of 28, 127
cultural argument 87, 89, 90
cultural bias 67, 68, 70, 71

Dastrup, S. 12
data analytics 82
data collection 80–84
data mining 82
Davis, A. 97
Davis, K. 13
Delgado, R. 35, 126
demographic characteristics 61, 62, 106
denominations 137–139
developmental disabilities 103–105, 107, 109
DeWitt, Larry 128
disabilities 5, 7–8, 68, 102–110, 124, 127
Disabilities Education Act 102, 104, 109
discrimination 22–25, 28, 34, 82, 84, 97, 104, 131, 136, 140
disproportionality 8, 68, 76, 82, 84
domestic workers 128
double jeopardy 5, 122–127, 129–132
DuBois, W.E.B. 51, 143
Duncan, G. A. 104
Duriez, B. 142

economic issues 41, 44, 47, 51
economics 13, 87, 90
economic sphere 23
education 3, 7, 28, 31, 32, 34, 37, 56, 68, 77, 102, 105, 109, 123, 124, 130, 136; disparities 30, 37, 61; levels 15, 36; opportunities 61, 69; policy 51, 61, 64–66, 69, 71; reform 65–67, 70
elderly African Americans 128
employer bias 23, 24
employment 4, 6, 7, 24, 25, 28, 36, 47, 48, 88, 91, 96, 97, 105, 108; status 23, 24, 93
engagement 79, 95, 139
episcopal Church 138, 141, 142
Esenstad, A. 78
ethnicity 15, 30, 31, 36, 37, 64, 68, 86, 103, 125, 141
expulsion 15, 67, 68, 70

family formation 87, 90, 94, 95, 97
family quality of life (FQOL) 102–104, 107, 108,110
Farber, N. B. 131
Farmer, M. M. 126
fatherhood 5, 6, 86, 88, 90, 93
Fenty, Mayor Adrien 50
Ferraro, K. F. 126
financial security 7, 34, 36
first African Church 138
Frazier, E. F. 89
Fry, R. 12
Furman, J. 128

Gaddis, S. M. 23
game changers 86
Gee, G. C. 125, 127
gentrification 4, 5, 39, 40, 44, 48, 50, 56–58
Gershenson, S. 67

Giovannoni, J. M. 75
Golden, H. M. 124
Gomes, P. J. 134
Gould, E. 12
Gourdine, R. M. 84
graduation 63
Gray, Mayor Vincent 51
Gupta, V. B. 105

habitual losers 39
Harrell, J. P. 16
Harrell, S. P. 16
Harris, A. P. 32
head start programs 62
healthcare 15, 36, 37, 105, 108, 109
health disparities 37, 105, 122
health inequities 6, 9, 126
Henderson, D. 15
Heyman, J. C. 9
higher education 61, 63–65, 71
higher quality of life 107
Hill, R. 5
historically Black colleges and universities (HBCUs) 65, 71, 139
Hoffman, A. J. 67
Holt, S. B. 67
housing 4, 6, 7, 28, 32, 34, 35, 37, 45, 47, 56–58, 108, 129; advocacy 39
housing policy 33, 41, 48, 54, 55, 58; advocacy 55
Howard, T. C. 32
Howard University School 2, 10, 132
human beings 3, 135–137
Hussey, C. 83
Hutsebaut, D. 142

Illinois Poverty 29, 32, 36
incarceration 5, 8, 35, 88, 93, 94, 96, 97, 113–117, 119, 120
Individuals with Disabilities Act 2004 (IDEA) 68
inequities 6, 32–37, 94, 96, 102, 104, 105, 108, 109, 126
institutional racism 88, 95, 128, 141
intrapsyche 12, 14, 16, 18
intrapsychic psychological binds 12–18
Issurdatt, S. 78

Jackson, B. B. 15
Jackson, J. L. 8
James, S. A. 16
Jim Crow 2, 28, 34, 96, 128, 131, 139
joblessness 88, 90–92, 96, 97
Jones, William G. 50
justice 2, 9, 32, 113, 117–119, 132

Kessler, R. C. 16
Kim, Y. J. 62
King, M. L. 122

King, S. V. 102
kinship care 79
Kleinbaum, D. G. 16
Kochhar, R. 12
Krieger, N. 16
Kurtz-Costes, B. E. 67

labor market participation 91
LaCroix, A. Z. 16
Ladd, H. F. 69
Ladner, J. A. 84
Ladson-Billings, G. 3, 32
Latinos 3, 32, 34–36, 67, 70, 105, 114
law enforcement 114–116
legacy of inequities 32
Lindsay, Inabel Burns 125
Lively, J. T. 23
Lourde, A. 6
low-income African Americans 57, 62

Manuel, R. C. 124, 125
Marion Barry insurgency 45
market-based reforms 68, 70–72
marriage 49, 86, 89, 90, 92–95
mass incarceration 5, 8, 32, 35, 88, 93, 94, 96, 97, 113, 115, 120
mayoral campaigns overtime 44
mayoral elections 39, 41, 44–46, 50, 53, 57
mayoral politics 55, 57, 58
McAdoo, H. P. 14
McCall, L. 13
McLeod, J. D. 14
media coverage 28, 30, 31
medicare 122, 131
mental health 4, 14, 83, 114, 127
Miller, K. M. 77
Miller, O. 78
Miller, R. R. 93
Milller-Cribbs, J. E. 131
Milner, H. R. 12
minimum wage 34, 54
minority families 105
Moore, J. 93, 94
Morrison-Rodriguez, B. 90, 93
Morton, J. 88
Mouzon, D. M. 127
Mullainathan, S. 12, 23

National Baptist Convention 139
National Urban League 5, 122, 123, 125
Navarro, O. 32
Neighbors, H. W. 16
No Child Left Behind (NCLB) 63, 66–68, 70
Nonnemaker, J. M. 14

older African Americans 5, 122–124, 130–132
Older Americans Act (OAA) 5, 122–123, 129

optimal health 6, 7
overrepresentation 76–78

Papageorge, N. 67
Park, R. 89
parolees 116, 117
Paul-Emile, K. 24
Pierce, C. M. 16
policy consideration 69
policy implications 108
policy recommendations 96
postsecondary education 61, 63–65, 67
poverty 4, 5, 12–14, 17, 18, 30, 31, 75–77, 122, 123, 125, 130–132; eradication 123
practice implications 108
preemployment discrimination 22, 25
primary education 62
prosecutorial bias 117
public health approach 69, 118, 119
public health model 118, 120
public health problem 6, 9
public health workers 108
public safety 119

quality of life 2, 5, 6, 9, 35, 102–105, 107–109, 127, 130, 132

race-based policies 8
race consciousness 42, 43, 47, 58
race equity 75
race-focused DC electoral map 41
race inequality 77
racial discrimination 5, 22, 25, 93, 138
racial disparities 36, 37, 91, 93, 94, 113–117, 120
racial disproportionality 78
racial equity 8, 78, 79; issues 78; standards evaluation project 78
Racial Equity Standards Areas (RESA) 75, 78–80
racialized game changing 87, 88
racial scoring gap 64
racism 2, 3, 5–10, 15, 16, 32, 88, 125, 126, 134, 136, 138, 139, 141, 142
redlining 29, 34
religion 5, 6, 8, 37, 110, 134, 136–138, 140, 142
revenue 65, 116, 128
Riveaux, S. J. 77
Roberts, D. 75
Rodgers, W. 103
Rynell, A. 32–34

Scazzero, Pete 140
school-based professionals 69, 71
school resegregation 65
school suspension 67, 68, 70
school systems 66, 68, 70
school vouchers 68, 70
secondary education 62

INDEX

self-concept 15, 17
Shafir, E. 12
Shah, A. K. 12
Simmons, K. 6
slavery argument 87, 89
slaves 89, 135–140
Smith, R. C. 10
social equity disparities 28
social factors 14, 88, 90
social policy-racism 6
social security 8, 31, 128
Social Security Act 94, 127–129
social welfare 2–4, 7, 9, 68, 69, 94, 95, 122–124, 127, 131, 132; policies 3, 4, 7, 90, 94, 95, 122–124, 127, 129, 131, 132
social work 2, 6, 7, 9, 10, 120, 125, 126, 129, 132
social workers 2, 4, 7, 9, 15, 78, 108–110, 125
Solomon, B. 139
special education 68, 102, 104
Spriggs, W. 128
Staples, R. 90
Stefancic, J. 35, 126
Stiehm, W. 15
Strogatz, D. S. 16
Sutherland, M. E. 16
systemic racism 16, 132, 140, 141
system stakeholders 82

Tate, W. F. 3, 32
Taylor, J. 15
Taylor, R. J. 127
Temporary Assistance to Needy Families (TANF) 24, 95
Terpstra, A. 32–34
Toldson, I. A. 88
traditional psychotherapy 18
trauma 13, 15–18
two-parent families 92, 95

unemployment 6, 14, 24, 36, 92, 97, 108, 120; rate 35, 90–92, 108, 110

Victor, D. 124
voter abstention 39, 53

Walsemann, K. M. 125
ward 41, 44, 45, 47, 48, 51–54, 56
Washington 39–41, 44–47, 55, 57, 65, 70
welfare reform 30, 88, 94, 95
Whitaker, T. 78
white Americans 6, 29, 32, 64, 114, 115
white Christian church 139, 142
white Christians 135, 136, 140, 141, 143
Whitehead, T. L. 93
white privilege 125, 136, 143
white racism 141
Williams, D. R. 16
Williams, Mayor Anthony 49
Wilson, William Julius 90
Wilson, W. J. 77, 83, 90, 91
Winnicott, D. W. 13, 14
Woodward, A. T. 127
workforce 3, 22–24, 91, 114
workplace 2, 22, 24, 25, 103; discrimination 22, 25

zero-tolerance policies 67, 68, 93